RECASTING:

Gone with the Wind
in American Culture

Edited by

Darden
Asbury
Pyron

A Florida International University Book
University Presses of Florida
Miami

University Presses of Florida is the central agency for scholarly publishing of the State of Florida's university system. Its offices are located at 15 NW 15th Street, Gainesville, FL 32603. Works published by University Presses of Florida are evaluated and selected for publication by a faculty editorial committee of any one of Florida's nine public universities: Florida A&M University (Tallahassee), Florida Atlantic University (Boca Raton), Florida International University (Miami), Florida State University (Tallahassee), University of Central Florida (Orlando), University of Florida (Gainesville), University of North Florida (Jacksonville), University of South Florida (Tampa), University of West Florida (Pensacola).

Library of Congress Cataloging in Publication Data
Main entry under title:
Recasting: "Gone with the wind" in American culture.

   Bibliography: p.
   Includes index.
   1. Mitchell, Margaret, 1900–1949. Gone with the
wind—Addresses, essays, lectures. 2. Southern
States in literature—Addresses, essays, lectures.
3. Gone with the wind (Motion picture) I. Pyron,
Darden Asbury.
PS3525.I972G687   1983   813′.52   82-20310
ISBN 0-8130-0747-X

Second printing, 1984
Typography by G&S Typesetters, Austin, Texas
Printed in U.S.A. on acid-free paper

Contents

This book is dedicated to my teachers William Leverett and William H. Harbaugh, and to the memory of Delbert Gilpatrick and of my father, A. H. Pyron, Jr.

Preface

Although I grew up on *Gone with the Wind*, all my first impressions were formed by the film rather than the novel; I paid little attention to Margaret Mitchell's original work. Not until 1974 did I read the novel for the first time, and then only as a lark: I was looking for a "light" assignment for a course I was teaching in Southern mythology. I got nothing I expected. I found it alien to the harmonious tales of late-nineteenth-century Southern romance and at odds with the largely conflict-free, aristocratic order of David Selznick's film. My strongest impressions were antithetical: I found conflict, disharmony, and irresolution.

Selznick's gentrification of the work fascinated me, but I was even more interested in the sources and meaning of the social structures in the novel. How and why did Margaret Mitchell revise and rewrite the plantation mythology of the South? What did the novel mean for Southern history, both of the nineteenth and of the twentieth centuries? How did the novel fit into the intellectual currents of the time in which it was written, specifically within the great revival of Southern letters in the twenties and thirties? With these and other problems in mind, I began to investigate how historians and literary critics had addressed these issues. I discovered that, by and large, they had not. The gap between popular acclaim and academic disdain piqued my curiosity still further, and eventually inspired this anthology.

I first conceived this collection in 1977 with two objectives: to collate some of the existing scholarship and to generate new critical opinion on the novel and the film. I have sought essays both old and new that return to the work itself and avoid the hoopla that has afflicted most discussion about it. I have looked for pieces that were based on close, fresh readings of the text itself within a well-defined disciplinary context. At the same time, the collection also reflects contemporary concerns of modern scholarship, particularly issues about race and sex or gender. I have been especially interested, too, in essays that deal with the Southern context.

I have not tried to balance the essays with pro and con arguments about the merit of the novel or film. The collection, however, is generally revisionist if only in pressing the idea that the work is worth studying. Some contributors like the work, some do not, even though these opinions may not always be apparent from the essays themselves. As for my own personal response (beyond my essay and the introductions to the three sections in this volume), Margaret Mitchell's work has often irritated and even angered me in its style and content; it has also always engaged me. After a score of readings, it has never bored me.

While this collection is intended for scholars and teachers of Southern and American literature and history, I have sought essays that will be accessible to a wider range of readers, too. I have tried to include pieces that will please as well as edify a more general audience.

As with any undertaking of this sort, I have incurred innumerable debts to a variety of people. To my friend and colleague Howard Kaminsky go special thanks. Besides putting *Gone with the Wind* into my intellectual consciousness, he has criticized every draft of my own work on the novel, has read the entire anthology, has offered both keen and sympathetic observations beyond the call of mere collegiality, and has encouraged this project throughout. I wish also to express my debts to my colleagues in the History Department and the faculty colloquium at my university. Professors Richard King and Richard Dwyer have also read and criticized the entire manuscript, with valuable suggestions on form and content. To King, I am especially grateful for our many conversations over many years that have enriched my understanding of Southern life and letters.

Florida International University has underwritten my work through Faculty Development Grants, and its administrators have been most supportive, especially Harry T. Antrim and Robert Fisher. I am deeply appreciative.

I would like to thank Judy Green, not only for her typing of this manuscript but also for her support and good humor throughout the making of this collection, and to thank also the staff of University Presses of Florida.

Finally, to the contributors themselves, especially the authors of the newest essays, who have patiently revised and rerevised and who have been willing to tailor their work to the larger objectives of this collection, I express my deepest gratitude.

Darden Asbury Pyron   **x**

Gone with the Wind is a phenomenon of American culture. Over a million copies were sold within the first year of its publication in 1936, and it has seldom sold less than 40,000 hardback editions per year since then, even in "low" years. It has been translated into twenty-five languages and is almost as popular abroad, especially in Germany and Japan, as it is in the United States. Indeed, it has spawned a cult in Japan, where it has been transformed into a long-running, all-female musical review in Tokyo.

The Japanese dramatization is only a bizarre expression of a general popular impulse: to have the novel in still more immediate and accessible form. David O. Selznick's 1939 film version is an integral extension of the *Gone with the Wind* "event." Even more people have seen the film than have read the book. Random samplings show that upward of 90 percent of the American population have sat through its four-hour screening. Almost as rare as the Americans who have not seen the film are those who have seen it only once. When shown on television at the extraordinary cost of $5 million in 1976, it drew 110 million viewers, up to that time the largest audience in television history.

But these raw figures hardly indicate the full impact of the novel and film. The phenomenon has proliferated an industry of its own, especially in publishing. Margaret Mitchell's biography by Finis Farr, originally published in 1965, still sells briskly in paperback. Two books on the single topic of the making of the film, one by Gavin Lambert (serialized before publication in the *Atlantic Monthly*) and another by Roland Flamini, appeared almost simultaneously in the early seventies; both sold very well. There are biographies of David O. Selznick and Vivien Leigh, and an autobiography by the Macmillan editor Harold Latham, who "discovered" Margaret Mitchell. Mitchell's published letters, edited by Richard Harwell, became a Book-of-the-Month Club alternate selection in 1976 and sold over 30,000 copies. Harwell also edited the script of the film, which Macmillan published in 1981.

Even distant cousins cash in on the magic. The Atlanta-born actress Evelyn Keyes, who played Suellen in the film, titled her autobiography (which has little actual material on the film) *Scarlett O'Hara's Younger Sister.* In 1977, Macmillan released the "ultimate" *Gone with the Wind* book: *Scarlett Fever,* by William Pratt and Herb

Bridges. A catalogue of facts about *Gone with the Wind* "collectibles," the novel, the film, and everyone connected with both, this volume is touted as "the fabulous 'wrap up' of the entertainment phenomenon of the century." Such finality seems premature. The Mitchell estate has allowed permission for a sequel to the novel to be written, and even such information as this finds a place in newspapers around the country.

The publishing industry reflects only a part of this phenomenon. During a recent Christmas season, one could buy three versions of a "Scarlett" doll—two actually bearing the name and a third stamped indelibly as the novel's heroine by the telltale green eyes and apple-green dress of the Wilkes's barbecue. The Atlanta restaurant "Pittypat's Porch," the Twelve Oaks offices of that city's radio-television station WSB, and even Atlanta itself reify Mitchell's fictions. And in the most unlikely places, antique dealers sell "Gone with the Wind lamps," and real estate brokers tout kitschy homes as "contemporary Taras." Indeed, the story's characters, places, and themes are so much a part of modern American culture that references not only to Scarlett and Tara but to not giving a damn, to thinking about things tomorrow, to knowing "nothin' 'bout birthin' babies," and so forth, all evoke ready-made responses.

If the one irrefutable fact of *Gone with the Wind* is its popularity, what that popularity means is another matter. It is problematic on at least two levels. It is taken by some, ipso facto, as the sign of the novel's artistic failure and inadequacy, but even those scholars interested in popular culture have drawn the most diverse and conflicting conclusions from the book's high sales. Is the novel progressive, or does it affirm tradition? Is it liberal or racist? realistic or escapist? The answers have hinged as much on one's values of democratic or popular culture as on the novel itself. As a result, analyses of *Gone with the Wind* as popular culture have focused on the novel's reception and have slighted the work itself. From this perspective, new or fresh analyses seemed impossible.

This situation began to change in the early 1970s, when there was a revival of academic interest in the novel. While some who reexamined it merely restated the dominant critical opinion —that the work was not worthy of scholarly inquiry—and others were bogged down by the meaning of popularity, still others offered fresh

2

insights and interpretations. This collection is itself a product of revived interest in the novel and the film as social or intellectual history and artwork. While it is farfetched to imagine "Margaret Mitchell" or "*Gone with the Wind*" study programs, this collection is another expression of the possibility that the novel, the film, their producers, and the *Gone with the Wind* phenomenon are capable of sustaining more detailed examination.

The fresh sense of critical examination might be signaling a new era in popular attitudes toward the novel. That the work can now be dissected with objectivity might mean that *Gone with the Wind*'s magic spell has been broken. But, as Richard Harwell suggests in his essay, one still has a vague feeling that Scarlett O'Hara—whom the eminent American historian David Donald once described as conjured rather than created—is more or less a permanent fixture in American life.

Critics were enraptured by *Gone with the Wind* when it appeared in the early summer of 1936, from the small-town Southern press to the great metropolitan dailies and literary journals. The *New York Sun* review related the work to "the great panoramic novel such as the English and the Russians and the Scandinavians have known how to produce"; it suggested that "in spaciousness, emotional power (and no American writer has approached Miss Mitchell in this respect) and in its picturing of a vast and complex social system in time of war, *Gone with the Wind* is most closely allied to Tolstoy's *War and Peace.*" Similarly, even while conceding the novel's flaws, Herschel Brickell was enthusiastic in the *New York Post*: "A good Southern novelist who is also an excellent critic wrote me the other day that he thought it was probably the greatest novel ever written in the United States. I am not willing to go this far, but . . . it is far and away the best novel that has ever been written about the Civil War and the days that followed." The *Saturday Review* and the *New Yorker* praised the book, and John Crowe Ransom expressed his "extreme" admiration "for the architectural persistence behind the big work."[1]

In this welter of enthusiasm, Henry Steele Commager's front-page review for the *New York Herald Tribune Books* is particularly outstanding and summarizes all of the virtues—and more—that most critics saw in the novel.

Commager was singular among *Gone with the Wind*'s reviewers in being a professional historian; he was, moreover, of the first rank among the young historians of his generation—and Mitchell's. Indeed, the two shared biases that certainly fostered Commager's sympathy with the novel. Reacting against the economic and class interpretations of the preceding generation of historians—typified in the work of Charles and Mary Beard—Commager's generation rediscovered history as tradition, as epic, as politics, and as the study of individual historical characters. The Civil War period offered a fertile field for this sort of inquiry: in its military, social, and even political aspects, heroes and heroines abounded and, with them, monumental actions. Such values helped define the form as well as the content of history written in the interwar years: there was an emphasis on biography and a revival of narrative history, or history as literature. With these also came a surge in popular his-

5

tory: historical fiction was one form of this—*Gone with the Wind* being only the most famous example; the other was genuinely popular and readable historical scholarship—not least among this work was Commager's own 1936 biography of the brilliant Boston abolitionist Theodore Parker (a book, not coincidentally, that engaged Margaret Mitchell as much as *Gone with the Wind* pleased Commager).[2]

History as dramatic confrontation, stirring narrative, vivid detail, heroic action, and flesh-and-blood characters were characteristics that Commager admired in the novel. His essay presents a very different view of the novel's history from that of most of the literary critics, indeed, from the author herself. For him, the novel's historical relevance does not lie where Mitchell considered it to be—in its historical authenticity and verisimilitude. On the contrary, Commager is keen to its falseness—its melodrama, sentimentality, and romanticism. But these shortcomings do not distress him, for he argues that Mitchell transcended her material and made *Gone with the Wind* "if not a work of art, a dramatic recreation of life itself." For Commager, its historical authenticity lies in capturing the essence of the regional experience rather than its details: a divisiveness or irresolution within the Old South itself.

Commager's review marked the zenith of academic or highbrow celebration of *Gone with the Wind.* Before the summer of 1936 had run its course, a reaction had set in.

Even enthusiastic reviewers had noted shortcomings in the book: its "prodigality," its melodrama and sentimentality, its stereotyped and shallow central characters, and a general "stagey-ness." Its Southernism was also said to be overdone. Thus even the "neo-Confederate" John Crowe Ransom criticized the book as overly Southern, particularly in its treatment of Reconstruction. He was unique in this regard, except for Communist reviewers; even Commager tacitly conceded the "horror" of Reconstruction, while one hostile critic actually recommended Claude Bower's execrable, Negrophobic *Tragic Era* as a more realistic treatment of the period.

The most consistently negative initial reaction to the book among mainstream literary critics (excluding the Communists of the *New Masses*) centered in the *New Republic.* John Peale Bishop's short review in July had dismissed the novel as merely "one more

6

of those 1000 page novels, competent but neither very good nor very sound."³ Much more directly, however, Malcolm Cowley's review, "Going with the Wind," two months later introduced attitudes that would dominate highbrow opinion toward the novel for over four decades. The first source of Cowley's disdain was the book's popularity and, related to that, the commercialization of literature. Two other issues provoked him as well: the novel's Southernism and its emphasis on female characters. Both of these issues would be noteworthy aspects of American intellectual culture for over a generation.

As to Southernism, national opinion has always been divided: distrust and disgust on the one hand, idealization and romanticization on the other. Between the late thirties and the mid-sixties, the negative view dominated among opinion makers of the American intellectual establishment. This trend became noticeable with Franklin Roosevelt's attempted purge of Southern conservatives like Senator Walter George in 1938. It was greatly accelerated by embarrassment over Southern racism and illiberalism as the nation fought a hot war against Nazi totalitarianism and a cold war against Communist oppression in the forties, fifties, and early sixties. One's stand on the South even became a measure of one's commitment to national values. Cowley's response to *Gone with the Wind* falls squarely on this side of the issue as he equates the novel with the political and ideological reaction of a false and pernicious Southern tradition.⁴

Cowley's third objection to the novel—its negative associations with women—relates both directly and indirectly to national attitudes about the South itself. Traditionally, the South has been identified with "female" characteristics, such as emotionalism, irrationalism, and a kind of overripe fecundity. These have stood in contrast to the traditionally "masculine" virtues of American Puritanism: discipline, control, and rationalism. One of the most interesting early examples of this linkage occurs in the writing of Thomas Wentworth Higginson.

An archetypal Puritan son of Brahmin Boston, Higginson was the abolitionist commander of an infantry unit of former slaves in the coastal area of South Carolina during the Civil War. The advent of spring in this area provoked classic Southern-woman-voluptuary images in his imagination: "Yet now, in the retrospect, there seems to have been infused into me through every pore the voluptuous charm of the season and the place. . . . It seemed to me also that the woods had not those pure, clean, innocent odors which so abound in the New England forests in the early Spring; but there was something luscious, voluptuous, almost oppressively fragrant, about the magnolias, as if they belonged not to Hebe, but to Magdalen." Such images contain a confusion of love and lust, desire and dread; they harken back to some of the most primitive notions in human society and masculine anxiety about women and female images.[5] Associating the region with female images was, then, one source of national historical ambivalence toward the South—and, by extension, to *Gone with the Wind.*

But there is another, more direct source of hostility to the novel as "female literature": the cultural and intellectual misogyny of Cowley's era. This reached a peak in the forties and fifties and constituted an important aspect of American intellectual history. As scholars such as Daniel Singal have noted, the young intellectuals of Cowley's generation had cut loose from the security of nineteenth-century Victorian civilization and had confronted the dangers and threats of a world without gods or order.[6] Theirs was a world of danger and anxiety—internal and external, real and imagined. One method of dealing with fear is to cut off feelings. Having feeling or sentiment was considered a female characteristic; given this association, the repudiation of one implied the repudiation of the other. And indeed the literary or intellectual stance of tough-minded, illusionless realism that characterized the postdepression era was self-consciously masculine and antifeminine. Through the sixties, the masculine term *hard-nosed* was a nicely Freudian, standard definition of virtue while the feminine *soft* was the antithetical term of opprobrium.[7]

Even friendly critics had connected Mitchell's novel to the world and work of women, but Cowley's essay adds a note of invidiousness to this criticism. However, he praises the novel's "splendid recklessness" and "simple-minded courage that suggest the great novelists of the past." His response was actually complex; his intellectual heirs made far fewer concessions.[8] Almost thirty years later—also in the *New Republic*—James Boatwright argued that

Cowley's was still the final word on *Gone with the Wind,* but he carried the gender-related condemnation still further. Margaret Mitchell was a tease: her book "titillates the audience" and "flirts with the terrible ambiguities of freedom without ever really believing in its possibility."[9]

Cowley's essay, then, is a monument to the cultural—if not strictly literary—criticism of the novel. It helps to illuminate the mystery of *Gone with the Wind*'s place, or "non-place," in American letters. The specific purpose of Richard Dwyer's essay, "The Case of the Cool Reception," is to understand *Gone with the Wind* in the context of the literary criticism of the late 1930s and, by implication, to place the work within the intellectual history of the Modernist movement. He does so by analyzing various sets of reviews, national and regional, highbrow and low, of Mitchell's work and other novels that appeared simultaneously. He concludes that the appearance of *Gone with the Wind* marks a watershed in American literary history; it constitutes a touchstone of the new literary criticism that dominated cultural history up through the mid-sixties. Finally, he notes how the dominant opinion, blinkered by larger social concerns, missed much of the latent meaning of *Gone with the Wind.* Fueled by psychological anxieties, domestic threats, and international insecurity, the social predisposition against the novel blinded critics, he suggests, to the ways in which Mitchell's work reflected and responded to the negativism and realism of the age.[10]

Notes

1. Edwin Granberry, "Book of the Day," *New York Sun,* June 30, 1936; Herschel Brickell, "Margaret Mitchell's First Novel, *Gone with the Wind,* a Fine Panorama of the Civil War Period," *New York Post,* June 30, 1936; John Crowe Ransom, "Fiction Harvest," *Southern Review* 2 (1936–37): 407; Louis Kronenberger, "Books," *New Yorker,* July 4, 1936, p. 48.

2. See Mitchell's letter to Commager, reprinted in *Margaret Mitchell's "Gone with the Wind" Letters, 1936–1949,* ed. Richard Harwell (New York: Macmillan, 1976), pp. 37–40.

3. John Peale Bishop, "War and No Peace," *New Republic,* July 15, 1936, p. 430.

Peale emphasized the novel's moral ambiguity and found little in the work to make it worthwhile, yet Margaret Mitchell thought his review "very good" and considered that because of it "the magazine had done rather well by me" (Harwell, p. 59).

4. While Cowley's review was actually more positive than Bishop's, it seemed to have particularly rankled Mitchell. See Harwell, pp. 66–67.

5. Higginson cited in Edmund Wilson, *Patriotic Gore: Studies in the Literature of the American Civil War* (New York: Oxford University Press, 1962), p. 653. For the use of such imagery in William Faulkner's work, see David Williams, *Faulkner's Women: The Myth and the Muse* (Montreal and London: McGill–Queen's University Press, 1977), especially through p. 59. See also Robert Graves's classic, *The White Goddess: An Historical Grammar of Poetic Myth,* 3d ed. (London: Faber and Faber, 1952).

6. Daniel Joseph Singal, *The War Within: From Victorian to Modernist Thought in the South, 1919–1945* (Chapel Hill: University of North Carolina Press, 1982).

7. In the presidential election of 1968, the use of such terms reached a comic climax in the exchanges between Vice-President Spiro Agnew and Senator Hubert Humphrey, whence came the modified charge of being "squishy soft on Communism."

8. Cowley never recanted any of his opinions, but the enthusiasm for *Gone with the Wind* in Europe, especially in high-culture circles, impressed him significantly. In a letter to Mitchell, almost ten years after his review, he cited Jean-Paul Sartre's commendation of her work and summarized "the highbrow French verdict" on her book by quoting Jacques Schiffrin, André Gide's friend and publisher: "He said to me," Cowley remembered, "'Now confess—it's better than Dos Passos, isn't it?' Dos Passos having a very high standing among the French highbrows." Cowley to Mitchell, August 7, 1945, in Margaret Mitchell Marsh Papers, University of Georgia Libraries, Athens.

9. James Boatwright, "'Totin' de Weery Load': A Reconsideration of *Gone with the Wind*," *New Republic,* September 1, 1973, pp. 29–32.

10. Dwyer argues that Mitchell's novel was an acute embarrassment to middlebrow, bourgeois critics, these being epitomized in Bernard DeVoto. Here again, Malcolm Cowley enters the picture. In 1944 DeVoto published *Literary Fallacies,* in which he carried his arguments against the "nihilistic modernists" even further than he did in the thirties. American writers of the interwar period had helped provoke the war, he insisted, by convincing the Europeans that the United States had lost its will to fight. Cowley answered the charge in "The War against Writers" (*New Republic,* May 4, 1944, pp. 31–32), analyzing the American novels that the Germans were reading in the thirties. *Gone with the Wind* was one of the most popular of these, which led him to a back-door defense of the work.

The Civil War in Georgia's Red Clay Hills

Henry Steele Commager

This novel is the prose to "John Brown's Body," and the theme is the same.

> Bury the bygone South,
> Bury the minstrel with the honeymouth,
> Bury the broadsword virtues of the clan,

wrote Benét, and Mrs. Mitchell takes for her story a similar and familiar text:

> As for man, his days are as grass;
> As the flower of the field, so he flourisheth
> For the wind passeth over it, and it is gone
> And the place thereof shall know it no more.

It is the Old South that is gone with the wind, but it is more. It is a way of life and of living, something deeply rooted and genuine and good, something—as the wayward heroine discovers—with "a glamor to it, a perfection and a completeness and a symmetry to it like Grecian art" [p. 529]. Sherman's army is the instrument of destruction, the hurricane, but that is only the superficial explanation. For what destroyed the South that Mrs. Mitchell describes with such tender realism was something from within, a weakness, an irresoluteness, a want of faith that is illustrated in character after character and thrown into sharpest relief by the contrasting virtues of the hero and heroine of the novel. Yet Mrs. Mitchell knows that victory can be purchased too dearly and that fortitude can wrest something from defeat. She knows the rest of the 103d Psalm, and it should be remembered, for it is essential to an understanding of the book:

> But the loving kindness of Jehovah is from
>   everlasting to everlasting upon them that fear him,
> And his righteousness unto children's children;
> To such as keep his covenant.
> And to those that remember his precepts to do them.

This essay originally appeared in *New York Herald Tribune Books,* July 5, 1936, pp. 1–2. The bracketed page references are keyed to the 1936 edition of *Gone with the Wind.*

For this is the story of a conflict of civilizations, and those civilizations are not necessarily the civilizations of the North and the South, but rather of the old South and the new. And though the material fabric of the old South is gone with the wind, something remains at the end that is shining and imperishable. The real victory is to such as keep the covenant and remember his precepts to do them.

What is remarkable about this book, however, is not the philosophy, so explicitly set forth, or even the historical authenticity of it all, but the richness of texture, the narrative vigor, the sweep and abundance and generosity of incident and of drama, piled up with carelessness and even with abandon, the ability to create characters and give them animation and reality. The men and women who glide so graciously or who storm so lustily through these pages are full blooded and full bodied and convincing. And the story, told with such sincerity and passion, illuminated by such understanding, woven of the stuff of history and of disciplined imagination, is endlessly interesting. It is dramatic, even melodramatic; it is romantic and occasionally sentimental; it brazenly employs all the trappings of the old-fashioned historical novel, and all of the stock characters of the old-fashioned Southern romance, but it rises triumphantly over this material and becomes, if not a work of art, a dramatic recreation of life itself.

The setting is in northern Georgia, on the plantation of Tara and in the bustling, pushing, vulgar city of Atlanta during the years of the Civil War and Reconstruction. We are introduced first to the County, to the Georgia version of *So Red the Rose* or of *The Battleground,* and if it is portrayed with less subtlety than Stark Young or Ellen Glasgow use, that is right, because the society of northern Georgia, only a generation old, lacked the finish, the polish, the graciousness of the Yazoo country or of the Valley. Yet there was beauty here, and a society, too, that was deeply rooted for all its youth. Families from Savannah and from Charleston had planted themselves here, and had taken on something of the strength and the crudeness of the red soil of Georgia that they came to love so well. This society is presented faithfully and understandingly—the great County families with their far-flung relationships, the crackers, the house darkies with their social distinctions. The County

12

families—the Tarletons and Fontaines, the Wilkeses and Munroes and Calverts—are cut out of a conventional pattern: the girls are all pretty coquettes or gentle ladies, the boys are tall and handsome and know how to ride and shoot. But not so with the O'Haras, and it is of the O'Haras that Mrs. Mitchell writes. And a grand family it is: Ellen, the mother, a great lady who meets all of the specifications that Benét laid down for that role in that wonderful description of Sally Lou Wingate; Gerald, the father, a stocky, red-headed, hard-drinking, hard-riding, violent Irishman, pushing and vigorous and rough and kind, proud of his Irish background and passionately fond of Tara, which he has made, and of his wife; the three daughters, weak little Carreen, and spoiled, pouting Suellen, and Scarlett herself.

Best of all is Scarlett, who wanted to be her mother's child but was inescapably her father's; Scarlett, who was vain and petty and jealous and unscrupulous and ruthless, but who had beauty and courage and fortitude. She had no mind, but she had a mind of her own; she had no subtlety, but she had a genius for getting below the surface of things and knowing their reality; she was full of pretense and of wile, but she was impatient of all sham, convention, shibboleth. Her depth was the depth of the earth; her realism, the realism of the soil; her gallantry was impersonal and almost unconscious. She was not a lady, though she wanted to be, but a magnificent woman, a vital, proud, passionate creature, undismayed by life or by death, tenacious of what was hers, acquisitive of what was not, hungry for admiration rather than love, ruthless but capable of tenderness, ambitious but capable of sacrifice, sentimental but without nonsense, deeply rooted in the soil of Tara, but uprooted, too, and lost.

It is the war that uproots her as it uproots them all, smashing to pieces not only the material fabric of their civilization but the spirit that produced and sustained it. "War is a man's business, not a woman's," says Scarlett bitterly, "a nuisance that killed men senselessly and cost money and made luxuries hard to get" (p. 173). But war was a woman's business, too, as she learned when her friends marched off to be killed or maimed or imprisoned, her husband and the man she loved among them. She fled to Atlanta, brash, exciting Atlanta, where the old families fought a losing fight against the new

13

people who crowded into the town, the soldiers and speculators and profiteers, men and women on the make, people without standards and without values. Here was Melanie, married to the man Scarlett loved, holding on to the old way of life, sustaining the tradition that Scarlett was ready to abandon, a great lady in her generation. And here, too, was Rhett Butler, black sheep of a Charleston family, a scoundrel and a wastrel, cynical, ruthless, unscrupulous, but utterly charming, making money hand over fist out of the society which had cast him out and which he scorned and understood and secretly loved.

It is the story of Scarlett and Rhett that furnishes the central theme of the book. They are two of a kind, and Rhett knows it, though Scarlett does not. She is dazzled by his audacity and intrigued by his mind and excited by his money, but she lives in the dream of the past and worships a dreamer, Ashley Wilkes, though she does not understand him. Rhett understands him, and his contempt is the contempt of the new for the old, of success for failure, but it is a contempt that is tinged with envy and admiration:

> Ashley Wilkes—bah! His breed is of no use or value in an upside-down world like ours. Whenever the world up-ends, his kind is the first to perish. And why not? They don't deserve to survive because they won't fight—don't know how to fight. This isn't the first time the world's been upside down and it won't be the last. It's happened before and it'll happen again. And when it does happen, every one loses everything and every one is equal. And then they all start again at taw, with nothing at all. That is, nothing except the cunning of their brains and the strength of their hands. But some people, like Ashley, have neither cunning nor strength, or, having them, scruple to use them. And so they go under, and they should go under. [p. 772]

This is the philosophy of materialism, and Rhett, who expounds it, does not really believe it, while Scarlett, who protests, believes it and acts upon it.

Soon Sherman is battering his way into Georgia and Atlanta is besieged. Never has a chapter of the war been more realistically recreated, more vividly described, not even in *Long Remember,* which used something of the same technique. We share the confidence of the Georgians as Joe Johnston holds Sherman at bay; we

14

sense the growing uncertainty, the fear, as flank movement after flank movement brings the Yankees ever closer to the doomed city; we are stirred by the gambler's hope as Hood replaces Johnston and prepares to take the offensive; we see the Home Guards, old men and boys and slackers, march out for the last defense, and know the hopelessness of it all. Then the city is abandoned, in a nightmare of confusion and agony. Rhett goes off to join the ragged Confederate army, while Scarlett and Melanie escape in the night, the rickety wagon jolting along the deep-rutted roads, Melanie lying on the rough boards with her new-born baby hugged to her breast, Scarlett prodding the emaciated mule while the words of a familiar song come back to her with a new meaning:

Just a few more days for to tote the weary load,
No matter, 'twill never be light.

But the blows of reconstruction were worse than the blows of war, for reconstruction wasted those impalpable values that had accumulated during generations of gentle living and hardened men as not even war had done. Scarlett, too, was hardened. She returned to Tara and for two years battled to save it from the triple threat of Yankee soldiers, Confederate commissaries, and carpet-bag tax gatherers. Her experiences furnished a justification, a logic, to her character and she determined that never again would she or hers know hunger or want, never again would Tara be in danger.

It was the struggle to save Tara that took Scarlett back to Atlanta and to Rhett Butler, the one man who had money. The old Atlanta was gone, the old families broken:

Their faces were little changed and their manners not at all, but it seemed to her that these two things were all that remained of her old friends. An ageless dignity, a timeless gallantry still clung about them and would cling to them until they died, but they would carry undying bitterness to their graves, a bitterness too deep for words. They were a soft-spoken, fierce, tired people who were defeated and would not know defeat, broken yet standing determinedly erect. They were crushed and helpless, citizens of conquered provinces. They were looking on the state they loved, seeing it trampled by the enemy. . . . And they were remembering graves. [p. 607]

15

But not Scarlett. She put graves resolutely out of her mind and parted company with the ghosts of the past. The new Atlanta, more bustling and more vulgar than ever, offered an opportunity for the display of her peculiar talents, and she seized it with characteristic audacity. She went into business, she used convict labor, she associated with carpetbaggers and scalawags and bought immunity from interference by her social grace and prestige. She won her way to financial security, for herself and for her family and for Tara, above all for Tara. But she lost everything that Tara stood for; she lost her standing in society, she forfeited the affection and respect of the old families and of her own family. Only Tara remained—Tara, symbol of everything that she had known and loved and forfeited, symbol of what she might have been and might still be.

> She thought of Tara and it was as if a gentle cool hand were stealing over her heart. She could see the white house gleaming welcome to her through the reddening autumn leaves, feel the quiet hush of the country twilight coming down over her like a benediction, feel the dews falling on the acres of green bushes starred with fleecy white, see the raw color on the red earth and the dismal dark beauty of the pines on the rolling hills. [pp.1036–37]

Going with the Wind

Malcolm
Cowley

I have to thank Miss Rosa Hutchinson of the Macmillan Company
for a series of press releases that is more impressive than any published review of the season's best seller:

June 19.—"Gone with the Wind," the forthcoming novel of the
real South in the sixties and seventies, by Margaret Mitchell of Atlanta, is having a record-breaking advance sale. Already—two
weeks before publication—this Macmillan novel has piled up the
largest advance sale of any book of recent years. It is the choice of
the Book of the Month Club for July.

Ellen Glasgow is enthusiastic about it. She writes: "The book is
absorbing. It is a fearless portrayal, romantic yet not sentimental, of
a lost tradition and a way of life. I hope it will be widely read and
appreciated."

June 29.—A fifth large printing of Margaret Mitchell's first novel,
"Gone with the Wind," has been ordered, although the book is just
out this week. The book may be out of stock at Macmillan's for a
few days, but booksellers throughout the country will have copies
available.

July 13.—A sixth printing of "Gone with the Wind," by Margaret
Mitchell, making a total of 140,000 to date, is being rushed through
the press and will be ready this week, so that all current orders may
be taken care of.

July 15.—Motion-picture rights in Margaret Mitchell's novel,
"Gone with the Wind," have been sold to Selznick International Pictures, Inc. The price is believed to be the highest ever given for a
first novel.

July 20.—176,000 copies of Margaret Mitchell's novel, "Gone
with the Wind," have now been printed by Macmillan in an attempt
to cope with the steady inrush of orders. The demand for the book
certainly reflects credit on the taste of the American reading public,
for "Gone with the Wind" has been likened by various prominent
critics to the work of Thackeray, Galsworthy, Tolstoy, Undset,
Hardy, Trollope and Dickens—and to "The Three Musketeers."

July 23.—What is believed to be a record in recent years has
been established by Margaret Mitchell's "Gone with the Wind." Al-

This essay originally appeared in *New Republic*, September 16, 1936, pp. 161–62.

though it has been published only one month, printings already total 201,000 copies.

In the first three days of this week alone, Macmillan shipped out on booksellers' reorders 16,468 copies.

July 24.—The Macmillan Company reports that orders booked yesterday for Margaret Mitchell's "Gone with the Wind" totaled 10,753.

Early in August.—"Gone with the Wind," by Margaret Mitchell—nationwide best seller in fiction lists—has as one of its chief characters Melanie Wilkes. Miss Mitchell writes Macmillan's that many people seem to be troubled as to the correct pronunciation of Melanie, some giving it the accent on the second syllable and with a long "a." The correct pronunciation puts the accent on the first syllable.

"Gone with the Wind" is now going into its ninth printing, bringing the total number of copies to 226,000.

August 17.—The sales department of the Macmillan Company is mathematically minded. It has figured out some interesting facts about "Gone with the Wind," the best seller by Margaret Mitchell. It appears that if all the copies of "Gone with the Wind" that have been printed were piled on top of each other the stack would be fifty times as high as the Empire State Building in New York City. Or if the pages of all these copies were laid end to end they would encircle the world at the Equator two and two-thirds times.

Some forty-five tons of boards and 34,000 yards of cloth have been used in the physical make-up of these books, and the paper already used would fill twenty-four carloads. Two printing plants are working on the book in three eight-hour shifts, and two binderies are fastening the sheets together.

September 3.—333,000 copies of Margaret Mitchell's novel, "Gone with the Wind," were printed to fill the demand up to August 30, two months after publication. Another large printing is now going through, which will bring the total up to 370,000.

September 8.—The feelings of a lady who sailed for Europe last week were somewhat mixed when, among her bon-voyage packages, she found nine copies of "Gone with the Wind."

That is the story to date of what promises to be the biggest publishing success since the good old days of "The Sheik" and "If Win-

ter Comes." Obviously Miss Mitchell's first novel meets the special-
ized demands of the book-buying public (as distinguished from the
larger and less prosperous public that borrows its books from the
library). It is written from the woman's point of view, and most
book buyers are women. It flatters people who like to think of
themselves as aristocrats, and this amiable weakness is more than
usually common among the patrons of bookstores. Moreover, it is
very long, and people who pay $3 for a novel like to think that they
are getting their money's worth, are getting entertainment that will
carry them through the idle moments for a whole fortnight. But beyond all this, an essential reason for its popularity lies in the big yet
comfortably familiar theme that Miss Mitchell has chosen.

"Gone with the Wind" is an encyclopedia of the plantation legend. Other novelists by the hundreds have helped to shape this legend, but each of them has presented only part of it. Miss Mitchell
repeats it as a whole, with all its episodes and all its characters and
all its stage settings—the big white-columned house sleeping under
its trees among the cotton fields; the band of faithful retainers, including two that quaintly resemble Aunt Jemima and Old Black Joe;
the white-haired massa bathing in mint juleps; the heroine with her
seventeen-inch waist and the high-spirited twins who come court-
ing her in the magnolia-colored moonlight with the darkies singing
under the hill—then the War between the States, sir, and the twins
riding off on their fiery chargers, and the lovely ladies staying
behind to nurse the wounded, and Sherman's march (now the
damyankees are looting the mansion and one of them threatens to
violate its high-bred mistress, but she clutches the rusty trigger of
an old horse pistol and it goes off bang in his ugly face)—then the
black days of Reconstruction, the callousness of the Carpetbaggers,
the scalawaggishness of the Scalawags, the knightliness of the Ku
Klux Klansmen, who frighten Negroes away from the polls, thus
making Georgia safe for democracy and virtuous womanhood, and
Our Gene Talmadge—it is all here, every last bale of cotton and
bushel of moonlight, every last full measure of Southern female devotion working its lilywhite fingers uncomplainingly to the lilywhite bone.

But even though the legend is false in part and silly in part and
vicious in its general effect on Southern life today, still it retains its

19

appeal to fundamental emotions. Miss Mitchell lends new strength to the legend by telling it as if it has never been told before, and also by mixing a good share of realism with the romance. She writes with a splendid recklessness, blundering into big scenes that a more experienced novelist would hesitate to handle for fear of being compared unfavorably with Dickens or Dostoevsky. Miss Mitchell is afraid of no comparison and no emotion—she makes us weep at a deathbed (and really weep), exult at a sudden rescue and grit our teeth at the crimes of our relatives the damyankees. I would never, never say that she has written a great novel, but in the midst of trite-ness and sentimentality her book has a simple-minded courage that suggests the great novelists of the past. No wonder it is going like the wind.

The Case of the Cool Reception | Richard Dwyer

For a large and diverse group of people, *Gone with the Wind* is the epic novel of our time, just as the jacket blurb says. The tens of millions who have read the book and the quarter of a billion who have seen the film more than love it; they own bedside, slipcased editions to which they turn for emotional, nostalgic, and even inspirational purposes. Yet in the teeth of this adoration, literary historians and critics have rarely mentioned it, and little serious academic attention has been paid to it. How did this paradox come about?

In an effort to find out, I have taken the sleuth's route of revisiting the literary scene of the first appearance of the novel, and the resulting essay might be thought of as an illustrated lineup of witnesses and suspects, some of whose academic members are still protesting the brutality of the victim. The trail of this hunt has led me from South to North, from the silence of Chapel Hill to the still deeps of the *Sewanee Review,* to warmer leads in the popular Eastern press, to pay dirt in the *Saturday Review* and its academic hinterland. Motive and modus operandi established, we end where we began, with the verdict of the vox populi.

As an unilluminating false start, I turned to Southern reviews first. The Southern academic context into which *Gone with the Wind* dropped was complex, but, simplified, it consisted of a polar opposition between Chapel Hill and Nashville. Two years before the appearance of Mitchell's novel, the University of North Carolina assembled a fundamentally sociological symposium on the Culture of the South, which downplayed regional distinctiveness and pictured the region as a legitimate part of the large nation. This progressive orientation is to be contrasted with a renewed appeal for regional uniqueness from that constellation of Fugitives, Agrarians, and New Critics hovering around the University of the South in Sewanee and Vanderbilt in Nashville. These writers declared a romantic political separateness in such works as *I'll Take My Stand* (1930) and *Who Owns America?* (1936) and a distinctive aesthetic in, for example, the tenth anniversary number of the *Virginia Quarterly Review* (1935), with articles by John Crowe Ransom on "Modern with a Southern Accent" and by Allen Tate on "The Profession of Letters in the South," that was to mature into the formalism of the New Critics of the *Kenyon Review.*

Ironically perhaps, the Southern literary establishment actually showed little interest in Southern letters in the interwar period. As late as 1935, George Atherton Chafee, in a cursory overview of "Four Novels of the South" for the *Sewanee Review,* expressed fatigue at the retold tales of Southern superiority over (and mistreatment at the hands of) the North in such works as *So Red the Rose*— "a tract in fiction of the Nashville Neo-Confederates"—and works by Carl Carmer and Caroline Gordon. It seems, however, that Margaret Mitchell's book acted as a catalyst that compelled Southern academicians to turn for a while from their customary concern with English literature—most particularly Jacobean—to regard their own backyard. Thus, in contrast to the absence of critical opinion about Southern letters (excepting Chafee's brief essay), the *Sewanee Review* commissioned Laura Krey to write a two-part review of "Southern Selections" in 1938 to counter such lists from other quarters. Krey's one reference to Mitchell's work is instructive: "In the past few years there has been no dearth of books on the South. Indeed, one reviewer, analyzing the contemporary publishing output, refers wearily to a 'rash of southern books' and another to a 'crop as numerous as dandelions in June'. Both reviewers are, I think, very nearly right, for almost every publishing house has quite naturally hoped to interest the million or more readers of *Gone with the Wind*" (October–December 1938, p. 550).

After looking vainly through Southern reviews for indications that anyone would admit to reading *Gone with the Wind*, it was refreshing to turn to the Eastern literary establishment, which reviewed it thoroughly and, at least at the outset, objectively. These early reviews foreshadow the problem that the novel would present to the American literary or intellectual establishment. An example is the useful distinction between two sorts of fiction that J. Donald Adams sketched in a pair of reviews in the *New York Times Book Review,* July 5, 1936. He finds *Gone with the Wind* "in narrative power, in sheer readability, surpassed by nothing in American fiction. *GWTW* is by no means a great novel, in the sense that *War and Peace* is, or even *Henry Esmond,* to name only novels which dealt, like this one, with past periods of time. But it is a long while since the American reading public has been offered such a bounteous feast of excellent story telling." He goes on to rate it above Mary Johnston's *The Long Roll* and *Cease Firing* and even

Ellen Glasgow's *The Battleground* and to observe that "Miss Mitchell's real triumph is Scarlett O'Hara, a heroine lacking in many virtues—in nearly all, one might say, but courage. She is a vital creature, this Scarlett, alive in every inch of her, selfish, unprincipled, ruthless, greedy and dominating, but with a backbone of supple, springing steel." Later in the month, Adams reviewed Aldous Huxley's *Eyeless in Gaza* and expressed with disarming candor his recognition that the house of fiction has many mansions:

> It is a strange experience to come to this book by Huxley fresh from reading Margaret Mitchell's *Gone with the Wind*, one of the most notable pieces of sheer story-telling in recent years, the picture of a way of life that is irrevocably vanished, a novel with slight values beyond that of entertainment—the other compact of thought, indomitably concerned with the here and now—two remarkable books that must be read for totally different reasons.
>
> Miss Mitchell never makes one uncomfortable, unless to feel shame at that black page of our history which was Reconstruction; Mr. Huxley does almost continually, and without mercy.[1]

Here, then, before the issue of popularity arises to confuse the judgments, is the clear perception of a literary opposition: narrative power versus satirical stance, generous story-telling, and simple characterization contrasted with the disciplined ironic sensibility betokening what we have come to call Modernism: a wintry discontent with heroes, large visions, and noble talk. Other reviewers felt the same strange effect as Mitchell's novel stayed in their minds and became a touchstone for revealing the guiles of Modernism. The elite artist's preference for working by indirection, for instance, is scored in Fred Marsh's review of *The Long Night* by Andrew Lytle: "Another first novel laid in the old and deep South, following in the wake of *GWTW*, which, like its predecessor, *So Red the Rose*, quickly reached the top of the bestseller lists, [exhibits] fancy allegorical overtones, carefully concealed, relating the desperate private war of revenge to the momentous issues of Civil War, in which the bloody and futile Battle of Shiloh, one may fancy, becomes a symbol. But such intimations of meanings, if intended (and there seems to be no other reason for bringing in the Civil War at all), have little to do with the worth of the novel and are quite beside the point, for it is as a story that the book is to be read or dismissed" (*New York Times Book Review,* September 6, 1936, p. 9). Later, when Harold Strauss came to review William Faulkner's *Absalom, Absalom!* he similarly found it "strange chiefly because of the amazing indirectness with which Faulkner has managed to tell a basically simple story. . . . the truth seems to be that Faulkner fears banality. Now that, since *Pylon* and his Hollywood residence, he has abandoned his more shocking themes, he is compelled to distinguish himself from the generality of authors in employing one of the most complex, unreadable and uncommunicative prose styles ever to find its way into print." [2]

Finally, Caroline Smith, in reviewing Caroline Gordon's *None Shall Look Back* for *The Nation* (March 20, 1937, p. 332), found it to be, in comparison to *Gone with the Wind*, "shorter, less verbose, less reckless, less spectacular; the narrative flows less freely; the details are not so lavish; and there is more intelligence." She finds Gordon's faults to be those of understatement and restraint but never of sentimentality or cheap melodrama, by implication the vices of Mitchell's work.

In these three reviews, we find professional readers puzzling over the artistic opposition of allegory, symbolism, complexities of plot and syntax, and even an insouciance toward craftsmanship on the part of writers addressing a sophisticated elite and maintaining their distance from, in the other corner, Margaret Mitchell's evident but quite different talent for swift narrative and clear characterization.

Given this trend of using *Gone with the Wind* as a touchstone against less commercially successful works, the terms in which that novel itself was to be judged did not long remain purely literary, and its publisher, Macmillan, must bear some of the blame. Macmillan maintained a running full-page stand, just inside the front cover of the *Saturday Review*. There, every week for the first months of the novel's life, the publisher ran a continuously updated box-score of sales, issues, and printings, literally rubbing its success into the commercial opposition, but also into the sensibilities of the literati. Macmillan's ad was offensive—a preview and analogue of McDonald's millions of burgers served—and it provoked competing publishers to take the hint. Bobbs Merrill's arch blurb for Andrew Lytle's *The Long Night* described it as "utterly different in both theme and treatment from other Southern novels being written today" (*New York Times Book Review,* September 6, 1936, p. 15).

In revealing these attitudes, the publishing industry was taking its cue from the established reviewers, who were being made increasingly uncomfortable by the massive popularity of a book whose good and bad qualities came to be overlooked in the face of commercial success. The contrast is neatly summed up in the opposition of two reviews in *New Republic,* one by John Peale Bishop (July 15) and the other by Malcolm Cowley (September 16). Although Bishop does not especially like the novel, he responds feelingly to its creation of place and personality. His objections to it are moral: by dramatizing two rogues who "assert indirectly the virtues of the society whose destruction they witness," Mitchell is unnecessarily trying to avoid sentimentality. Tolstoy, on the other hand, "is not afraid of Prince André's enthusiasm for the Tsar." The basic problem, however, was that "Scarlett wants only to last and takes any terms life offers. Miss Mitchell seems to approve of her persistence. But she also implies that civilization consists precisely of an unwillingness to survive on any terms save those of one's own determining." Apart from the fact that both of these views are completely foreign impositions on the novel, it is interesting to see an early reviewer responding principally to aesthetic and moral issues raised.

Malcolm Cowley begins his longer, later review by quoting an obnoxious series of Macmillan Company press releases that harp on the sales of the novel; he then turns to what really bothers him: its calculated appeal to and flattery of the masses of book buyers, mostly female, in contrast to the more refined "and less prosperous public that borrows its books from the library." Cowley spends the rest of his review burlesquing the plantation legend.

Other professionals in the industry reacted with similar defenses. By December 1936, the issue of popularity had become paramount. In his editorial "What Makes a Bestseller?" Edward Weeks writes: "I confess that I began reading *GWTW* with misgivings. It irritated me to see any book so showered with superlatives as this one was." He finds the charm of the book in the vitality of its four central characters, whose appeal he locates in their almost mythic simplicity, but he concludes with the familiar distinction between great books and best-sellers.

Increasingly, critics ignored the narrative qualities of the novel and focused exclusively—and bitchily—upon its popularity. For example, I. A. R. Wylie in "As One Writer to Another" (*Harper's Magazine*, February 1937, pp. 268–74) wonders "why should we practice five-finger exercises with the English language when a young woman sells a million copies of her first novel (which, if we believe rumors, wasn't even written for publication)." The issue was not even between two kinds of books, rather simple envy at too much too soon—MM's fortune as a medieval exemplum.

But we must leave the anxieties and prejudices of these witnesses of the industry and turn to their academic wellsprings. As a representative of the Eastern liberal establishment, Bernard De Voto characteristically took *Gone with the Wind* deeply to heart and came up fibrillating. At the time of the appearance of the novel, he had just moved from a two-year post as lecturer at his alma mater, Harvard, to become editor of the *Saturday Review*. As a novelist and Pulitzer Prize–winning historian, De Voto was challenged by Margaret Mitchell's book. For the next two years, he turned out high-minded judgments in which *Gone with the Wind* figured constantly as a cautionary tale. De Voto wanted novels to be both historically accurate and ideologically liberal—affirming of a masculine democracy. Perhaps taking his cue from *Saturday Review*'s flattering review of *Gone with the Wind* by Stephen Vincent Benét, in which Benét had discussed the novel in part as a woman's achievement, De Voto took aim at the woman's fiction marketplace: ". . . the slick writers of the highest bracket (they are practically all women) believe firmly in the moral overtones of their stuff, which are what give it cash value. . . . In all ages these simplicities are what the popular audience has most wanted from literature and what it has most rewarded. The women's magazines, and the slicks in general, merely canalize the popular taste" ("Writing for Money," *Saturday Review,* October 9, 1937).

De Voto then adopted the academic response to any issue—to fire back a bibliography, a canon, as it were, of more acceptable authorities than the opponent's. In a lecture he had given at Harvard,

which he condensed into an article for *Saturday Review* ("Fiction
Fights the Civil War," December 18, 1937), De Voto sets forth,
though not in perfect clarity, a sequence of four stages in the treatment of the Civil War in fiction. There is overlap and the odd omis-
sion of works like Winston Churchill's *The Crisis*, but De Voto's
basic intention is realized—to point readers away from Tara. He describes an initial period of Northern moralistic, conciliatory love
stories, followed by a period of Southern Lost Cause fiction (in the
works of Thomas Nelson Page and others) that lovingly displays a
perishing aristocracy, family slaves, merry yeomen, and no po'
whites. Realism set in about 1895 and slipped into current modes
that De Voto values: realistic, psychologically valid, socially aware,
and philosophical varieties. He cites the Yankees MacKinlay Kantor
and Royce Brier and such Southerners as Caroline Gordon, Andrew
Lytle, Stark Young, and Clifford Dowdy, but he reserves his highest
praise for James Boyd's *Marching On,* for its portrait of a collapsing
social system and its power of speculative realization. But it is clear
by the end of the lecture that De Voto has been itching to get at
Margaret Mitchell, and so he does: "*Gone with the Wind* is important as a phenomenon but hardly as a novel. It has too little thought
and no philosophical overtones. It documents very well the daily
life of a society at war and under reconstruction, but its ideas are
rudimentary. Its author has no eye and no feeling of human character, and its page by page reliance on all the formulas of sentimental
romance and all the effect of melodrama is offensive. The size of its
public is significant; the book is not" (p. 16).

In a 1938 *Saturday Review* editorial, "Shallow Waters," De Voto
took a parting shot at *Gone with the Wind* and the popularity of
women's fiction in the form of a response to a letter from Holmes
Alexander, author of *Aaron Burr, the Proud Pretender.* De Voto had
just returned from a convention of the Modern Language Association where he had heard Alexander Cowie read a paper on women
writers of the mid-nineteenth century. Fresh from this inspection of
the weapons of literacy, thoughtlessly handed over to these belles
sauvages, De Voto responded to Holmes Alexander's chivalrous defense of Margaret Mitchell: "He thinks that melodrama is all right.
We do too, but we don't like such a high concentration of it in a
novel which undertakes to present the realities of human experi-

ence. We don't like so much of it in any single book, and we don't like Miss Mitchell's inclusiveness. . . . The novel's sentiments are strong and lively but also commonplace and frequently cheap. Its total effect is a falsification of experience" (*Saturday Review*, January 8, 1938, p. 8).

De Voto's confrontation with *Gone with the Wind* was actually no more than a diversion—albeit a revealing one—from a larger struggle: his liberal commitment to progress, social responsibility, and useful literature contrasted with Modernism, what he saw as the enervating nihilism of such writers as Pound, Eliot, and Joyce. To one engaged in the titanic struggle between the rival elites Liberalism and Modernism, Miss Mitchell could only be a distraction. But her very popularity with the book-buying audience, which De Voto wished to win for the higher causes of positive thinking, proved galling. And her case brought out of the defender of the democratic dogma all of the internal contradictions of De Voto's position. What he could not see is that such authors as Eliot, Yeats, and Lawrence shared a reactionary outlook that was deeper and more valid as an artistic response to the crises of bourgeois capitalism than that made by its liberal defenders. The ultimate irony of De Voto's reaction is that Margaret Mitchell's hustling urban Irishry are the most authentic representatives of the bourgeois liberal tradition in action. While they and she may be utterly unreflective and intellectually imperceptive of their own ideology, they do reflect it. And it is De Voto who compromises it by drawing back from the full implications of laissez-faire democracy, of the please-yourself marketplace and winner-take-all.

It seems, then, that the response to the novel was determined by nothing so much as its marketplace success, its very popularity. Amid a concentric series of world, national, and regional contexts in which popularity could be seen as dangerous or contemptible, reviewers let the sales reports determine their judgments. They, and the academic commentators, were quick to associate the relative popularity of the book with Mass Culture at a time when the specter of mass movements like European and Asian Fascism and Communism could provoke such classic elite reactions as *The Revolt of the Masses,* by the Spanish humanist José Ortega y Gasset, or F. R. Leavis's *Mass Civilization and Minority Culture* (1930), which warned: "In any period it is upon a very small minority that the discerning appreciation of art and literature depends: it is (apart from cases of the simple and familiar) only a few who are capable of unprompted, first-hand judgment. They are still a small minority, though a larger one, who are capable of endorsing such first-hand judgment by genuine personal response. . . . the minority capable not only of appreciating Dante, Shakespeare, Donne, Baudelaire, Hardy (to take major instances) but of recognizing their latest successors constitute the consciousness of the race (or a branch of it) at a given time."[3]

In the thirties, these terrible duties of serving as the racial consciousness weighed differently on shoulders in Cambridge, Nuremberg, and Nashville, but the tensions operating on a planetary scale did make lesser reverberations everywhere. An entertainment like *Gone with the Wind* fell somehow in that vast ground between the political extremes of Left and Right and the social poles of Elites and Masses, on that preserve of the very bourgeois getters-and-spenders celebrated in the novel and addressed by the publishers. And its glittering presence there turned out to be, for reviewers from *Saturday* to *Sewanee*, the worst thing that had happened to them for some time.

These various academic establishments, whether Southern conservative or progressive or Eastern liberal, agreed alike in judging *Gone with the Wind* by standards—whether of social consciousness, ironic tone, or textual intricacy—that are irrelevant to the engaging qualities of good narrative. As the phenomenal popularity of the novel surged ever higher, the academics resorted to a variety of rhetorical strategies that serve, in hindsight, to reveal nothing so much as their elitist ideological biases against the nonacademic majority of the American public as consumers of convenience, comfort, and mindless diversion. Today, long after the agonies of the thirties, a reference such as Louis D. Rubin's *A Bibliographical Guide to Southern Literature* (1969) has only a brief, wholly biographical comment about Mitchell, but it also includes among its general topics a section on Southern popular literature by Floyd Watkins. After noting that information about popular writing may be found listed in studies of such individual authors as Margaret Mitchell, he says, "The popularity or the sales of a book, according to the critic who rightfully decries mass advertising of literature and mass taste, should be one of the last factors in evaluating it. For this reason, when this topic overlaps with others (the Civil War, local color, periods of Southern literature, periodicals), this category has been the first to yield" (p. 90).[4] To me, it is quite apparent, in the absence of such topics as narrative power and sheer readability, that its popularity is the *only* criterion by which *Gone with the Wind* is still being judged here and elsewhere.

The opposite of popularity is exclusiveness. In a democratic bourgeois society, elites who seek to maintain a distinct identity must reach for their rationales. The better-off have received some exposure to the university, where, at least since the time of Veblen or of Henry Adams's *Education,* one keynote has been an affectation of irony, a tone that is a complex of intimacy, servility, and disguised arrogance. When the irony becomes cosmic, as in the case of the world view elaborated by the Modernism of Eliot, Auden, and Huxley, we find a self-exile to greener wastelands from which to behold the mob:

> No one of them was capable of lying,
> There was not one which knew that it was dying
> Or could have with a rhythm or a rhyme
> Assumed responsibility for time.
>> [W. H. Auden, "Their Lonely Betters"]

As long as such ironic attitudes toward even irony itself prevail in the modern academy, mere college-educated book reviewers will always leave the scenes of their encounters with narrative power and unsurpassed readability confessing that it was no big deal. And we who teach will be left to ponder why the Great Books we offer in their place so often seem to our students like instruments of oppression.

Notes

1. *New York Times Book Review*, July 19, 1936. *Gone with the Wind* impressed Adams so deeply that he continued to write about it for the next twenty-five years: in

NYTBR, August 28, 1949, he quotes MM's letters on the writing of the novel; on June 24, 1956, he notes its phenomenal success; and on July 23, 1961, he defends it in a letter against its critics.

2. *New York Times Book Review,* November 1, 1936, p. 7. Cf. Clifton Fadiman's observation that Faulkner had invented "the Non-Stop, or Life, Sentence" a method of "Anti-Narrative, a set of complex devices used to keep the story from being told." See J. W. Matthews, "The Civil War of 1936: *GWTW* and *Absalom, Absalom!*," *Georgia Review* 21 (1967): 462–69.

3. F. R. Leavis, *Mass Civilization and Minority Culture* (Cambridge, England: The Minority Press, 1930), pp. 3–5.

4. Watkins takes more direct aim in "*GWTW* as Vulgar Literature," *Southern Literary Journal* 2 (1970): 86–103, where he observes, for example, that the novel is factually wrong concerning the rate at which baled cotton burns.

Gone with the Wind as Art |

After the initial round of reviews in 1936 and 1937, *Gone with the Wind* almost disappeared from highbrow literary consciousness in the United States—except as a negative reference point. Bernard DeVoto's assessment, as cited by Dwyer, conquered the field: "The size of its public is impressive; the book is not." In this context, questions of how the novel works as art became irrelevant. They were indeed rarely asked. Yet by the early seventies, and with increasing frequency as the decade progressed, the novel's art became a lively topic of debate in academic circles.

How does *Gone with the Wind* work stylistically? How does it function structurally? Where does it fit into literary history or the history of the novel? What are the sources of its dramatic power? Is there any relationship between its literary merit and its popularity? Is it a legitimate part of the Southern Renaissance of the 1920s and 1930s? The record is almost blank. The essays in this section propose some answers to these questions.

Few people know *Gone with the Wind* more intimately than Richard Harwell. He edited Margaret Mitchell's letters, the film script of *Gone with the Wind,* and other documents relating to the novel and the film; he has also served as curator of the Mitchell manuscripts at the University of Georgia. His essay in this volume is an examination of Margaret Mitchell's literary style.

One of the general literary criticisms of the novel is that the work *has* no style. A related assumption is that its author, an Atlanta housewife, whipped off the manuscript between stints of housecleaning and dishwashing. By examining Mitchell's personal biography, literary reviews, and the novel itself, Harwell suggests that both assumptions are misguided. However apparently artless the writing in *Gone with the Wind,* Harwell argues, this was the very effect for which its author strove and she achieved it only through a disciplined, professional sense of the writing craft. Belying the fable of the lucky housewife, the creation of *Gone with the Wind,* according to Harwell, was no more than the culmination of Mitchell's lifetime commitment to writing, as well as the product of native gifts. Finally, in analyzing Mitchell's personal style, Harwell reveals much about the author's character and personality that informs the values in the novel itself.

Helen Deiss Irvin takes on another of the most persistent critical

33

objections to *Gone with the Wind,* its ostensible lack of content. Most generally, scholars seem to have accepted Miss Mitchell at her word when she insisted that she was simply spinning a tale without any meaning beyond the surface narrative. Whether or not Mitchell consciously intended it, however, the novel does possess a sub-structure of myths and images. These, according to Irvin, are based on both the form and the content of the classic myth of the great Earth Mother.

Irvin suggests for *Gone with the Wind* a thesis that David Williams has recently applied to the greatest writer of the American South in his *Faulkner's Women: The Myth and the Muse.* Williams argues that Faulkner repudiated both Christianity and Apollonian or Olympian values in favor of devotion to the mystery cult of the Great Goddess or the force of the Archetypal Feminine. Represented in various forms in history and mythology—Kore, Demeter, Hebe, Hecate, Isis, the Holy Mother—the Great Goddess always possessed dual characteristics: she was the source of life but the repository of death, the nurturer but also the avenger. In Williams's treatment, Faulkner's characters—and even Faulkner himself as artist—are compelled to acknowledge the irrational combination of life and death embodied in the form of the Eternal Female.

Irvin finds the same forces at work in Margaret Mitchell's novel. Earth is the primal force who consistently renews and vitalizes her devotees. Mitchell compares Scarlett specifically to Antaeus, who regained his strength each time he touched his mother; but Irvin also finds the content as well as the forms of the myth throughout the novel—for example, in Scarlett's collapse and renewal in the garden patch at Twelve Oaks after Sherman's passage. Within this structure, Mitchell's Earth punishes heretics and disbelievers, as well, however. All of the characters stand or fall by Earth's measure.

All this touches upon another problem in *Gone with the Wind* which Williams's work may help to illuminate. Even when they acknowledge the authority of the "Great Goddess," Faulkner's novels are determinedly masculine and generally avoid the female perspective. They are structured naturally around the theme of the accommodation of a male character's reason or masculine abstraction to the feminine presence. Lucius Apuleius's odyssey in *The Golden Ass* is one of the earliest literary models for this kind of structure.

34

What happens to this natural form, however, when the primary character is not a Lucius but a Lucia, when the point of view is as insistently female in *Gone with the Wind* as it is male in Faulkner? Perhaps the amorality on the one hand or the ambivalence on the other for which critics have often faulted the novel are actually dictated or structured into the work by the logic of the female point of view toward the life-and-death mysteries of the Great Goddess.

While Irvin does not address this issue, she does suggest (insofar as the images of Earth Mother mythology relate to universals within the human experience) that Mitchell's reliance on this mythic substructure might offer one key to understanding the fundamental appeal of the novel and to appreciating it fully.

James Michener, one of the greatest living practitioners of the popular epic novel, has a different context from Harwell's or Irvin's for understanding the work. As does Harwell, he begins with a defense of Mitchell's style, her craft, and her discipline and professionalism. His main point, however, is to suggest that *Gone with the Wind* is best appreciated in the tradition of the great nineteenth-century European novelists. In this regard, he echoes the nearly universal opinion of the first reviewers, even Malcolm Cowley. He compares *Gone with the Wind* with Thackeray's *Vanity Fair,* Flaubert's *Madame Bovary,* and Tolstoy's *Anna Karenina,* and he finds that Mitchell's fiction holds up well even in this distinguished company. Although he criticizes Mitchell for her restricted social vision, particularly in regard to Negro emancipation, he returns to the observation of John Crowe Ransom and insists that Mitchell actually excels these other authors "in her ability to devise and control intricate dramatic structure."

Like Cowley and Irvin, Michener finds themes about women crucial in understanding all four works. Arguing that the development of "a new type of heroine" in rebellious conflict with traditional society is the principal motive in each work, he proposes that this is a common source of their merit as artistic and cultural documents. In this regard, he insists that, of the four, it was Mitchell who created the female rebel "who lives most vividly and with the greatest contemporary application."

This insight relates to the theme of the essay by Louis Rubin, Jr., one of the premier critics of the Southern Renaissance. He begins

35

by setting the novel within Southern history and society. His specific point of reference is William Faulkner's *Absalom, Absalom!*, which contains striking parallels to Mitchell's novel. In this comparison Rubin is especially critical of Mitchell's specific detail of the regional past. Like Michener, he faults her treatment of black people and Reconstruction. Like Commager, however, who also notes the falseness in the book, Rubin insists that, in the final analysis, Mitchell's errors of historical emphasis are irrelevant. For him, Mitchell's Civil War is only a stage setting for "a very modern heroine dressed in lace and crinolines," and it is through Scarlett O'Hara that the novel achieves its historical authenticity—and more. The novel becomes historically true insofar as this "very modern heroine" represents or personifies what individual Southerners, and the whole region, did after the war.

This relates to an even more universal appeal and meaning. Scarlett represents not only the Southern response to one historical episode but what "middle class, democratic capitalistic society always does." By this measure, the character becomes a kind of female, bourgeois Everyman. Moreover, Rubin maintains that the work is psychologically authentic as well. He argues that the sense of loss and frustration that pervades the novel relates to the generalized sense of regret or "ambivalence about doing what we have to do instead of what we have been taught we should do." While beginning with the South and heroines, Rubin moves beyond them in his conclusion: *Absalom, Absalom!* and *Gone with the Wind* are tales that are both in and of the South but that speak most fundamentally to universals within the human condition.

The concluding essay of this section, Anne Jones's "'The Bad Little Girl of the Good Old Days'," is also concerned, as Michener's and Rubin's are, with the "new type of heroine." Rubin sees this interpretation as a means of understanding bourgeois culture in general, but Jones's focus is on regional society, specifically its peculiar emphasis upon sex and gender. Her theme resonates with Irvin's. Where Irvin finds female archetypes at the mythic core of the novel, Jones finds gender or sexual themes equally pervasive on the surface of the work. She argues that rigidly defined sexual roles and gender restrictions constitute an obsession within the narrative and characterization. As they relate to the realities of the Southern so-

36

cial order, these roles and restrictions provide the most consistent source of social and psychological identity, but also of conflict, in the work. Jones's essay is an examination of the meaning of the internal and external gender constraints described by Mitchell.

Margaret Mitchell had not read *Vanity Fair* when she wrote her book, and she did not know Thackeray's double-edged subtitle, *A Novel without a Hero.* But Jones suggests, in effect, that Mitchell's characters live the ambivalence of Thackeray's irony. Her males are prohibited perfectly heroic status because they are all ultimately dependent upon women; her women are likewise denied heroic action because of the public/male definition of heroism. Within a rigid regional framework of social and gender distinctions, life becomes a trap, and one of the sources of dramatic action and psychological tension in the novel is the characters' efforts to accommodate or transcend these limits, to establish their personalistic integrity while maintaining their social identity. The task is morally, psychologically, and physically debilitating for them. In Mitchell's Southern setting, to be a "new type of heroine," hardly less the new type of hero, has fatal consequences. Whereas Rubin ends with an essentially optimistic reading, for Jones the novel documents fictionally the historic inability of the Southern social order to absorb new sources of action and modes of behavior.

In August of 1936 a Midwesterner who described himself as a glue salesman wrote a fan letter to Margaret Mitchell. Like thousands of others of her correspondents he had just read *Gone with the Wind* and wanted to share his enthusiasm for the novel with its author. His letter stands out among the hundreds that Miss Mitchell was receiving daily at that time. The glue salesman was a bit more than that; he and his brother owned the manufacturing company for which he traveled. More importantly, he was Morris H. Williams who, as Billy Williams, had known Peggy Mitchell while she was a freshman at Smith College in 1918–19. Mr. Williams wrote:

> I recall that many years ago you said to me in Northampton, "when I get through here, I'm going to find out if I really can write." I must confess that I thought it was the usual youthful phase, and that it would be forgotten soon enough. But where did you ever develop such a style, and such an intimate knowledge of the cerebral processes of both sexes? It's terrifying.[1]

Williams briefly reviewed his career in the years since his college days. He had had a more typical experience than hers in finding out whether or not he could really write. "I tried my hand at writing several years ago," he said, "had two gags published in Life, a letter in . . . Liberty . . . and 1750 rejection slips. I guess you either have it or you don't." He closed his letter asking for more novels from Miss Mitchell: "No matter how much the success of *Gone with the Wind* may have flabbergasted you, none of this 'never again' stuff. I'm looking forward to your next one with eagerness."[2]

She said in her reply: "Your 'voice from the dim past' brought back vividly the last time I saw you in 1919 in Northampton. We sat on the steps of the boathouse in a driving rain and the rain sloshed down the steps in a Niagara upon us. How primitive were the dating facilities at Smith College! I remember too we were both young and a little forlorn in that queer aftermath of the War."[3]

There are few records of Margaret Mitchell's schoolgirl days. A few grade school report cards escaped the general destruction of her personal, private papers that she requested of the executors of

This essay originally appeared in *Atlanta Historical Journal* 25 (Summer 1981): 21–38.

her will. And there are her entrance papers for Smith; not many southern girls went to Smith in those days and her application was made on a Randolph-Macon Woman's College form with the college's name changed in ink. Smith did—and does—pride itself on being the equal of any Ivy League college in its curriculum and not just another school for young ladies. But the most blue-stockinged feminist college would not have intimidated the youngster from Atlanta.

A lady who was, briefly, her roommate says in an unpublished recollection of Peggy Mitchell's days in Northampton [written in 1939]:

> During the last months of the World War, Peggy arrived at Smith as a freshman. . . . "Scarlett O'Hara was not beautiful, but men seldom realized it when caught by her charm." That sentence which starts off the grand, exciting story of *Gone with the Wind* gives you an excellent idea of Peggy as I first saw her in 1918. . . .
>
> Unlike Scarlett, the Mitchell charm extended definitely beyond men and she promptly became the most popular girl in the house. The rest of us were awed by the bulk of her overseas mail and enslaved by her sense of humor which was considerably broader than you'd expect to find in a frail flower of the South. Moreover, we respected her scorn for campus rules. . . .
>
> We were all movie fans, cutting classes to see the latest pictures starring Charlie Ray, Norma Talmadge or Wallace Reid. And one evening every week was put aside for play-going at the local stock company where the dangerously irresistible leading man was one William Powell. . . . Ah, but that was many years before the same smooth Powell became a candidate to play Rhett! In the evenings, no one ever thought of studying. Instead, there was usually S.R.O. in our room, listening to Peggy talk—for she was then, and is today, an even better talker than writer—so you can imagine the A quality of the conversation which ranged somewhere between the standards of Noel Coward and the Marx Brothers.
>
> When topics took more serious turns, you could pretty safely depend that Peggy would get them around somehow to the Civil War, for her indignation over Sherman's March to the Sea was just as much a part of her as her [flashing] eyes or her joyful laugh. She would sling you off a well-rounded tabloid description of the Second Battle of Bull Run with the same eager sparkle that another girl might tell you

about last night's bridge hand. . . . Whenever she got mad enough at her roommate to call me a "Damn Yankee," I knew our home life was threatened!

But suddenly the grim realities of a war close at hand engulfed Peggy in their tragedy, just as that other war trapped Scarlett. Her fiance was killed in France an ironically short time before the Armistice and she had scarcely comprehended that stunning blow before she was called home early in 1919 by the death of her mother, a victim of the influenza epidemic.

At the end of her freshman year, Peggy left college to keep house for her father and brother, both Atlanta lawyers, in the [family home] on Peachtree Street which looks like nothing so much as Tara on a street-car line. But no one could ever picture Peggy content with a sewing basket and a bunch of keys to the linen closet, and before long she was feature-writing for the *Atlanta Journal.* . . .[4]

Miss Mitchell included in her letter to Billy Williams in September 1936:

For my own present history—I did not finish at Smith, as my mother died and I had to come home and keep house for my father. I made my debut here in Atlanta shortly afterwards, ate chicken salad for a year, had a big time and then got a job as a reporter on the Atlanta Journal. I married in 1925. My husband is John R. Marsh, a former newspaper man but now Manager of the Advertising Department of the Georgia Power Company. We have no children. Due to a number of mishaps and accidents, mostly automobile accidents, my health was not very good and I was forced to give up reporting. I started *Gone with the Wind* when I had a broken ankle and couldn't walk. I finished it several years ago and never even tried to sell it. Therefore you can imagine my complete consternation when an editor came along, dug it up, published it and made a best seller of it.[5]

The world knows it was not the publisher who made a best seller of *Gone with the Wind.* It was the story and characters and the hard work Margaret Mitchell put into writing it that made it a best seller. The book became a part of the America of her generation, and—book and film—*GWTW* continues to be a large and delectable slice of Americana for each succeeding generation.

One of Margaret Mitchell's teachers at Washington Seminary, Atlanta's fine and fashionable girls' school of her time, was Mrs. Eva Wilson Paisley. By the time *GWTW* was published Mrs. Paisley was living in North Lovell, Maine. In October 1936 she wrote her reactions to her pupil's book:

> Before I opened the covers I knew I would find straightforward thinking and great dramatic quality, but I was unprepared for the exquisitely fine perceptions of light and shade against which the characters stand out so sharply. My little girl, you have worked hard and done a lot of long thinking.

She added:

> I remember in the old days of English II & III, when you and Courtenay [Ross] used to sit at my right elbow in the long narrow classroom down stairs—and not always as attentive as I could have wished—something your mother said. She had come out to the Seminary to see one of the other teachers and stopped to talk with me. "Margaret puzzles me. I don't know whether she is headed for success or failure, but in any event she will be her own honest self." I wish she might know how well you have been that honest thinking self.[6]

To this Miss Mitchell replied:

> Although I have had hundreds of letters in varying hand writings, when I saw your letter my heart stopped a beat and I was once more a student at Washington Seminary. Only the last time I saw your handwriting it was in red ink on the margin of a theme which I thought showed authentic genius. But your note remarked tersely that after three years I had not absorbed even the elements of unity and coherence. While as for emphasis and proportion, I would not know them if I met them in the road.
>
> I have had you on my mind for many months. Ever since I sold the book I have wanted to write you and thank you for all you did for me, but from the time the book was sold until now, I have worked like a galley slave, sometimes twenty hours a day, for weeks and weeks, but back in the back of my mind was the memory of how hard you had labored over me and how unappreciative I must have seemed to you. So often when I was writing and rewriting, I suddenly thought, "This, then, is what Mrs. Paisley meant by unity. This is what she meant by

sentence balance." So many things you used to try to pound through
my thick skull became so very clear. I wonder how you ever had the
patience to put up with me. I recall that Mother frequently expressed that same thought. . . .

Praise from you is just about the highest praise I can get. You will
never know how hard I used to struggle to get praise from you. Now
I thank the Lord that you were sparing of it for it would have ruined
me. I recall my sense of shock when I went to college and a good-
hearted professor proclaimed me a youthful genius on the strength
of the world's worst theme. I knew it was a rotten theme. I knew she
should have realized how rotten it was. Most of all, I knew you would
have realized it and would have read it before the class with appropriate remarks about just how bad it was. So I didn't have any respect
at all for her and I learned precious little from her.[7]

On New Year's Day 1937 Mrs. Paisley wrote a long, chatty letter
in which she noted:

Only one thing concerns me in your great success. When the sales
begin to go down, as they must sometime, your publishers will be on
your trail. Let them cool their heels! *Gone with the Wind* is a piece of
dramatic perfection. Don't ever let me hear of your being persuaded
to follow it up in any way [with a sequel]. After a few years—and
remember this book has taken far more than the "ten years" of the
reviews—you will write another great book. And you will begin to
think about it now.[8]

The novelist's brother, Stephens Mitchell, a veteran Atlanta lawyer as expert in his own field as his sister was in hers, recalls: "Margaret began to write stories as soon as her fingers could guide a pencil and join letters into words. She didn't wait to be able to spell.
The stories were forming fast in her head. As soon as she finished
one she started another." He points out that writing was her main
diversion, not a device to show off but a method of entertaining
herself and those she loved. In this sense, says Mr. Mitchell, her
childhood efforts "were written in exactly the same spirit as she
wrote *Gone with the Wind*."

"The stories," he says, "were written on little school tablets, the
first ones in pencil, later ones in ink. Mother read them and put
them away in a large, white-enamelled breadbox. I don't know how

43

soon the first bread-box was filled, but by the time Margaret went off to college there was an imposing row of bread-boxes on a shelf in the storeroom. She never stopped writing."[9]

When the family moved into a new house on Peachtree there were spacious rooms which opened into areas big enough for staging plays. Margaret turned her hand to writing dramas in which the neighborhood children played out the roles she created. Concerning one of these, she wrote Thomas Dixon in August 1936 in answer to a letter from the author of *The Clansman*, the book from which "The Birth of a Nation" was adapted:

> For many years I have had you on my conscience, and I suppose I might as well confess it now. When I was eleven years old I decided that I would dramatize your book "The Traitor"—and dramatize it I did in six acts. I played the part of Steve because none of the little boys in the neighborhood would lower themselves to play a part where they had to "kiss any little ol' girl." The clansmen were recruited from the small-fry of the neighborhood, their ages ranging from five to eight. They were dressed in the shirts of their fathers, with the shirt tails bobbed off. I had my troubles with the clansmen as, after Act 2, they went on strike, demanding a ten cent wage instead of a five cent one. Then, too, just as I was about to be hanged, two of the clansmen had to go to the bathroom, necessitating a dreadful stage wait which made the audience scream with delight, but which mortified me intensely. My mother was out of town at the time. On her return, she and father, a lawyer, gave me a long lecture on infringement of copy-rights. They gave me such a lecture that for years afterward I expected Mr. Thomas Dixon to sue me for a million dollars, and I have had a great respect for copy-rights ever since then.[10]

Margaret Mitchell many times pointed out that while *Gone with the Wind* took over ten years from first putting words on paper to publication, most of it was written by 1929 and that work on it after 1928 was sporadic and mostly rewriting. Mrs. Paisley was right, however. The origins of the book were far older than ten years. In an appreciative letter thanking Henry Steele Commager for his fine review which caught the essence of the book's theme in a key paragraph about survival, Miss Mitchell wrote, "How happy I was that you were impressed enough by Rhett's remarks about the upside-down world to quote them in full. For in that paragraph lies the genesis of my book and the genesis lies years back when I was six years old and those words minus the reference to Ashley Wilkes were said to me." She told Mr. Commager how her mother had impressed on her the value of an education as a woman's tool for survival. "I never could learn the multiplication tables above the sevens," she wrote, "but I was frightened and impressed enough by her words to learn enough rhetoric to land a job on a newspaper some years later."[11]

Her stories, her plays, her themes at Washington Seminary and at Smith prepared her for her job on the *Atlanta Journal* that began in December 1922. There, writing for the Sunday magazine and doing occasional feature stories for the daily paper, was her real training ground. Part of her training, probably a very important part, came through self-imposed discipline during her and John Marsh's courtship. Marsh was a graduate of the University of Kentucky and had taught English there before serving in World War I and then moving to Atlanta and a copyediting job on the *Atlanta Georgian*. The two became friends before Margaret joined Atlanta's circle of young and ambitious newspaper people. After she went to work for the *Journal*, Marsh reviewed article after article printed in the magazine section, criticizing each with the eyes of English teacher and copyeditor. It takes a firm friendship to survive such a test, but their friendship grew into courtship and, in July 1925, into marriage. Margaret worked about a year longer on the paper, resigned because of recurring ill-health, and then read herself into boredom to such an extent that she began in 1926 to put on paper the novel that had been formulating in her mind since 1907 when her mother drove her along "the road to Tara" and explained to the six-year-old girl Rhett Butler's philosophy of survival.

William S. Howland's assessment of Peggy Mitchell as a good reporter is widely known. Her boss on the *Journal Sunday Magazine*, Angus Perkerson, called her "one of the best reporters I have ever seen" and compared her to such well known *Journal* staffers as Ward Greene, Ward Morehouse, and William B. Seabrook.[12] At the *Journal* she was a veteran when Erskine Caldwell worked there as a beginner. Just how good she was was spelled out in *Scribner's* in October 1936 by Elinor Hillyer, then on the staff of *Delineator.* Miss Hillyer had been a schoolmate of Peggy's and took over her job on the paper when she left it. As she described it,

> Peggy Mitchell had just decamped from the *Atlanta Journal* when I came to inherit her desk, typewriter (Underwood antique) and an impossible standard. As rookie reporter and feature writer, I was told to get out files of the last year, read the Mitchell efforts and go and write likewise. Of course nobody ever really stepped into her shoes, and on his bad days, the editor [Perkerson] would tear his hair and yell "If only Peggy Mitchell were here to make a silk purse out of a sow's ear of a story."[13]

In her short career on the *Journal* Margaret Mitchell became a competent newspaper woman. In the ten years between leaving her job on the paper and the publication of *Gone with the Wind* she became a very competent writer indeed. She wrote that *GWTW* could have been written in "a fairly short while, had I had uninterrupted time," but what beginning novelist has uninterrupted time? She undoubtedly put the interruptions to good use as thinking time and spent much of her stretched-out writing time in rewriting and revising. She wrote thankfully in answer to a letter from Stark Young in which he "disclaimed the 'ease in writing'" which she had attributed to him. "I had thought," she declared, "that only luckless beginners like myself had to rewrite endlessly, tear up and throw away whole chapters, start afresh, rewrite and throw away again." She continued in a typical hyperbole:

> I knew nothing about other writers and their working habits and I thought I was the only writer in the world who went through such goings on. After I had written a chapter ten or twelve times and had what I thought was a workable "first draft," I'd put it away for a month. When I dug it out again I'd beat on my breast and snatch out my hair, because it was so lousy. Then the chapter would be thrown away, because the content of it had not been reduced to the complete simplicity I wanted. Simplicity of ideas, of construction, of

words. Then there would be another awful month of substituting Anglo-Saxon derivatives for Latin ones, simple sentence constructions
for the more cumbersome Latin constructions.[14]

And she wrote to a correspondent in Rhode Island:

There are many parts of my book which I will never be able to read
because I become sick with the memory of the number of times I re-
wrote them. One chapter for instance was re-written seventy times,
many chapters at least thirty times. I do not write with ease, nor am I
ever pleased with anything I write. And so, I re-write. There are,
however, a few chapters which never were altered from the first way
in which they were set down. If you are interested, I made no change
in the text from page 398, when Scarlett is struggling home to Tara,
to page 421, when she decided to take up her load and carry it. There
were a few other passages which I did not change. For the most part
however, the book was sweated over.[15]

The last chapter of *Gone with the Wind* was the first written.
After that Miss Mitchell worked on her story at whatever point she
chose, having already set its conclusion and having the whole tale
firmly in her mind. Its beginning gave her much pause and the first
chapter as it appears in *Gone with the Wind* was written after she
had decided to let Macmillan's Harold Latham read her manuscript
and even then there was still one unbridged gap—getting Frank
Kennedy out of the story and Scarlett married to Rhett Butler. To
achieve this, Miss Mitchell wrote two versions, one in which Frank
died of pneumonia and the other in which he was killed in the raid
on Shantytown, and submitted both to her editors. They naturally
chose the more dramatic version.

Another part of her work done after the manuscript had been accepted for publication was the careful verification of facts that had
been written from a remarkably good memory. As Evelyn Scott
pointed out in her review in *The Nation:* "Margaret Mitchell gives
us our Civil War through Southern eyes exclusively, and no tolerant
philosophy illumines the crimes of the invaders; she writes with the
bias of passionate regionalism, but the veritable happenings described eloquently justify prejudice." [16] *Gone with the Wind* was in

effect that mythical desideratum of southerners, "an unbiased history of the war from the Confederate point of view." It thereby has an independent importance as an accurate record of what the children and grandchildren of the Confederates believed. History is subject to revision by each new generation, but how these first two generations after the Civil War viewed it is as much fact—and almost as influential—as the events of the war itself. Revisionists can alter their own views but they can no more alter the views of the past than they can alter the facts of the past.

A third task was the honing of her style in a final revision. And the last, of course, was a massive job of reading edited copy and proof.

Book reviewers have little space to waste. They must get to the point. The point of *Gone with the Wind* was, and is, its gripping story. An assessment of its style was secondary. Often it was not mentioned and when it was, the care that Margaret Mitchell had lavished on making her style as simple as possible, on avoiding the appearance of being a stylist, on controlling her writing so that it never impedes her story was generally overlooked. The winter after *GWTW* was published she wrote to Olin Miller, a veteran Georgia newspaperman:

> How much I thank you for what you said about my sentence structure and the rhythm of it. You cannot imagine what balm your words were to me. So many critics have said nice things about my plot, narrative and characters, and then they finish off with remarks about my "undistinguished style," or they say the story gets across in spite of the way it was written. I do not mean that I am not grateful for the nice things they wrote about characters et cetera, but I did work so hard on the style. I wanted it to be simple enough for a child of five to understand, and I did not want the style to intrude upon the story. I worked to secure a style which I called "Colloquial" for want of any other term. I have a fairly good ear for voices and the intonations of voices, and it has always seemed to me that there is beauty and poetry in the Georgia voice and the Georgia way of expressing things. It shows up even in the conversation of people who have little or no formal education. I thought, as I was writing a book about Georgia people, that I would write it in the style a Georgian would use in speaking the story. I do not mean just in conversation but in the ex-

48

pository parts as well. To this end I labored, frequently shifting words and making sentences somewhat ungrammatical, but shifting them just the same because to my inner ear the accent of a Georgian's voice would fall at that place.[17]

Miss Mitchell magnified the lack of critical response to the style of *Gone with the Wind.* Its first recorded critic, Professor Charles W. Everett of the English Department of Columbia University who gave the manuscript a professional reading at the request of the Macmillan Company, emphasized one of the points noted by Mr. Miller. "It has a high degree of literary finish," he wrote. ". . . It is perhaps in this control of tempo that the book is most impressive. When the writer wants things to seem slow, timeless, eternal, that is the way they move. But her prestissimo is prestissimo, and her fortissimo is FFF."[18]

When *GWTW* came before the professional reviewers, they quite rightly emphasized the narrative power of the novel, but its style was certainly not unnoticed. Joseph Henry Jackson, the first newspaper reviewer to write of it, said in his book column in the *San Francisco Chronicle*:

As for its literary quality, you will be surprised to see, when you read this book, how its simplicity will affect you. Miss Mitchell's directness, her sensible avoidance of "literary" tricks, have a cumulative effect, so to speak. They pile up on you. And you won't be very far along in the book before you realize that this frank, honest storytelling is impressing you far more than all the fine writing that the more consciously artistic novelists sometimes attempt. Indeed, one New York critic, for whose judgement I have the greatest respect, said to me a day or two ago that he believed that this was at last the great American novel people have been waiting for.[19]

(Jackson deserves some sort of special award for prescience. In that column datelined "New York, May 9," seven weeks before *Gone with the Wind*'s publication date, he declared: "Without doubt, 'Gone with the Wind' is already being read and considered in Hollywood. If it isn't, some enterprising producer had better get after it in a hurry. I don't believe I ever read a novel of which I was more certain that it had in it not only the makings of a best seller, but a genuinely magnificent motion picture.")

Aaron Bernd wrote in the *Macon Telegraph*:

> In a sense, Gone with the Wind is an old-fashioned novel. It gives the reader no mental work to do—each person and place is set out in detail. The Hemingway and Faulkner devotees who have tortured their brains figuring out relationships and picturing personalities, will find relief in a straight forward narrative.[20]

Edwin Granberry raised a question in his review in the *New York Sun:* "This book is going to give a lot of novelists much to think about. . . . Could it be possible that it might make it difficult hereafter for the pinched, strangulated novel which pays more attention to manner than to matter?"[21] On this score Miss Mitchell commented in a letter of July 11, 1936, to Dr. Mark Allen Patton: "When I sit down to read I don't want to have to read about muddled minds even if the muddled minds *are* muddling along in lovely prose!"[22]

Margaret Mitchell's letter to Dr. Patton was in response to one to her complaining about some of Fanny Butcher's remarks in the *Chicago Tribune.* He took offense at Miss Butcher's comparing unfavorably *Gone with the Wind* to *War and Peace*! In her lead paragraph Miss Butcher noted: "It [*Gone with the Wind*] is everything that a truly great book should be except stylistically great." Later in her review she wrote:

> If Miss Mitchell had the genius of Tolstoi, "Gone with the Wind" would have been a literary classic destined to be read as long as any one reads English as "War and Peace" must always be a part of any rich literary knowledge. She writes with great skill, infinite patience, a sense of what has a place and what hasn't in her narrative. The book is fascinating and unforgettable. But it is not the work of a real genius, and to give the reader [as nothing in the book or in its dust-jacket does] the impression that he is to find another "War and Peace" is to be unfair to the author.[23]

What more praise could an author want of a first novel? Miss Mitchell, sensibly, did not take umbrage, as Dr. Patton did, but wrote Miss Butcher a very appreciative letter of thanks.

Malcolm Cowley, in the 1930s an angry young man of letters instead of the dean of American critics he later became, did not care
for *Gone with the Wind* and made that fact very plain in an article
in the *New Republic.* He called *GWTW* "an encyclopedia of the
plantation legend" and declared:

> Miss Mitchell lends new strength to the legend by telling it as if it had
> never been told before, and also by mixing a good share of realism
> with the romance. She writes with a splendid recklessness. . . . In the
> midst of triteness and sentimentality her book has a simple-minded
> courage that suggests the great novelists of the past.[24]

Kenneth A. Fowler, whose reviews were published in a number
of suburban New York papers, wrote:

> A few of the commentators on "Gone with the Wind" have men-
> tioned its style as "undistinguished." We should like to say to that if,
> to provide a book as absorbing and exciting as this, it is necessary to
> give it an "undistinguished style," we are all for more of this kind of
> style in American letters. As a matter of fact, Miss Mitchell's style is
> deceptive—so simple and smooth-flowing that, lulled by its very per-
> fection, one may easily overlook many passages of exceptional merit.
>   In sum, a superb new story-teller has arrived to prove to American
> letters that pure narration is not a lost art, and this, her first book,
> bears a striking resemblance to a masterpiece.[25]

Eugene Mitchell, the author's father, said what should have been
the last word about his daughter's style—but, of course, wasn't.
Miss Mitchell quoted him in her response to Dr. Patton: "'What do
they mean, "undistinguished style"? Good heavens, I can actually
understand every word you write without having to read it twice!
In this day and time that amounts to sheer genius!'"[26]

Harold Latham took Margaret Mitchell's massive manuscript with
him when he left Atlanta in April 1935. When he arrived in New
Orleans the day after she gave it to him, a telegram from her was
waiting for him: "Send it back, I've changed my mind."[27] Mr. Latham
had started reading the manuscript on the train. He was already
convinced he had something important and the draft did not go
back to Mitchell until early August, after a contract for its publica-

tion had been signed. Then came six months of the hard work of revision. She later wrote Stark Young: "Before I went to press I snatched out double hand fulls of copy, whole chapters. Snatched them out under such pressure that I didn't have time to tie up the severed arteries. In my eyes the book will bleed endlessly and reproachfully." [28] The manuscript was finished and typed for the printer on January 22, 1936, but the author insisted that her father have the privilege of reading it before it went to New York for publication. By January 27 Mr. Mitchell had read his daughter's work and the manuscript was in the mails for New York.

An author's work seems never to be done. Margaret Mitchell now had a careful and conscientious copy-editor's work to approve. The copy-editor was a lady with a name that could have been straight out of Dickens, Susan Prink. Miss Prink did not know Southern speech and was not aware, at first, of the careful ways in which Miss Mitchell had used varying dialects and sometimes unorthodox punctuation to achieve the effects she desired. There began an adversary relationship which was annoying to an author who had been a good and careful editor of her own material. Mr. Latham wrote: "Margaret knew her business; she had her facts; there was little that required attention in the copy that she delivered for typesetting." [29]

Margaret Mitchell was a great conversationalist and a brilliant raconteur. She could make a good story out of the tiniest incident and she delighted the Macon Writers Club in a pre-publication speech in April 1936 with her tales of how *Gone with the Wind* came into being. Of her contests over copy-editing she told, according to Marian Elder Jones, how she had to fight with the editors and proofreaders to get them to leave things as she had put them down. She recounted some of her struggles to keep the Southern customs, costumes, speech just as she had them. Proofs came back, she said, with such words as cape jasmine, sweet potatoes, and lemon verbena hyphenated; there were thousands of colons where she had none. There were arguments about subjunctives, split infinitives, and dangling participles. "Finally the battle was a draw and I got half the colons out, kept six infinitives, and they won on the dangling participles." [30]

All arguments were settled and all proof returned by mid-March.

52

The book which had first been announced for publication on April 21 at $2.50 was now expected to be ready in May and to sell at $3.00 (or at $2.75 until the official publication date of May 31). On April 15 the Book of the Month Club agreed to make *GWTW* "an early selection" and soon settled on July as the month for distributing it to its members. By then Macmillan's executives were sure they had a record breaker on their hands. Publication date was pushed back to June 30 and a larger than usual quota of review copies was distributed. The first printing was 10,000 copies. (It is marked "Published May 1936" on the back of the title page.) There were two more printings in June, plus the book club's own printing, so that by publication date *Gone with the Wind* was already a best seller.

Its further history needs no elaboration here. It has been praised by countless reviewers, attacked by the devotees of higher criticism, and enjoyed by readers in six decades. *Gone with the Wind* is probably the most widely read—and loved—novel ever written. Its popularity has at last—hesitantly in the late sixties, more assuredly in the seventies—caused the critics to reassess it. Their new look convinces them that *Gone with the Wind* has more breadth and depth than they once perceived, something the public knew all along. It now begins to fall into the clutches of the explicators. It is a good guess that *Gone with the Wind* will survive the investigations and explanations of the explicators as happily as Margaret Mitchell parried the forays of Susan Prink.

Mrs. Paisley wrote her own novel, *Sanctuary,* after *Gone with the Wind* was published. The younger author wrote the newer one in a Christmas note in 1940:

> I read Sanctuary and loved it, not only for the content but because so many phrases and turns of thought brought your voice back to me as clearly as if I were in a one armed desk at the Seminary. For you did not teach only unity, coherence, emphasis and proportion, you taught the fortitude of the human mind, the bottomless resources of the spirit. They are in your book and I cherish them and your book.[31]

They were also in Margaret Mitchell. And in her book.

What is important to the world about Margaret Mitchell is her book. It continues to captivate new generations of readers. Stephen Vincent Benét described *Gone with the Wind* as "like the books one reads when one is young" in which the characters take hold and make the story go on and on in the reader's mind.[32] Each reader, perhaps, composes his own sequel. This reader still feels roughly like the bookseller in Nashville (and booksellers are hard readers to please) who wrote Margaret Mitchell weeks before *GWTW*'s publication date:

> Finished the book last night and when I tried to read the morning paper I couldn't; it seemed not to matter, to be unreal. I have lived in Atlanta, Georgia, during the war and Reconstruction for the past week and can't begin to feel that anything else is important yet. The world without Melanie is a desolate place and I wonder where Rhett is and what he is doing. I seem to know that Scarlett is making the most of Tara but I can't help knowing that she feels desolate when the moon shines and the mockingbirds sing.[33]

Notes

1. Williams to Mitchell, ALS, 2 p., Conneaut, Ohio, August 25, 1936. This and all other manuscript materials referred to in this article are in the Margaret Mitchell Marsh Papers in the University of Georgia Libraries, Athens. The letters by Margaret Mitchell are quoted with the permission of Stephens Mitchell.

2. Ibid.

3. Mitchell to Williams, TL (copy), 2 p., Atlanta, Ga., September 3, 1936.

4. Virginia (Morris) Nixon, unpublished typescript, pp. 2–3 (filed under Morris).

5. Mitchell to Williams, TL (copy), 2 p., Atlanta, Ga., September 3, 1936.

6. Paisley to Mitchell, ALS, 4 p., North Lovell, Me., October 19, 1936.

7. Mitchell to Paisley, TL (copy), 2 p., Atlanta, Ga., October 23, 1936.

8. Paisley to Mitchell, ALS, 2 p., North Lovell, Me., January 1, 1937.

9. Stephens Mitchell, unpublished MS, pp. 65–66.

10. Mitchell to Dixon, TL (copy), 2 p., Atlanta, Ga., August 15, 1936.

11. Mitchell to Commager, TL (copy), 2 p., Atlanta, Ga., July 10, 1936.

12. Perkerson to Walter Winchell, TL (copy), 2 p., [Atlanta,] March 15, 1940 (filed under Winchell).

13. *Scribner's* 100 (October 1936): 14.

14. Mitchell to Young, TL (copy), 3 p., Atlanta, Ga., September 29, 1936.

15. Mitchell to Mrs. Alfred L. Lustig, TL (copy), 1 p., Atlanta, Ga., January 19, 1937.

16. *The Nation* 143 (July 4, 1936): 14.

17. Mitchell to Miller, TL (copy), 2 p., Atlanta, Ga., March 3, 1937.

18. Quoted in Finis Farr, *Margaret Mitchell of Atlanta* (New York: William Morrow, 1965), p. 101.

19. *San Francisco Chronicle,* May 13, 1936.

20. *Macon Telegraph,* June 30, 1936.

21. *New York Sun,* June 30, 1936.

22. Mitchell to Patton, TL (copy), 3 p., Atlanta, Ga., July 11, 1936.

23. *Chicago Tribune,* July 5, 1936.

24. *New Republic,* September 16, 1936.

25. *Mount Vernon* (N.Y.) *Argus,* July 11, 1936. Fowler's review appeared in July and August 1936 also in the *New Rochelle Standard,* the *Tarrytown News,* and the *Yonkers Herald-Statesman.*

26. Mitchell to Patton, TL (copy) 3 p., Atlanta, Ga., July 11, 1936.

27. Harold S. Latham, *My Life in Publishing* (New York: Dutton, 1965), p. 52.

28. Mitchell to Young, TL (copy), 3 p., Atlanta, Ga., September 29, 1936.

29. Latham, p. 53.

30. Marian Elder Jones, "Me and My Book," *Georgia Review* 16 (1962): 186.

31. Mitchell to Paisley, ALS (copy), 1 p., Atlanta, Ga., December 23, 1940.

32. Benét to Mitchell, TLS, 3 p., New York City, [July 1936].

33. Elsie W. Stokes to Mitchell, TLS, 3 p., Nashville, Tenn., June 2, 1936.

Reviewing *Margaret Mitchell's "Gone with the Wind" Letters,
1936–1949,* Blair Rouse observes that critics have faulted *Gone
with the Wind* "for lack of depth, or lack of symbolical or philosophical intricacy. . . ."[1] This observation is apt. In fact, although
the novel's narrative power is generally conceded, critics have indeed failed to see beyond the surface narrative. The novel does possess, however, a consistent mythic undergirding: that of the Great
Mother, the archetypal feminine or Gea—the Earth Mother of classical antiquity.

In *Gone with the Wind*, Earth is treated consistently as this Great
Goddess. She is the source of strength and endurance but also the
jealous one who punishes those who scorn her rites and values. All
the characters relate to this imagery, but Scarlett O'Hara's life is
structured around it. She is the child of Earth. As Rhett Butler says,
"Sometimes I think she's like the giant Antaeus who became
stronger each time he touched Mother Earth."[2] And so she is. Like
the battling Antaeus, child of Gea, Scarlett draws her strength from
Earth. But she also strays after false gods—the Apollonian Ashley
Wilkes and the urban cult of acquisition in commercial, industrial
Atlanta. These themes and conflicts form an underlying mythic sub-
structure for the entire novel.

Earth-worship is an ancient and powerful religious impulse dating back for millenia through Western Asia, Asia Minor, and the
Aegean. From India to ancient Greece and Rome, worshipers were
well aware of the two-sided nature of the goddess: giver of fruitfulness yet queen of death. Across the centuries, literature speaks of
the compelling power of Earth and implies, as well, her power as
avenger. Worship of Earth appears in biblical accounts. It supports
the myth of Cain, for, according to Genesis (4: 9–12), shedding a
brother's blood insults the Earth:

> Then the lord said to Cain, "Where is Abel your brother?" He said, "I
> do not know; am I my brother's keeper?" And the Lord said, "What
> have you done? The voice of your brother's blood is crying to me
> from the ground. And now you are cursed from the ground, which
> has opened its mouth to receive your brother's blood from your
> hand. When you till the ground, it shall no longer yield to you its
> strength; you shall be a fugitive and a wanderer on the earth."

57

When troubles mount for Scarlett O'Hara, she thinks that she may "curse God and die too. Somebody in the Bible had done just that thing. Cursed God and died" (p. 395). That "somebody"—Job— had prayed to Earth to fulfill her ancient role as avenger: "O earth, cover not my blood, and let my cry find no resting place" (Job 16: 18).

As art and history record, the ceremonial salute to Earth is a gesture of enduring power in Western culture. In Roman times, according to Livy (I, 56), an oracle proclaimed that the man among those present who first kissed his mother would receive the *summum imperium.* Immediately, Brutus prostrated himself and kissed the Earth. In the nineteenth century, Dostoevsky, in *Crime and Punishment,* has Raskolnikov show repentance for murder by seeking forgiveness from the Earth: "He knelt down in the middle of the square, bowed down to the earth, and kissed the filthy earth with bliss and rapture. He got up and bowed down a second time." [3] Earlier in that novel a stranger who believes he has falsely accused Raskolnikov asks forgiveness, bowing down twice and touching the ground with his finger. With this salute, he offers propitiation to the sacred Earth. And in the twentieth century, in Stravinsky's ballet *The Rite of Spring,* the central experience of the section entitled "The Celebrant" is the ceremonial kiss to the Earth. Here the salute is one of praise and celebration rather than of expiation.

Thus Scarlett O'Hara has ample precedent when she salutes the Earth, lying face down in the dirt of a life-sustaining garden patch. There she finds "the earth as soft and comfortable as a feather pillow" (p. 427), and she draws strength from the soil so that she can support her helpless dependents. Like the battling Antaeus, who took on all challengers, she rises to fight again. At the turning point of her life, in a scene set in the heart of the novel, Scarlett salutes the Earth and is rewarded by it.

Earth's other aspect, that of avenger for offenses, is implied in the opening pages of *Gone with the Wind.* As Scarlett sits on the veranda at Tara with the Tarleton twins—paradigms of devoted brotherhood—the sun sets on the peaceful scene "in a welter of crimson" that foreshadows the shedding of the blood of brothers upon the outraged Earth: "Already the plowing was nearly finished, and the bloody glory of the sunset colored the fresh-cut furrows of red Georgia clay to even redder hues. The moist hungry earth, waiting upturned for the cotton seeds, showed pinkish on the sandy tops of furrows, vermilion and scarlet and maroon where shadows lay along the sides of the trenches" (p. 7). The menace of the Earth is always present in the threat of the nearby wilderness: ". . . mysterious, a little sinister, the soughing pines seeming to wait with an age-old patience, to threaten with soft sighs: 'Be careful! Be careful! We had you once. We can take you back again'" (p. 8). It is this unending struggle between productive and destructive nature that the myth of Antaeus and his battle with Hercules is said to represent: the Nile versus the desert sands that constantly threatened to take it over. In Scarlett's Georgia, the struggle is one that many plantations, after the war, must lose.

To Scarlett, this land is Mother Earth. On four occasions she is linked to the Earth as mother. As a spoiled sixteen-year-old, she is lectured by her father, Gerald: "to anyone with a drop of Irish blood in them the land they live on is like their mother" (p. 36). Years later, when the war has taken away everything but the red earth of Tara, she recalls her father's words "the land they live on is like their mother" (p. 435). Even as a young girl Scarlett feels as her father does, without acknowledging her devotion: "She loved this land so much, without even knowing she loved it, loved it as she loved her mother's face under the lamp at prayer time" (p. 28). At evening prayers, what Scarlett really worships is her mother, Ellen O'Hara; as a child, Scarlett "had confused her mother with the Virgin Mary . . ." (p. 60). To equate that love with her love for the land implies the depth of the religious dimension in Scarlett's feeling for Tara. Later, she experiences the Earth's powerful maternalism vividly as she flees the destruction of Atlanta with an old wagon carrying helpless refugees. As she nears Tara, she finds the countryside "like the familiar and dear face of a mother, beautiful and quiet at last, after death agonies" (p. 398).

Scarlett's worship of Mother Earth sustains her when Catholicism no longer does. Eroded by the sorrows of the war, her Catholicism—never more than lip service—fails her. But her devotion to the Earth remains a vital part of her being. Like her Irish father, Scarlett is a pagan, and appropriately so: the original Tara, seat of the kings of Ireland, was cursed in the sixth century as a site of Druidism and idolatry.

Scarlett's own idolatry, however, lies not in worshiping the Earth but in deviating from this religion to follow false gods. The jealous Earth is not to be affronted lightly, and Scarlett will suffer for her defection.

Her first deviation from Earth worship is her long adoration of Ashley Wilkes, whom she mistakes for a god. At Ashley's first appearance in the novel, Scarlett observes that "the sun gleamed on [his] gold hair . . ." (p. 108), and his sunlit hair is a motif throughout the novel; like a sun god, an Apollo, he dazzles the earthy Scarlett. She thinks of Ashley's home, Twelve Oaks, as "the beautiful white-columned house that crowned the hill like a Greek temple" (p. 25). Years later she still thinks of him as the sun; after the war he embraces her, and "when he withdrew . . . it was like the warm sun going down . . ." (p. 530). Ashley, too, relates himself to ancient Greece. Speaking with regret of the lost prewar life, he says that it had "a perfection and a completeness and a symmetry to it like Grecian art" (p. 529). Further, he is aware that "we Southerners did think we were gods" (p. 527). But another Southerner, the realistic Rhett Butler, sums him up satirically as "the godlike and wooden-headed Mr. Wilkes" (p. 340).

Scarlett's devotion to Ashley Wilkes is destructive because he is antithetical to Earth. After the war, when all must work at Tara to survive, he farms ineptly and unhappily. The neighboring Fontaine brothers, former dandies who had never soiled their hands with work, learn to be successful dirt farmers. Ashley will not. Physically coordinated enough to ride and hunt before the war, he is ineffectual at all farm tasks, from splitting kindling to plowing. Someone must feed Ashley and his family, and that someone is Scarlett. Chopping wood in the orchard, Ashley is dressed in the trousers of his old Confederate uniform and a tattered, ruffled shirt, a leisured gentleman's shirt that once was Gerald's. When he puts his coat on Scarlett's shoulders, it is also clear that she must assume responsibilities traditionally considered his. Unwilling to serve the Earth, he is tortured by powerlessness.

Devoid of natural vitality, Ashley fears Scarlett's earthy qualities.

On the day that her fruitless love for him begins, he wears "the head of a Medusa in cameo on his cravat pin" (p. 25)—perhaps an indication of his fear of powerful females. Certainly he fears Scarlett's power. In the library at Twelve Oaks on the day of the barbecue, he rejects her, reminding her that she "can love and hate with a violence impossible to me" and that she is "as elemental as fire and wind and wild things and I—" (p. 117). He leaves the comparison unfinished. The disparity between them is indeed marked, as their very names indicate: Scarlett, vivid, colorful, alive; Ashley, pallid, burned out. He is aligned with the products of artifice rather than nature. Even in his love of books and music, he is a consumer, not a creator, and when he longs for the life of the old South as one of "perfection . . . like Grecian art," he disregards the fact that this art, as in ancient Greece, was made possible for a few by the slavery of many. Elegant and nonfunctional, Ashley is like the object Scarlett smashes after he refuses her in the library: "a tiny china rose-bowl on which two china cherubs smirked" (p. 119)—an object that represents, as well, her feelings for him which are grounded in sentimentality and artifice.

Ashley's rejection of her brings Scarlett to her second deviation from Earth worship: her abandonment of Tara for Atlanta and her subsequent conversion to its cult of acquisitiveness. Although Atlanta is a raw, violent city where Earth is desecrated, she gives this profane site her love and admiration. The city's very origin involved Earth's violation: "an engineer drove a stake in the red clay to mark the southern end of the [railroad] line, and Atlanta, born Terminus, had begun" (p. 141). Arriving at the Atlanta depot, Scarlett fears that she will soil her slippers and skirts in the mud, a concern she has never had at Tara. Here Atlanta's warlike people worship Ares and are at odds with Earth: "In the open space around the depot, the soft ground had been cut and churned by the constant flow of traffic in and out until it resembled an enormous hog wallow, and here and there vehicles were mired to the hubs in the ruts. A never-ceasing line of army wagons and ambulances, loading and unloading supplies and wounded from the trains, made the mud and confusion worse as they toiled in and struggled out, drivers swearing, mules plunging and mud spattering for yards" (p. 143). Even notices in the Atlanta newspaper associate the city with death, disease, and impotence with their advertisements for "cures for private diseases, abortifacients and restoratives for lost manhood" (p. 236).

In Atlanta's wartime moral climate, where ties with Earth are forgotten or profaned, a benefit ball—foremost rite of the social season—is itself a perversion of Earth worship. In contrast to the barbecue held outdoors at Twelve Oaks, this ritual is held indoors, in a crowded, dusty drill hall, where the natural fragrance of flowers is overpowered by artificial odors. At Twelve Oaks, the celebrants sat under natural arbors; in Atlanta, they sit beneath artificial ones.

As an Earth worshiper, Scarlett is apparently alone in objecting to the perversion of what should be a midsummer celebration of life. Instead, the ball is dedicated to war and death, as her own pleasure-denying black dress reminds her and the flag-draped portraits of Confederate leaders attest:

> Even the banked flowers below the pictures of Mr. Davis and Mr. Stephens displeased her.
> "It looks like an altar," she sniffed. "And the way they all carry on about those two, they might as well be the Father and Son! . . . Everybody carries on like they were holy and they aren't anything but men, and mighty unattractive ones at that." [p. 173]

Far from these social rounds, the war escalates and Earth plays a role in the conflict. Lee's army invades the fertile fields of Pennsylvania; his men die on the sun-parched grass. To the anxious and self-deluding people of Atlanta, the Southern soldiers seem miraculous products of Earth itself: "Even now the Southern ranks might be falling like grain before a hailstorm, but the Cause for which they fought could never fall. They might be dying in thousands but, like the fruit of the dragon's teeth, thousands of fresh men in gray and butternut with the Rebel yell on their lips would spring up from the earth to take their places" (p. 256). In their desperation, they look to Earth for rescue, but no miracle occurs and the South is doomed.

As Sherman's army advances on Atlanta, ambulances roll down Atlanta's streets. Farm wagons, and even oxcarts, are packed with wounded from the defeated army, "dripping blood into the red dust" (p. 321). Earth has its own wounds, from fresh trenches: "red gashes surmounted by red mounds, waiting for the men who would fill them" (p. 323).

The offense to sacred nature is evident, as the morning skies are "profaned with cannon smoke" (p. 330). Green picnic places Scarlett remembers are now defiled, and clear streams run crimson. She thinks of "the soft green grasses where she had sat . . . cut to bits by heavy cannon wheels, trampled by desperate feet when bayonet met bayonet and flattened where bodies threshed in agonies. . . . And the lazy streams . . . redder now than ever Georgia clay could make them . . . graves where friends lay buried . . . tangled underbrush and thick woods where bodies rotted unburied. . ." (p. 344). As Atlanta begins to burn, the Earth shakes and trembles.

Fleeing to Tara, Scarlett sees for herself the devastation visited on the land: a familiar plantation house burned, crops stripped, gardens destroyed. Although Tara is still standing, Scarlett's mother is dead, her father deranged, and her sisters desperately ill.

At this point, in the heart of the novel, she turns to the Earth in the central experience of her life. Searching for food for her helpless household, she finds at last the only source overlooked by the invaders—the garden patches of the Wilkes's former slaves. There she collapses onto the "soft dirt," and the Earth sustains her: "She lay weakly on her face, the earth as soft and comfortable as a feather pillow. . ." (p. 427). Her griefs and terrors attack her "like buzzards"—or like Furies: "The thoughts circled and swooped above her, dived down and drove tearing claws and sharp beaks into her mind. For a timeless time, she lay still, her face in the dirt. . . ." Strengthened and renewed by Earth, she takes up a heavy burden for herself and others: "When she arose at last and saw again the black ruins of Twelve Oaks, her head was raised high. . . . And as Scarlett settled the heavy basket across her arm, she had settled her own mind and her own life" (p. 428).

During this profound experience, Scarlett reaffirms her real religion. Although she was trained carefully as a Catholic, she never thinks of the prayers of the Church. When she calls on God, it is only as a witness to her claims upon life.

The price for Scarlett's commitment is high, for in the garden patch, "potential tenderness had gone out of her face forever" (p.

428). And even as Earth strengthens her will to survive and defend her own people, it exacts a further penalty, for her very hardness and determination are reflected in her nightmares in which the Earth turns on her: "She was in a wild strange country so thick with swirling mist she could not see her hand before her face. The earth beneath her feet was uneasy. . . . There were things in the fog reaching out fingers to pluck her skirt, to drag her down into the uneasy quaking earth on which she stood. . ." (p. 474).

As long as Scarlett remains at Tara, her hardness serves the community. Trained only as a belle and unaccustomed to any responsibility, she is able to see to the needs of no fewer than eleven dependents suffering from hunger, shock, and bereavement. Not until she moves permanently to Atlanta, abandoning the Earth, does her new hardness become self-serving.

Originally, Scarlett returns to Atlanta to serve Tara. She is willing even to sell herself to secure tax money to keep Tara from falling into irreverent hands. By stealing Frank Kennedy, her sister's beau, she accomplishes her goal, but she is soon seduced by Atlanta's cult of acquisition. She forgets her worship of Earth and joins in its desecration. She plans to "put up a cheap saloon out of poor-grade lumber I can't sell . . ." (p. 638). She sells poor lumber as good, she blackguards other lumber dealers, and she drives into bankruptcy an honest poor white who has said openly that she is a liar and a swindler. Worse, she leases overworked convicts and acquiesces in starving them, when she and her family have themselves known starvation and her own recurring nightmare is of hunger.

Scarlett enjoys Atlanta's extravagant new "mongrel society" (p. 876), far removed from Tara's standards. She builds a pretentious house, while her former friends feel the pinch of want and often of actual hunger. Unlike the house at Tara with its simple design and its openness to air and sunlight, Scarlett's Atlanta house is antithetical to nature. Even the adornments on the lawn are metal objects: iron benches, iron summerhouse, two iron statues of animals, a stag and a mastiff, prey and predator. In the house itself "plum-colored plush hangings . . . shut out most of the sunlight" (p. 868).

Atlanta's malign effect upon Scarlett, in contrast to Tara's beneficent influence, is illustrated by two incidents that occur within a few months. In these, she interacts with two similar persons, Uncle

64

Peter and Pork, both respected, intelligent, devoted former slaves of advancing years. In Atlanta, she permits the Northern wives of occupation officers to insult Peter, bringing him first to tears, then to anger. He never drives for her again. At Tara, in contrast, Scarlett is sensitive to Pork's grief at the death of her father, Gerald. Gently, she presents him with Gerald's handsome watch, praising him for all he did for her father. In Atlanta, Scarlett acquiesces in stripping Peter of his dignity; at Tara, she supports Pork's self-esteem.

Throughout the novel, the most admirable and attractive characters are those close to Earth. When Scarlett is at Tara, she is one of these. Her naturalness is established early in the novel: "She was as forthright and simple as the winds that blew over Tara and the yellow river that wound about it . . ." (p. 26). A healthy, vigorous child, she resents the repressive code imposed on her behavior. As a sixteen-year-old, she objects indignantly: "I'm tired of everlastingly being unnatural and never doing anything I want to do. I'm tired of acting like I don't eat more than a bird, and walking when I want to run and saying I feel faint after a waltz. I'm tired of saying, 'How wonderful you are!' to fool men who haven't got one-half the sense I've got . . ." (p. 79). And three times she is described directly as "earthy."

Scarlett's appearance and very clothing reinforce her role as creature of nature and Earth worshiper. Her skin is magnolia-white. Her eyes, in her father's opinion, are as "green as the hills of Ireland" (p. 81), and the father and daughter sing "The Wearin' o' the Green." At Tara, the green clothes she wears are linked to nature—a green-flowered muslin, an apple-green ball dress. In Atlanta, emerging from the black of widowhood, she accepts a green silk dress and hat from Rhett Butler. To excuse this breach of propriety, she invents a natural association for these green garments: she will wear them to take flowers to convalescent officers. But after the war, attempting to get money from Rhett to save Tara, she once more wears a green dress that has associations with the Earth: improvised from Tara's curtains, the dress is of "moss-green velvet" (p. 545). Years later in Atlanta, the change in her clothing implies her inner alteration. Here she wears a dress of jade green, evoking not a natural setting but artifice, as in the mounting of jewelry. Not only is jade cold, costly, and hard, but the word is also a term for a disreputable woman. Scarlett has come a long distance from the simple green-flowered and apple-green dresses that she wore in the naturalness of Tara.

Other characters in *Gone with the Wind* are also defined by the standards of naturalness, nurturance, and association with the Earth. Although Rhett Butler has no attachment to the land, he has natural attributes. His name has the same color association as Scarlett's—Rhett/red. He is frequently compared to an Indian, a savage, a pagan, and a panther, but he is also a gentle nurturer of children. Both Gerald O'Hara and Will Benteen love the land, and Will, the kindly cracker who manages Tara after the war, takes care of children and babies almost as deftly as Mammy does. Although Melanie Hamilton Wilkes lacks vitality and strength, she has a natural simplicity: "She looked—and was—as simple as earth, as good as bread, as transparent as spring water" (p. 101). Like Scarlett's mother, Ellen O'Hara, she dedicates herself to nurturance. Stronger than Melanie and Ellen are two women who survive: Beatrice Tarleton and Grandma Fontaine. With the loss of her four sons and her thoroughbreds in the war, Beatrice also loses her spirit, but eventually she acquires a new mare and its colt and begins to recapture her natural vitality. Grandma Fontaine is the wise woman/witch. Able to remember pioneer-Indian days, the old lady is attuned to the primitive and the natural. Prophesying that some will survive the South's devastation and some will not, Grandma Fontaine provides an example from nature to explain survival: "We bow to the inevitable. We're not wheat, we're buckwheat! When a storm comes along it flattens ripe wheat because it's dry and can't bend with the wind. But ripe buckwheat's got sap in it and it bends. And when the wind has passed, it springs up almost as straight and strong as before" (p. 717).

Alienated from Earth, others will not thrive. As Grandma Fontaine predicts, Ashley Wilkes is one such person, and his sister India is another. Still another neighbor, Cathleen Calvert, surrenders unconditionally, as the fields surrender to the surrounding wilderness and the Southern army to the Northern. She marries her family's overseer as a way out and soon becomes a slattern. Scarlett's sister Suellen is also alienated from nature, refusing to work in the fields at Tara when she is needed. Others who lack natural qualities are

Scarlett's Atlanta friends of the carpetbag aristocracy, among them a former barmaid, chambermaid, and whore: "They were so lately come from nothing and so uncertain of themselves they were doubly anxious to appear refined. At all costs they must be ladies. . . . To hear them talk one would have thought they had no legs, natural functions or knowledge of the wicked world" (p. 879). Like the genuine aristocracy who lack natural qualities, these too will decline.

Despite the racist reputation of *Gone with the Wind* almost all of the slaves and former slaves in the novel are attractive, natural characters. Only Prissy fails to sustain others. The men are nurturers, Pork caring for Gerald, Uncle Peter guiding the childlike Aunt Pittypat, and Big Sam protecting Scarlett from attackers. Dilcey, the part-Indian wife of Pork, is an Earth mother, working hard in the fields as a voluntary offering and willingly nursing the fragile Melanie's white baby along with her own black one.

But the primary Earth mother in the novel is Mammy. We see her early in the novel forcing needed food upon Ellen and laying down the laws of dress and decorum to the willful Scarlett. She doses Confederate soldiers walking home from the war, rebukes what she calls "black trash" loitering on Atlanta streets, and comforts sick or unhappy babies with a magical touch. Close to the primitive, she has "ears like a lynx" (p. 833) and can move with "savage stealth" (p. 546). As she sets her will against Scarlett's, she shifts "from one foot to another like a restive elephant" (p. 547)—not only a very large animal, but an intelligent, dangerous, and powerful one. And Mammy has power. Hers is the only voice that Scarlett heeds, and Rhett claims that Mammy is "the real head of the house" (p. 869). Stronger and closer to the Earth than even Scarlett, Mammy is the one to whom Scarlett turns as the novel ends, seeking at Tara to renew life from the Earth.

Will Scarlett touch the Earth and rise again? Apparently. One reason for the novel's great appeal lies in its suggestion not only of a second chance in life, but even more: *Gone with the Wind* is open-ended, hinting at a last chance after bitter losses. This implication is supported by the myth that Rhett Butler associates with Scarlett O'Hara. Held in midair in his struggle with Hercules, Gea's child Antaeus dies because he cannot touch the Earth. But Scarlett is still able to regain strength from Tara, and to receive solace from the Earth as mother and as sacred place: "She thought of Tara and it was as if a gentle cool hand were stealing over her heart. She could see the white house gleaming welcome to her through the reddening autumn leaves, feel the quiet hush of the country twilight coming down over her like a benediction" (p. 1036). With this benediction, the novel that opened at Tara in a harsh spring closes at Tara with a subdued autumnal promise.

The mythic evocations in *Gone with the Wind* may be one source of the novel's long-lasting popularity—not, of course, the myth of Antaeus in itself but rather the significance of the Earth as a powerful, nurturing mother. In the depression years, when America's fruitfulness had failed its people, a reminder of Earth's abundance was an appealing, if romantic, avenue of escape. In the present and future as well, these evocations may enhance the novel's attraction. As Earth's resources themselves dwindle, the ancient myth of enduring fecundity holds a nostalgic appeal. Carefully, consistently developed by Margaret Mitchell, *Gone with the Wind*'s mythic dimension not only supports the narrative but gives the novel depth that its critics have ignored.

Notes

1. Blair Rouse, "Gone with the Wind—But Not Forgotten," review of *Margaret Mitchell's "Gone with the Wind" Letters, 1936–1949,* ed. Richard Harwell, *Southern Literary Journal* 10, no. 2 (1978): 172–79.

2. Margaret Mitchell, *Gone with the Wind* (New York: Macmillan, 1936), p. 968. All subsequent page references to this work appear in the text.

3. Ed. George Gibian, trans. Jessie Coulson (New York: W. W. Norton, 1964), p. 505.

The Company of Giants James Michener

Within the space of eighty-nine years, four novelists from four widely divergent national literatures published books focused on a new type of heroine: free spirited, attractive, immoral and totally ingratiating.

In 1847 in England, William Makepeace Thackeray offered the first of the unforgettable portraits, Miss Becky Sharp of *Vanity Fair.*

In 1857 in France, Gustave Flaubert related the banal yet tragic events engulfing *Madame Bovary.*

In 1875 in Russia, Leo Tolstoy unfolded a long and majestic portrait of *Anna Karenina* and her associates.

And in 1936 in the United States, Margaret Mitchell published a novel which was to have a shattering impact, *Gone with the Wind,* centering upon the fortunes of Scarlett O'Hara. A few comparisons will help the reader already familiar with these books to appreciate their relationships.

The three male authors were proved, professional literary talents when they published their books. Margaret Mitchell was an untested housewife living in what each of the European authors would have described as "a provincial city."

It is notable that Thackeray, Flaubert and Mitchell published their books when they were thirty-six years old. Tolstoy, having published *War and Peace* at that watershed age, did not publish *Anna Karenina* till eleven years later, when he was forty-seven.

The four books are alike in that they deal with liberated women, but Emma Bovary and Anna Karenina, faced by the consequences of their radical deportment, commit suicide. The novels named after them are classic tragedies. Becky Sharp and Scarlett O'Hara survive and, indeed, prosper. Their books, not named after them, are certainly not tragedies and might best be considered comedies of manners.

Vanity Fair, Anna Karenina and *Gone with the Wind* deal essentially with the upper classes of their societies, often with compassionate side glances at the state of the peasantry. Because of this,

This essay originally appeared as the introduction to the anniversary edition of *Gone with the Wind* (New York: Macmillan, 1975); it is reprinted here by permission of the William Morris Agency, Inc., as agent for the author. The bracketed page references are keyed to the 1936 edition of *Gone with the Wind.*

they sometimes seem outmoded today, focusing as they do upon the gentry. *Madame Bovary,* on the other hand, makes a specific virtue of dealing with an average French village and its population.

Anna Karenina and *Gone with the Wind* have the virtue of dealing with a great nation in time of crisis and gain added strength and interest because of their wide historical scope and relevance. The other two works lack this breadth.

Artistically each of the books has its unique virtues, which account for the high regard in which it is held. For pure literary control few novels in any genre have ever equaled *Madame Bovary;* its crystalline purity remains a standard and an enchantment. For comic invention few novels excel *Vanity Fair;* its style of expression may have fallen from fashion, but its sardonic insights never will. *Anna Karenina* has a magisterial quality, its many characters offering variation and challenge. And *Gone with the Wind* displays high skill in its interweaving of narrative passages describing historical events and dramatic scenes in which characters confront one another. To achieve a satisfactory balance between narrative and scene is a major obligation of the novelist.

Psychologically each writer displays a clear vision of his or her central character. Flaubert has been excessively praised for his analysis of Emma Bovary, but she is observed within a limited range of situations and emotions. Tolstoy did a splendid job on each of his four major characters, but Thackeray tended to gloss over his. Margaret Mitchell had great success with Scarlett O'Hara, less with Rhett Butler; but of the four major women in this assembly of novels, it is Scarlett who lives most vividly and with the greatest contemporary application.

> Frank, in common with all men he knew, felt that a wife should be guided by her husband's superior knowledge, should accept his opinions in full and have none of her own. He would have given most women their own way. Women were such funny little creatures and it never hurt to humor their small whims. Mild and gentle by nature, it was not in him to deny a wife much. He would have enjoyed gratifying the foolish notions of some soft little person and scolding her lovingly for her stupidity and extravagance. But the things Scarlett set her mind on were unthinkable.
>
> That sawmill, for example. It was the shock of his life when she

70

told him with a sweet smile, in answer to his questions, that she intended to run it herself. [pp. 636–37]

Structurally the novels of Thackeray and Tolstoy fall apart in their final pages, the former disastrously so, as if Thackeray had no clear understanding of what he was about, the latter because Tolstoy was trying to force his story of Anna into a larger mold to which it was not suited. (In the final nineteen chapters Anna cannot appear, for she has already committed suicide; indeed, she is scarcely spoken of by the characters who survive.) *Madame Bovary* holds together beautifully, like a Greek tragedy, but this is because Flaubert is working on a very restricted canvas not likely to provide any tempting diversion. Miss Mitchell's very long novel, however, offers many temptations for the author to go astray, but she keeps it vital, relevant and interesting right up to the last page. In her ability to devise and control an intricate dramatic structure, she excels the other three by far.

In critical acceptance, judging these novels alone, Flaubert stands supreme with Tolstoy not far behind. This is partly because these two presented their portraits as tragedies, which the public has been trained to accept as a higher level of art. Thackeray has been much diminished in recent years because of his flippancy, his outmoded style and his lack of high intention, but I would expect his fortunes to revive. Margaret Mitchell was excessively praised at publication, numerous critics comparing her novel favorably with *War and Peace,* and was excessively deflated in the 1950s and 1960s because of her parochial viewpoint and the lack of development in her characters. I am certain that her reputation will grow in the future, because critics will have to grapple with the problem of why her novel has remained so readable and so important to so many people.

Popular acceptance was accorded each of the first three novels. Thackeray became the sensation of London; Tolstoy was already the glory of Russia. However, it was *Gone with the Wind* which the entire world would embrace.

It is difficult even now to comprehend what a staggering event *Gone with the Wind* was in that post-depression year of 1936. Today a good novel that sells 40,000 copies can lead the best-seller lists, and a sale of 200,000 copies is a veritable sensation. So great was the word-of-mouth publicity on *Gone with the Wind* that within twenty days of publication 176,000 copies had been sold. Over the summer months, when bookstores customarily fell into doldrums, sales rose to 700,000 copies, one New York store ordering 50,000 on one day. Within a year of publication, 1,383,000 copies had been sold. Today, sales stand at about 21,000,000.

The impact on American society was memorable. Appearing at the end of a Depression during which many families had faced great loss, this story of a saucy French-Irish girl of sixteen facing up to the Civil War and holding her family together through the post-war reconstruction became more than a mere novel. It became a symbol. Editorials were written, pointing out the relevancy. Sermons were preached in churches across the nation directing parishioners to lessons learned. Politicians used the novel as an allegory pointing the way to national survival. And individual readers wrote thousands of letters to Miss Mitchell, assuring her that in this novel they read the story of their own lives.

The Macmillan Company, which had the good fortune to publish the book, saw to it that a constant stream of interesting stories circulated. One woman, leaving New York on a boat trip to Europe, found that she had received nine copies as bon-voyage presents. A maiden lady in Boston who had never been south of the Hudson River started reading the novel one morning and kept at it through the night. When her Boston *Transcript* landed on her porch next afternoon, she staggered to the door, looked out with bloodshot eyes and cried, "Get out of here, you damned Yankees!"

For two years Miss Mitchell lived at the center of a publicity spotlight more fierce than that known by any writer since the day on which Lord Byron could say, after publication of *Childe Harold*, "I awoke one morning and found myself famous." Newspaper publishers and magazine editors besieged her, praying for any scrap of writing. She was offered fantastic sums if she would write even a portion of a page, on any subject that came to mind. Wherever she went she was encircled by people begging autographs. Every worthy cause in the South implored her to make a statement or an appearance in its behalf. Uncounted invitations to speak piled in. The pressures became almost intolerable.

72

Then, in 1938, the pace accelerated. Hollywood had purchased her novel, at the ridiculously low figure of $50,000 for all movie rights, and a great publicity brouhaha was generated over which actors and actresses were best qualified to play the leading roles. The heady nonsense that ensued might have derailed a weaker person, but with unwavering determination Miss Mitchell kept herself clear of it. She would participate in no sensationalism. If she had been a practiced author, with a score of earlier books to her credit, her sagacious behavior under such pressure would have been remarkable. For an untested young woman to receive such adulation on her first book, and to accept it with such stately restraint, was a miracle.

I met Miss Mitchell twice in those hectic years. I was a minor editor at Macmillan and my cubbyhole stood next to the second-floor office of Mr. Brett, head of our company. I remember the awe with which word flashed through our rooms that "Margaret Mitchell is coming in for lunch today!" We waited with more than ordinary respect, because we were aware that the generous Christmas bonuses we had been receiving were due solely to the profits she had made possible. I remember an official of Macmillan's telling me, "It was Mr. Brett who made one of the significant decisions in American publishing. At our final meeting on price we showed how this very long book could just possibly be published at the traditional price of two dollars and fifty cents . . . if it turned out to be a big success. It would be safer, however, to publish at the radical price of two seventy-five. Mr. Brett leaned back in his chair and asked, 'Can this book be as good as everyone says?' We told him yes and he said, 'If it's that good, people will want it. The price is three dollars.'"

My secretary called excitedly, "Here she comes!" And I went to my door to watch as the solemn procession, much like the marching priests in *Aida*, moved past. There was Mr. Brett, the young and impulsive head of our company, and Harold Latham, the stout and gracious head editor, and Alec Blanton, the charismatic businessman, and Jim Putnam, the Oxford-type gentleman editor—all surrounding a very tiny woman, not five feet tall and weighing much less than a hundred pounds. The four men looked fiercely protective, aware of the gravity of this day, but Margaret Mitchell looked from side to side, nodding to the secretaries and the junior editors.

I thought, then, and I would like to think now, that when she reached my cubbyhole she smiled with special graciousness.

Later that day, and on her second visit, I was allowed to shake hands with her and I could not get over how small she was. One of the Macmillan men whispered to me, "When she attends a formal dinner she takes along a copy of *Bartlett's Quotations.* Puts it on the floor so her feet can touch." I have often thought, in recent years, of those queenly visits and what happened to the participants. Marvelous Alec Blanton, the certain hope of the publishing industry, dead in an unfathomable suicide. Gentlemanly Jim Putnam, moved on to a good job in another company. George Brett, gone from the historic company, which he sold. And Margaret Mitchell, killed in one of the most senseless tragedies in American literature. Gone with the wind, all of these.

Certain myths associated with the novel ought to be dispelled, and the seventy-fifth birthday of the author is an appropriate time to do so.

That Margaret Mitchell was a simple-minded Atlanta housewife who fumbled her way into the writing of a famous novel. False. She came from a distinguished Atlanta family, all of whose members read widely. At ten she was writing novelettes and plays which astounded her contemporaries. She inclined toward vigorous dramatization and conscripted a repertoire company of neighborhood children who acted out her writing. In her *Phil Kelly, Detective,* she played the role of "Zara, a female crook and one of the gang." She attended Smith College in Massachusetts, then landed a job on the *Atlanta Journal*, where she followed in the footsteps of Laurence Stallings, Grantland Rice and Roark Bradford. She was an alert, street-smart, irreverent, popular little reporter who married a typical southern sharpie, then had the good sense to divorce him almost immediately.

That she was a naïve woman who was hoodwinked by smart New York publishers. False. Her father and brother were smart lawyers and legal scholars who checked every clause in her contract. Her second husband was a knowledgeable businessman who gave her excellent advice.

That scores of publishing houses read and rejected her novel before Macmillan grudgingly accepted it. False. It took Margaret

74

Mitchell ten years to write her novel, and during most of that time she had as her close personal friend Lois Cole, Macmillan's representative in Atlanta. Miss Cole sent repeated brief notices that a very clever young woman in her territory was in the process of writing a novel which might be good. Harold Latham, Macmillan's senior editor, looked Miss Mitchell up during a scouting trip to Atlanta, and was the first professional publisher to see the material. The manuscript was in dreadful physical condition and was almost the size of its author. Latham crammed it into a large suitcase he purchased for that purpose and carried it off with him, but Miss Mitchell, having fears that he might think it unsuitable, telegraphed him: SEND THE MANUSCRIPT BACK. I'VE CHANGED MY MIND. Prudently, he refused. Instead, he sent her word that Macmillan wanted to publish it. At that time the novel was called *Tomorrow Is Another Day,* and it was not until just prior to casting the manuscript into type that its heroine's name was changed from Pansy O'Hara to Scarlett.

That Miss Mitchell, being a woman and Southern to boot, could not possibly have written such a novel; it was done by some male friend. False. It is true that prior to her death she directed that her manuscript and all papers related to it be burned, and this was done; but a few sample pages, research notes and other documents were put aside to prove, should the need ever arise, that she alone had written the novel. On this point the testimony of brother, husband, editor and proofreader is overwhelming.

That the book is merely another Civil War novel. False. The book contains 947 [1037] pages and 63 chapters. The Civil War ends on page 444 [487], in the first sentence of Chapter 29. The remaining pages and chapters deal with post-war events, and these are often the most interesting and provocative. Thus 54 percent of the pages and 56 percent of the chapters are not, strictly speaking, Civil War. In time span the same is true. The first 28 chapters deal with events occurring between the dates of April 1861 and April 1865. The last 35 chapters deal with the years 1865–1873. Scarlett is sixteen when the book opens, twenty-eight when it closes.

That the book was copied from Vanity Fair. I think that anyone informed in world literature would have to notice the parallelism between Scarlett O'Hara/Melanie Hamilton and Becky Sharp/ Amelia Sedley, and in the first major review of the book, by J. Donald Adams in the *Sunday New York Times Book Review,* this similarity was pointed out, as it should have been. But Miss Mitchell was firm in rejecting the imputation:

> I see that Scarlett, the central character, is coming in for comparison with Becky Sharp. Nothing could be more flattering but the fact remains that I never read *Vanity Fair* till about a year and a half ago, after my auto accident. When I read *Vanity Fair* at last, I was charmed beyond words and howled with delight; but it never occurred to me that there'd be a comparison between Becky and Scarlett.

Actually, the analogy with *Vanity Fair* is not the most apt, for Thackeray's two women do not have associated with them men as interesting or as important as those in *Gone with the Wind.* A much more appropriate comparison is with *Anna Karenina*, for here the analogous structure is almost identical. Anna and Vronsky are extremely similar to Scarlett and Rhett, while the lovely Princess Kitty Scherbatskaya and her rural husband Konstantin Levin are dead ringers for Melanie Hamilton and Ashley Wilkes. Miss Mitchell never commented on this parallelism, for it seems unlikely that she had read Tolstoy's masterpiece. However, almost any novelist depicting a woman like Scarlett would want to counterpoise against her a woman like Amelia or Kitty or Melanie. Honoré de Balzac had done just this in 1841 when he wrote what may have been the progenitor of all these novels, his delightful *Memoirs of Two Young Married Women,* in which an impetuous Louise follows a stormy path strewn with handsome men while the more sober Renée finds matronly happiness with her more stodgy lover, who winds up a count. But I doubt that sources for *Gone with the Wind* need be sought elsewhere than in the mind of an impressionable child listening to family recollections of the Civil War and its aftermath.

The essential fact about this novel, however, is its extraordinary readability. May Lamberton Becker, a major critic when the book was published, delivered the permanent verdict: "It is the shortest long novel I have read in a long time." It is filled with stunning scenes: Mammy lacing Scarlett into her corset; the wounded at the railway station; Scarlett shooting the Union straggler; the girls making Scarlett a dress from the moss-green velvet draperies; Rhett carrying his wife upstairs to the long-unused bedroom.

But the novel does not depend merely upon super-dramatic confrontations. Contrary to what some critics have argued, the two major characters do grow—Melanie and Ashley do not—and I have always felt that the central paragraph comes toward the middle of the book, in Chapter 29:

> Somewhere, on the long road that wound through those four years, the girl with her sachet and dancing slippers had slipped away and there was left a woman with sharp green eyes, who counted pennies and turned her hands to many menial tasks, a woman to whom nothing was left from the wreckage except the indestructible red earth on which she stood. [p. 490]

In the final pages there is a similar portrait of Rhett at forty-five:

> He was sunken in his chair, his suit wrinkling untidily against his thickening waist, every line of him proclaiming the ruin of a fine body and a coarsening of a strong face. Drink and dissipation had done their work on the coin-clean profile and now it was no longer the head of a young pagan prince on new minted gold but a decadent, tired Caesar on copper debased by long usage. [pp. 1024–25]

Primarily, however, it is the South that changes, altered by war and defeat and social upheaval and stark determination to reestablish itself. The abiding merit of this novel is not that it has given us the portrait of a headstrong young woman, but that it has depicted with remarkable facility the spiritual history of a region.

The book's weakness is that it focuses so uncompromisingly on Atlanta, ignoring the rest of the South, the nation and the world. One is struck, when reading Miss Mitchell's private letters, by her obsession that the better class of people in Atlanta should like her book. This led her to a highly restricted view of Negro liberation and permitted her to offer a paragraph like this; she is speaking, not a character:

> The former slaves were now the lords of creation and, with the aid of the Yankees, the lowest and most ignorant ones were on top. The

better class of them, scorning freedom, were suffering as severely as their white masters. Thousands of house servants, the highest caste in the slave population, remained with their white folks, doing manual labor which had been beneath them in the old days. Many loyal field hands also refused to avail themselves of the new freedom, but the hordes of "trashy free issue niggers," who were causing most of the trouble, were drawn largely from the field-hand class. [p. 654]

A more comprehensive and compassionate view of freedom was possible, but she ignored it.

Finally, the book contains single sentences and paragraphs which positively sing. Some are extravagant; some are nineteenth century in style; but all add to the essentially romantic quality of this much-loved novel:

She thought wildly: Let the whole Confederacy crumble in the dust. Let the world end, but you must not die! I couldn't live if you were dead! [p. 275]

Hunger gnawed at her empty stomach again, and she said aloud: "As God is my witness, as God is my witness, the Yankees aren't going to lick me. I'm going to live through this, and when it's over, I'm never going to be hungry again. No, nor any of my folks. If I have to steal or kill—as God is my witness, I'm never going to be hungry again."
[p. 428]

He swung her off her feet into his arms and started up the stairs. Her head was crushed against his chest and she heard the hard hammering of his heart beneath her ears. He hurt her and she cried out, muffled, frightened. Up the stairs, he went in utter darkness, up, up, and she was wild with fear. [p. 939]

It is with a sense of deep personal loss that I write this paragraph. On August 11, 1949, Miss Mitchell, who had been born in the opening year of this century, was walking across Peachtree Street to attend a movie, *A Canterbury Tale,* when a taxicab, running wild, struck her brutally, knocking her into the gutter. Five days later, without regaining consciousness, she died. The driver was found to have a record of twenty-four arrests for speeding, recklessness, disorderly conduct and other violations. On the day after his trial he was involved in yet another crash.

It seems highly doubtful that Margaret Mitchell, had she lived, would have written other books. An editor at Macmillan who knew her well told me prior to her death that she had indicated to him that she would not, and we have various letters in which she stated positively that she would write no more: "As you can gather from my novel, I'm a verbose creature, but I feel that nothing short of insanity will ever make me write another line." She is best considered, I think, a unique young woman who before the age of ten loved to tell stories and who at twenty-six began a long and powerful recollection of her home town. That it was destined to become a titanic tale of human passions, loved around the world, was a mystery then and remains one now.

Scarlett O'Hara and the Two Quentin Compsons   Louis Rubin, Jr.

In the year 1936, which happened to be the seventy-fifth anniversary of the outbreak of the American Civil War, there were two works of fiction published which dealt importantly with that war, and which are still actively in print today. One of these novels is by all odds the best-selling popular historical novel ever published in America; the sales of *Gone with the Wind* have run into the tens of millions. The other, though it has never achieved the general popularity of Margaret Mitchell's novel, is the book which many consider the finest historical novel ever written by an American, and one of the great works of modern literature, William Faulkner's *Absalom, Absalom!*

My guess would be that for every person who has read *Absalom, Absalom!* fifty have read *Gone with the Wind.* I have run into people who go through Miss Mitchell's novel almost annually—all 1,037 printed pages of it—and who could no more accept the suggestion that it has faults or blemishes than that the Holy Scriptures err. Such devoted readers grow angry at any criticism of their favorite novel: it is the work only of nitpickers, or even worse, of college professors.

Quality, of course, is no reputable index either of a book's literary merit or of its capacity for lasting beyond its immediate occasion; otherwise the year 1850, for example, would be literarily memorable not for the publication of Hawthorne's *The Scarlet Letter* but of I. K. Marvel's *Reveries of a Bachelor, a Book of the Heart,* which outsold it many times over, while it would be Maria Cummins' *The Lamp-Lighter,* now remembered only as the subject of a wicked stylistic parody by James Joyce, and not Thoreau's *Walden,* which would cause us to look back with interest at the publishing season of 1854. All the same, I do not believe that *Gone with the Wind* was or is no more than a mere popular amusement; it has endured for four decades, and for all its literary clumsiness it is an important work of the imagination, with genuine insight into its time.

Of the literary excellence of Faulkner's *Absalom, Absalom!* there now seems little question. Yet at the time of its first publication it

This essay originally appeared in Evans Harrington and Ann J. Abadie, eds., *The South and Faulkner's Yoknapatawpha: The Actual and the Apocryphal* (Jackson: University Press of Mississippi, 1977).

was only modestly noticed and even more modestly read; by the 1940s it was out of print, and remained so until "discovery" of Faulkner by the academic literary community in the 1950s. The response of two of the more influential middlebrow critics to the publication of the two novels in 1936 is illustrative. A well-paid lightweight such as the late J. Donald Adams could declare of Miss Mitchell's novel in the *New York Times* that "in narrative power, in sheer readability," it was "surpassed by nothing in American fiction."[1] Meanwhile in the *New Yorker,* the somewhat more sophisticated but certainly no more intelligent Clifton P. Fadiman could unleash a tirade against *Absalom, Absalom!* Missing the chief structural point of the story, the search for the meaning of the past, Fadiman could assert sarcastically that Faulkner "gets quite an interesting effect, for example, by tearing the Sutpen chronicle into pieces, as if a mad child were to go to work on it with a pair of shears, and then having each of the jagged divisions narrated by a different personage. . . ." He concludes with the following ringing insight into twentieth-century literature: "Seriously, I do not know what to say of this book except that it seems to point to the final blowup of what was once a remarkable, if minor talent."[2]

Absalom, Absalom! sold very poorly. William Faulkner found, shortly after it was published, that he would have to go back out to Hollywood, which he hated, to work as a screen writer in order to pay his bills and buy a little time for writing fiction. It was not until the 1950s, when he had won the Nobel Prize and his books were being reissued in the hundred of thousands, that he was able to support himself on his literary income and so could abandon his stints in Hollywood and concentrate on the one thing he wanted to do in his life: write good fiction. By contrast, Margaret Mitchell made vast sums from her *Gone with the Wind*: the screen rights alone brought her $50,000. One of the provisions in her contract with David O. Selznick was that under no circumstances would she be expected to go out to Hollywood or have anything to do with the conversion of the novel into film. The public prominence into which the novel and then the movie forced her was such that she declared emphatically that she was through with writing fiction forever, and glad of it. In later years she appears to have changed her mind, but not to the extent of ever actually beginning another novel. When she died on August 16, 1949, after being struck by an automobile, she was a one-book novelist: a single book that has been translated into twenty-five languages and sold in the tens of millions.

If Margaret Mitchell ever read William Faulkner, I do not know of it; if nothing else she must have encountered his stories in the *Saturday Evening Post.* Faulkner would seem to have left no comments on *Gone with the Wind*. At the time of its publication he said he hadn't read either it or *Anthony Adverse* because of their inordinate length: ". . . no story takes 1,000 pages to tell," he said.[3] Faulkner was not a notably jealous man, but it must have galled him to realize that a book such as *Absalom, Absalom!,* which he told a friend was "the best novel ever yet written by an American,"[4] should have so poor a sale, while another Southern novel with roughly the same Southern subject matter was so extravagant a best seller. Faulkner didn't write merely for money, but at the time he needed money very badly indeed.

No matter; the two novels have had different audiences, will doubtless continue to do so. Faulkner's fiction is "highbrow" fiction, written in the tradition of Dreiser, Hawthorne, Melville, James; Miss Mitchell's novel is and was intended to be "middlebrow" literature, of a piece with *Anthony Adverse, To Have and To Hold, Ben Hur, The Last Days of Pompeii,* and so on. So we have treated them, and with some justification. As well compare the painting of Pablo Picasso with that of Norman Rockwell, or the mind of the late Sigmund Freud with that of Dr. Joyce Brothers, Ph.D., or the theology of Karl Barth with the Rev. Billy Graham.

Yet is it so simple as that? I think not. My hunch is rather that these two novels, published in the same year by two Southern novelists, and dealing with the same period of Southern history, not only make an interesting comparison, but that each emerges from such a comparison with considerable honor. Moreover, there are certain startling similarities in *Absalom, Absalom!* and *Gone with the Wind,* and we might well consider what they signify about the time and place from which both novels sprang—the Deep South of the Depression 1930s, with the Confederate veterans almost all dead by then, and the one-time agricultural region a full working partner in an industrializing, urbanizing American society, though

83

still with enough significant differences to keep it politically the Solid South.

Consider, first of all, the personality of the central protagonist of each novel, and that protagonist's relationship to the community. Thomas Sutpen is a strong, ruthless, single-minded man, intent upon setting up his dynasty, and with neither an interest in nor even an awareness of the feelings of those with whom he comes into contact in his relentless drive for his goal. Scarlett O'Hara is similarly quite contemptuous and heedless of the manners, mores, and feelings of her fellow Atlantans in her quest for success. She horrifies her friends and enrages her foes as she flouts the conventions of well-bred Atlanta society both during and after the war; nothing—her family, her honor, her sex, her several husbands' needs or wishes—is allowed to stand in her way. Both Sutpen and Scarlett are hard-headed, tough-minded self-seekers, who refuse to allow the niceties of social custom to retard their consuming ambition. Neither of them is remotely concerned with public opinion; both view the human beings they encounter merely as commodities to be expended in pursuit of their objectives.

When the Civil War comes to Georgia, Scarlett O'Hara resents it because it will interfere with her social life; and when as a young war widow she is expected to remain in mourning she uses Southern patriotism, about which she has no feelings at all, as an excuse to permit her to go out in public, dance with Rhett Butler, and resume her prematurely blighted social career. Thomas Sutpen rides off to war as a Confederate officer, but there is never any doubt about why he is in the army: he wishes to protect his investment. When after the war he is urged by his neighbors to join in nightriding activities he tells them he is too busy; the proper course of action for the South, he says, is to get back to work and restore its fortune—admirable advice in this instance, but given not from a feeling for the welfare of the South but because he doesn't wish to be diverted from his sole and consuming private goal. Sutpen has no wish to get involved in overthrowing the Yankee-enforced Reconstruction government; any government that will keep things sufficiently orderly so that he can concentrate upon his design is presumably acceptable to him. Similarly, Scarlett O'Hara doesn't care for the Klan because it means disorder, and for all her troubles

84

with Yankee bummers and Scalawag politicians while she was trying to save Tara, she is quite willing to socialize with the recent enemy after the war if it will promote her lumber business.

Both Thomas Sutpen and Scarlett O'Hara, in short, live and function within a complex and sharply drawn community, yet they are
not members of that community in any true sense. They are almost
completely passionless concerning the things about which the
community feels most strongly, and for identical reasons: they have
their own private goals and will expend no passion or emotion on
anything that does not advance those goals. Though nominally citizens, they are outsiders; moreover, their single-mindedness and
their ruthless acquisitiveness embody just the elements that will
eventually destroy the societies in which they live and flourish.

Of the last comment, more later; for now I should like to note
certain interesting similarities in the stratification of social classes
in the two novels. Here, because of chronology, it is appropriate to
shift the comparison with Thomas Sutpen from Scarlett O'Hara to
her father Gerald, who is roughly Sutpen's age. Sutpen, of course, is
a parvenu, a man of no breeding, who as a poor white youth in Tidewater Virginia aspires to the status of a planter-aristocrat and will
not rest until he can own the big house with the formal gardens and
have the family that will give him his dynasty. Though the northern
Mississippi country he seeks out in order to secure his land and begin his dynasty has itself been settled by whites for only a very few
years, already there are upon the land men who have made themselves into something of a local squirearchy: the Compsons, Ben-
bows, Sartorises, De Spains. Members of these families, if they did
not trace their lineage back to the grandees of plantation Virginia,
could even so say as Rosa Coldfield did, that "our father knew who
his father was in Tennessee and who his grandfather had been in
Virginia and our neighbors and the people we lived among—that
we knew and we knew they knew we knew . . . ."[5]

When Sutpen gets his ten miles of bottom-land and brings in the
slaves and builds his mansion—the source of his wealth being
highly suspect—he then seeks respectability, and goes to town in
search of a wife who can provide him with that status as well as be
the mother of his son and heir. His choice of Ellen Coldfield, as we
are told, is deliberate and unerring, and though it shocks the town

85

to learn that this daughter of a Methodist elder has accepted him, the eventual result is that together with Sutpen's land and money, her presence as mistress of Sutpen's Hundred is sufficient to give Sutpen the status he requires. There is, in any event, no question of the right of his son Henry to be considered—to use the words of the letter that Quentin Compson and Shreve McCannon imagine the New Orleans lawyer as addressing to Henry Sutpen, Esquire, at the University of Mississippi—a "young gentleman whose position needs neither detailing nor recapitulation in the place where this letter is read . . ." (*Absalom!,* p. 315).

In very much the same situation, the Irish immigrant Gerald O'Hara "with a ruthless singleness of purpose . . . desired his own house, his own plantation, his own horses, his own slaves."[6] Upon discovering that the Tidewater region of Georgia "was too firmly held by an entrenched aristocracy for him ever to hope to win the place he intended to have," he seeks out the new lands of northern Georgia (*GWTW,* p. 46). He wins a plantation in a carefully arranged poker game, buys his slaves, and builds his mansion. Next he too recognizes the need for a wife, who "must be a lady and lady of blood" (*GWTW,* p. 52), and so goes back to Savannah and wins the hand of his Ellen—a Robillard, of an old French family. Their children, growing up among Wilkeses, Calverts, Tarletons, and Fontaines, are indisputably members of the resident gentry; they belong to what the slaves are made to refer to as "the Quality," and they look down upon the Poor White Trash.

Now of course there are important differences between Thomas Sutpen and Gerald O'Hara, and so far as qualities of human warmth go, these are all to the advantage of O'Hara. However intense his ambition, he is affable and generous, kind to his slaves, and despite his roughness of manner and style is generally accepted and liked by his neighbors. There is nothing in Gerald O'Hara's makeup comparable to the passion for abstract perfection of design, devoid of human considerations, with which Thomas Sutpen pursues his dream. When O'Hara goes in search of a bride, he seeks a wife he can love and cherish, not merely a breeder of children who will perfect a design; human love, not dynastic perpetuation, is what produces O'Hara's children and characterizes his conduct as their father.

86

We can see the difference in the houses the two men build; the mansion at Sutpen's Hundred, designed by an imported French architect, rises in the Mississippi wilderness as an empty symbol of planter magnificence, a palace, for which the necessary dynastic occupants must then be secured. By contrast Gerald O'Hara's Tara is an ample, rather plain affair of no particular style, added to as the family's needs require. Thomas Sutpen lives *in,* but is not *of,* the community of Yoknapatawpha. Gerald O'Hara, the Irish-born immigrant, becomes a member of the north Georgia community and shares its loyalties, hatreds, loves, and sorrows. Not Gerald O'Hara but his daughter Scarlett stands aloof from the human beings around her.

Thomas Sutpen's dynastic ambitions fail when his unacknowledged son by his first wife, Charles Bon, is shot to death by Henry Sutpen, his son by his second wife, in order to prevent Charles, who is presumably part black, from marrying his half-sister Judith Sutpen. Despite Henry's admiration and love for Charles Bon, he proves obedient to the community's racial mores; we recall that when Henry urges Charles not to go through with the marriage plan because he is Judith's brother, as well as his own, Charles replies, "No I'm not. I'm the nigger that's going to sleep with your sister" (*Absalom!,* p. 358). The issue is stated succinctly: Faulkner deliberately has a Confederate soldier use an anachronistic expression, characteristic of the South of Faulkner's own day. In shooting his own brother, Henry does his father's bidding, but not in any attempt to further Thomas Sutpen's abstract design of perfection; rather he acts out of the racial prejudices of his community, which decree that racial "purity" comes before all else.

There is little or no evidence that his father shares any such personal racial prejudice. Thomas Sutpen twice destroys his plans for dynastic continuity when he learns that its absolute perfection of design would be tarnished by the likely presence of black blood. Yet when the dynasty is not involved, he displays no racial prejudice whatever, raising his daughter by a slave right there in the house with his family, and even engaging in public fist fights with his slaves. His insistence upon an immaculate racial heritage for his children is abstract: because in the *society* (not the *community* as such) in which his design is to be executed, black ancestry is held

87

to be a flaw, he cannot tolerate it. By contrast his son Henry shares the community ethos, kills the man he admires most in the world because finally, as Charles himself tells him, "it's the miscegenation, not the incest, which you can't bear" (*Absalom!,* p. 356). The crime is the same; the motives for it are importantly different.

In *Gone with the Wind* Scarlett O'Hara is no dissenter from community standards on racial matters, nor for that matter is Margaret Mitchell; but otherwise it is she, and not her father, who pursues a design for success without reference to its relationship to the community. The ostensible reason for Scarlett O'Hara's single-minded quest for financial fortune is the destitution she experiences at Tara during the final months of the war; she is determined to save Tara at any cost, and has recurring nightmares of being hungry and cold and of fleeing from some nameless terror. This explanation has always seemed rather unconvincing to me. Well before the wartime ordeal at the devastated plantation home, she has demonstrated that she is deeply out of sympathy with the social and familial status quo, abidingly unhappy with her lot, contemptuous of the patriotic feelings of the community, and unwilling to acquiesce in the traditional standards set for the Southern lady of her station and her time.

Supposedly this is because she is in love with a man she cannot have. But what is Ashley Wilkes' appeal for her? It is not Ashley's actual personality; when finally she realizes what he is really like, she does not want him. He seems to be a kind of symbol of well-born grace, culture, sophistication, aristocratic bearing: the perfect Southern gentlemen. "He never really existed at all, except in my imagination," she realizes at the end. "I loved something I made up, something that's just as dead as Melly is. I made a pretty suit of clothes and fell in love with it. And when Ashley came riding along, so handsome, so different, I put that suit on him and made him wear it whether it fitted him or not. And I wouldn't see what he really was. I kept on loving the pretty clothes—and not him at all" (*GWTW,* p. 1016). She realizes then that she had wanted him only because she could not have him, and that if ever she had gotten him she would no longer have desired him. Ashley Wilkes, as he existed for her in the long years before Melanie's death, was thus in his own way an abstraction, an ideal design as unanchored in real life as Sutpen's dream of dynasty.

Why such an abstraction? Because, I would think, Ashley Wilkes symbolizes the dream of the Old South: the ideal of plantation perfection. Even the home he will someday inherit, Twelve Oaks, partakes of the ideal for Scarlett: "They topped the rise and the white house reared its perfect symmetry before her, tall of columns, wide of verandas, flat of roof, beautiful as a woman is beautiful who is so sure of her charm that she can be generous and gracious to all. Scarlett loved Twelve Oaks even more than Tara, for it had a stately beauty, a mellowed dignity that Gerald's house did not possess" (*GWTW,* p. 94). And after Sherman had come through, it is precisely the sight of the gutted and ruined Twelve Oaks that directly triggers the vow she makes that "As God is my witness, as God is my witness, the Yankees aren't going to lick me. I'm going to live through this, and when it's over, I'm never going to be hungry again. No, nor any of my folks. If I have to steal or kill—as God is my witness, I'm never going to be hungry again" (*GWTW,* p. 428).

The loss of the war, the destruction of the plantation way of life, the coming of the Yankees, the Carpetbaggers, and Reconstruction supposedly represent deprivation, the loss of the beauty and comfort that might have been, the end of a Golden Age, and Scarlett O'Hara's subsequent career as businesswoman and entrepreneur in postwar Atlanta is depicted as the response of one who, determined not to be borne down to destruction by living in the past, squares her shoulders and makes the most of a new and more elemental world. As she says of the women of postwar Atlanta, "The silly fools don't seem to realize that you can't be a lady without money!" (*GWTW,* p. 609). For Ashley Wilkes it may be the Götterdämerung; Scarlett will live in the present.

The novel, Miss Mitchell once said, is about the theme of survival; because Scarlett has Gerald O'Hara's toughness within her bones, she will not be defeated by the cruel circumstances in which she finds herself, but will make the best of it. Isn't the truth rather that the debacle of the war and the breakdown of the old plantation society serve to liberate Scarlett? They enable her to do what she could never have thought of doing in the antebellum plantation society: live a life of her own, own property, go into business, make money. The notion that what Scarlett does after the fall of the South is merely a matter of making the best of a disadvantaged situation is neither psychologically nor historically convincing. She does not *wish* to be a lady. If we think of the Scarlett of Tara and compare her with the Scarlett who married first Frank Kennedy and then Rhett Butler, and is making money and thriving in Reconstruction Atlanta, we can only recognize how far more satisfactory she finds the postwar South than the old. She even says as much to Ashley Wilkes: "I like these days better" (*GWTW*, p. 924). Supposedly she doesn't really mean that, but given the energy, the determination, and the desire for material advancement that characterize her every action, it is difficult to see why not, or to imagine what charms the antebellum life would ever have held for her that could come close to equalling the active entrepreneurial existence she leads in postwar Atlanta. It is not without significance, I believe, that one of the more memorable scenes in the opening chapters of the novel, as Scarlett prepares to attend the festivities at Twelve Oaks, is that in which Scarlett is laced up into a whalebone girdle; her body as well as spirit rebels against the constricted role of the plantation belle.

Margaret Mitchell went to considerable length to identify Scarlett O'Hara with the city of Atlanta. For Atlanta, too, the coming of the war meant opportunity rather than misfortune. As the chief rail junction connecting the east with Tennessee and the Gulf states, the city swiftly expanded in size and population, developed manufactures, and attained a boomtime prosperity until its defenses fell and Sherman's army burned and pillaged it. The setback was only temporary; Atlanta rose from its ashes like a fully certified phoenix and was very soon the commercial and manufacturing capital of the New South. The antebellum political domination of agricultural interests was broken by the war, and Atlanta most of all the cities of the New South took advantage of it. It was unhampered by the conventions and attitudes of the old tradition; it could make money and grow in size and strength without any of the aristocratic disdain for trade that had been part of the antebellum social stance. Atlanta had what it took to survive and flourish in postwar America; it had less to forget, it was open to the methods and ethics of industrial society, it recognized that—to echo Scarlett—to be a lady or a gentleman takes money, and it put what it considered first things, which is to say financial things, first. The implications of Scarlett O'Hara and her career for the community in which she is reared and thrives are, I think, quite far-reaching. But before we explore them, I should like to turn again to *Absalom, Absalom!* and Thomas Sutpen. Faulkner's protagonist, as we know, runs roughshod over the customs and attitudes of antebellum Mississippi. Indeed, Miss Rosa Coldfield's outrage is well known. As Quentin Compson thinks while listening to the old woman telling him about Sutpen's career, *"It's because she wants it told . . . so that people whom she will never see and whose names she will never hear and who have never heard her name nor seen her face will read it and know at last why God let us lose the War: that only through the blood of our men and the tears of our women could He slay this demon and efface his name and lineage from the earth* (*Absalom!,* p. 11). Miss Rosa is, of course, to say the least rather biased. But Quentin Compson's father is considerably less personally involved with Sutpen's personality, and he remarks almost the same thing, if with less demoniac imagery. Speaking of Miss Rosa Coldfield's father and his withdrawal from all contact with the life of the community of Jefferson when the war broke out, he advanced, as Quentin tells Shreve, this interpretation of Coldfield's action: "He knew that he would either be killed or die of hardship, and so he would not be present on that day when the South would realize that it was now paying the price for having erected its economic edifice not on the rock of stern morality but on the shifting sands of moral brigandage" (*Absalom!,* p. 260). Now that is what Quentin says that his father said about Goodhue Coldfield's view, not what William Faulkner necessarily thought: but surely the comment describes, in quite accurate moral fashion, the social implications of Thomas Sutpen's career. There seems little doubt that this is one of the meanings (not the only one) of Thomas Sutpen's story, and it is not accident that the language that Quentin is made to use is that of the teller of the tale, the central rhetorical and moral consciousness wherein the events of Faulkner's novel and the interpretation of those events are presented.

But Thomas Sutpen is not a "typical," or even a "representative" antebellum Southern figure. There is little doubt of that. The ab-

stract nature of his design, the contempt for the community he in-
habits, the utter ignorance and lack of feeling for tradition, his very
pragmatic attitude toward race (*he* doesn't share in the prejudice,
but because the society is prejudiced he must shape his design so as
to keep his dynasty pure white)—surely none of these attributes is
characteristic of the Old South. Whatever else may be said of the
antebellum planter, lack of community passion was not one of his
shortcomings! Sutpen, as Cleanth Brooks insists, scarcely makes a
uniquely Southern figure: "Thorsten Veblen would have understood
Sutpen's relation to traditional culture. Sutpen is on all fours with
the robber baron of the Gilded Age building a fake Renaissance palace on the banks of the Hudson."[7]

Brooks is led to emphasize Sutpen's relation to American, and not
peculiarly to Southern, society, in response to various glib asser-
tions by critics that Sutpen's rise and fall is somehow an allegory of
the rise and fall of the Old South, with the easy equation of Sutpen's
rejection of Charles Bon with the South's employment of Negro
slavery. The point is well taken, and I share Brooks' impatience with
that kind of superficial generalization. But there is more to the
problem than the question of Sutpen's "typicality," I think. One cannot separate *Absalom, Absalom!* from its relation to Southern history simply because its protagonist is not "typically" or "represen-
tatively" Southern. The issue is rather that in the antebellum South
a Thomas Sutpen *was* possible, and it is this that so appalls Quentin
Compson. Brooks' point, that Sutpen's career has its counterparts in
the robber barons of the Gilded Age, only demonstrates its universality. In any society, one might say, there are such men (and
women, if we are to believe Miss Mitchell) who can bend it to their
personal desire, exploit its institutions, seize upon its openings,
capitalize upon its weaknesses for their own purposes. Given the
antebellum South as it was, with its attitudes toward land, its structures of caste, its reliance upon human slavery, this is what the ruthless ambition of a Sutpen could do, and the cost in human degradation that such ambition could exact. Such is Faulkner's story, or part
of his story.

Indeed, there is a rather striking parallel to Sutpen's particular career, I think, in the history of the Mississippi from which William
Faulkner's imagination sprang. For as historians know very well, an-

tebellum Mississippi settlement and development was not a matter of the slow evolution, over several centuries, of an ordered plantation society. It happened almost at once. When the Indian lands were opened up in the 1810s, 1820s, and 1830s, men came pouring in from the older South to seize the chance to raise cotton and grow rich. There are numerous instances of planters from Virginia and South Carolina transporting their entire establishments from the exhausted soil of the east to the new land, and setting up not merely farms and homes but ornate mansions in the cleared wilderness. More often the newcomers were not established planters seeking greater advantage, but men on the make, middle-class farmers and others who coveted, in the new land to the west, the opportunities denied them in the more settled seaboard South, and emigrated to the Mississippi country with the definite purpose of acquiring land, buying slaves, raising cotton, and becoming gentlemen-planters. The older aristocracy of the east called them "cotton snobs," the planter equivalent for newly rich opportunists in search of social status. Surely there was an important element of preconceived design, of abstraction, in the way in which the old Southwest was transformed almost overnight from wilderness to a society of white-columned mansions, plantation lords and ladies, broad acres of cotton worked by hundreds of slaves. And just as surely it was the ownership and exploitation of human beings as property that made such a life possible, and ultimately brought it down to defeat and ruin when the war came. And if so, is not Thomas Sutpen, in what he was and what he exemplified, only an intensified delineation of the potentialities within the society itself?

Were there any Thomas Sutpens in Margaret Mitchell's antebellum Georgia? To ask the question is to answer it: there are always Thomas Sutpens, and always will be, for there is something of the self-serving user of other persons in all of us, which is what gives *Absalom, Absalom!* the profound historical insight that it displays. We have seen how within the much more benevolently limned characterization of Gerald O'Hara there are elements of Sutpen's single-mindedness, his desire for status and dynasty, just as in Gerald's daughter Scarlett there are ruthless ambition, opportunism, contempt for tradition, barely masked aggressiveness.

The difference between Thomas Sutpen's antebellum Mississippi and Gerald O'Hara's antebellum Georgia lies in the willingness of William Faulkner to recognize the moral implications that Thomas Sutpen's career held for his society. By contrast, the depiction of plantation Georgia in *Gone with the Wind* is romantic, uncritical, eulogistic. Slavery is a benevolent institution, only poor whites and Yankee overseers are ever immoral or ambitious, life is beautiful, Eden is retold. There is no evil in Margaret Mitchell's antebellum Southern garden; it comes from outside with Sherman's army. In Floyd Watkins' apt description, "there is no mention of sweat, of exhaustion, of the arduousness of field work. *Gone with the Wind* is a world without sweat, except for that caused by the Yankees."[8] The only hint that the antebellum society might contain within itself the possibility of self-destruction lies in its naïveté, as seen in its facile assumption that any Southern boy will be able to whip ten Yankees, that Southern independence can be secured merely by a declaration to that effect, and so on. From the standpoint of recorded history, Margaret Mitchell's depiction of prewar plantation society is romanticized and false. Miss Mitchell liked to think of herself as a historical realist, but when it came to antebellum life she was as whole-souled a perpetuator of the plantation myth as Thomas Nelson Page or Stark Young at their most eulogistic.

But with wartime and postwar Georgia it is another matter. Any reputable historian can attest to the one-sidedness of Margaret Mitchell's depiction of the Reconstruction in Georgia; she accepts uncritically all the folklore of Reconstruction, depicts the Ku Klux Klan as a noble institution of the best people chiefly concerned with discouraging black sexual assault upon white women, portrays Reconstruction government as being made up exclusively of scheming Carpetbaggers and deluded blacks, magnifies the political disqualification of white Georgians, fails to recognize the extent to which ex-Confederates and other Southerners of good family and social status took part in Reconstruction politics and finances and yet managed to retain and even enhance their positions when Reconstruction government was ousted. As one Georgia editor admitted soon after Reconstruction ended, "It is a mortifying fact that the extravagance of Bullock's administration—we say nothing as to the corruption—benefited about as many Democrats as Republicans."[9] Anyone familiar with the postwar career of Governor Joseph C.

94

Brown, the commercial and financial alliances developed among such leading Georgians as John B. Gordon and Alfred Colquitt, the way in which "Carpetbaggers" such as H. I. Kimball and even Governor Rufus Bullock himself were received into the best society of post-1876 Atlanta, will recognize the element of falseness in Margaret Mitchell's supposedly realistic depiction of post-1865 Atlanta.

Yet despite the one-sidedness and the mythology of Miss Mitchell's elaborate documentation, in an ultimate sense her presentation is both remarkably accurate and deeply moving, for the simple reason that Scarlett O'Hara is what matters, and in the vicissitudes and triumphs of her career as entrepreneur and opportunist, we have a notable glimpse into the times. The most profound statement in *Gone with the Wind*, I think, is the one which I have several times quoted. Let me place it in context. Scarlett O'Hara, back in Atlanta after the desperate days at Tara at the close of the war, attends a dance. The ladies and gentlemen of Atlanta society, resuming the social regimen amid diminished circumstance, seem to Scarlett to be different from her. "Everything in their old world had changed but the old forms," she thinks. "The old usages went on, must go on, for the forms were all that were left to them. . . . No matter what sights they had seen, what menial tasks they had done and would have to do, they remained ladies and gentlemen, royalty in exile—bitter, aloof, incurious, kind to one another, diamond hard, as bright and brittle as the crystals of the broken chandelier over their heads." Scarlett realizes the difference, as she sees it, between them and herself. She cannot bravely ignore loss and misfortune, cannot wear a mask to disguise her feelings, "survey the wreck of the world with an air of casual unconcern." Not until she has once again acquired the comfort, the wealth, the material possessions of the prewar days will she rest easy: ". . . she knew that she would never feel like a lady again until her table was weighted with silver and crystal and smoking with rich food, until her own horses and carriages stood in her stables, until black hands and not white took the cotton from Tara." And then, "'Ah!' she thought angrily, sucking in her breath. 'That's the difference! Even though they're poor, they still feel like ladies and I don't. The silly fools don't seem to realize that you can't be a lady without money!'" (*GWTW*, pp. 608–9). Whereupon she goes in pursuit of Frank Kennedy, her sister's suitor, and secures him and his money for her own. Her career as sawmill operator, lumber salesman, investor, and entrepreneur follows.

The attitude may be materialistic, but historically it is also remarkably accurate, and in it lie the psychological strength and the historical insight of *Gone with the Wind*. The statement has often been made, by the author herself among others, that Scarlett O'Hara does what she does in order to survive, with the implication that had it not been for the need to sweat and scheme in order to survive, she would have been better off, happier, more contented. I have earlier suggested that rather the reverse is more like the truth: she was deeply dissatisfied under the old regime, and the effect of the war and the destruction of the plantation system was to liberate her from the constriction of her traditional role as Southern lady. And I have noted that in linking Scarlett with the spirit of postwar Atlanta, Miss Mitchell was quite accurate.

What Scarlett O'Hara does in postwar Atlanta—marrying for money, becoming a hard-nosed businesswoman, collaborating with the Carpetbag-Scalawag government, employing convict labor to work her mill, marrying the wealthy Rhett Butler when Frank Kennedy dies, building an ostentatious Victorian mansion, and so on—is, though perhaps exaggerated at times, no more and no less than what the South as a whole did in the late nineteenth century and is still doing in the twentieth century. It is what a middle-class, democratic, capitalistic society always does: try to make money and improve its position. Like Thomas Sutpen, Scarlett O'Hara is not peculiarly Southern, but American *and therefore Southern.* She does not merely do those things; she enjoys doing them. One couldn't and can't be a lady—in Scarlett's definition—without money, because being what Scarlett means by a lady depends upon leisure, which is possible only when there is someone else to do the physical labor. When Scarlett refers to being a lady, she is not talking about morality, codes of honor and virtue, grace and courtesy and the like; she is talking about social status. And not merely Scarlett but Margaret Mitchell is aware of the inescapable relationship between leisure and money, between position and power—between, in short, worldly Success and worldly Ambition. And however the reader of *Gone with the Wind*, like the author, may be appalled at times by the price that must be paid to achieve Success, there is no doubt that in a post-Edenic world such a price is always going to be paid, regretfully perhaps but willingly. Scarlett O'Hara has no choice, really: just as historically Atlanta and the South had no choice after Appomattox but to seek fulfillment on the terms offered it, which were those of postwar industrial America. But there is always a bit of remorse that goes along with such a transaction: Americans (like other people) do what they must to make a good living and to achieve success, are pragmatic and reasonably efficient, yet at the same time tend to feel somewhat guilty over their efficiency and practicality, and look with a certain amount of wistful regret at the vanished grace and leisure of earlier and simpler days. This has historically been one of the charms of the plantation image in our literature: the ideal of an ordered, leisured, settled life, free of striving and the pursuit of the almighty dollar, with time for relaxation and enjoyment of one's days. It has been a staple of Southern literature at least since Kennedy's *Swallow Barn*. Thomas Nelson Page rang the changes on it; consider the opening paragraphs of "Marse Chan," in which a postwar gentleman rides along a Tidewater Virginia road, notices the rundown and decaying mansions of the old regime set back half-hidden from the road, and remarks as follows: "Distance was nothing to these people; time was of no consequence to them. They desired but a level path in life, and that they had, though the way was longer, and the outer world strode by them as they dreamed." [10]

But it *is* the past, it *is* a dream, not reality: and Margaret Mitchell shows her Scarlett O'Hara as preferring the present, doing what she must do because she believes in real life and not in playing a role in a game of charades. Historically she represents the spirit of enterprise, of ambition, of practical achievement; she is what the South felt that it *had to be* after 1865, and what Atlanta in particular wanted to be and did so well. But she is not happy. She does not recognize who it is that she loves, and when she finally does, it is too late, for she has driven him away: "Captain Butler—be kind to him. He loves you so" (*GWTW*, p. 1011). Only he doesn't anymore. So it is right; if the moral of the story is to come out right, the price must be paid, and yet it is very sad. This is melodrama, but melodrama of a very high sort, for psychologically it is authentic, and historically quite accurate, ten thousand postwar eulogies to the

Days Befo' De Wah and invocations of the Purity of Southern Womanhood to the contrary notwithstanding.

The difference between *Gone with the Wind* and *Absalom, Absalom!* is that William Faulkner realized, both in dismay and fascination, what Margaret Mitchell could face only partially and intermittently: that it is not history that makes human beings but that human beings *are* the history. To put it another way, it was the Fall of Man, not the fall of Atlanta, that was responsible for Scarlett O'Hara's career. Thomas Sutpen pursued his design and wreaked his destruction in the Old South, but historically he could as appropriately have been Duke or De Bardeleben or Candler or Cannon or Reynolds (or for that matter, Carnegie or Rockefeller). In Faulkner's Yoknapatawpha County there is no Golden Age; there are only men in history. Or to express the difference still another way: there is no Quentin Compson in *Gone with the Wind*. There is no point of historical consciousness from which to view the past as the living past, and in so doing to recognize that the men and women who lived in it functioned within a moral circumstance no less complex or difficult than our own, facing not History but life, wearing not costumes but clothes, achieving success or failure in as ambiguous and compromised a form as must we.

Consider, for example, the problem of race and slavery. Faulkner cannot sentimentalize or sidestep its moral consequences as did Margaret Mitchell, because, growing up as and when he did, he knew that people back in the antebellum period were men and women, too, and he could not create his art without exploring the implications of that fact in a society in which slavery and race were fundamental considerations. Human complexity and the necessity for moral judgment did not begin in the year 1865.

Dealing as Margaret Mitchell also did with the single most cataclysmic moral and social event in this region's history, William Faulkner saw history as a problem of moral knowledge, not of documentary authenticity. So he created a character who could be of his own time—just ten years older than himself—and he let this character be the center of consciousness, to whom the story is told by eyewitnesses and others and by whom it is sorted out, understood, and, finally, judged. He recognized that the reason why the particu-

lar history was so much a part of his own consciousness was that
emotionally, morally, in shame as well as pride, it was a problem of
self-knowledge, and that in order to deal with it authentically it was
essential to recognize it in terms of its impact upon himself as a
twentieth-century Southerner and Mississippian, as well as to recite
what happened. He knew that in his mind and heart, as in the consciousness of any Southerner of his generation possessed of imagination and compassion as well as pride and anger, the two were
inseparable.

So he invented Quentin Compson, or utilized him (since he had
already conceived him when he wrote *The Sound and the Fury* a
half-dozen years earlier) and not only that, but he divided him into
the two Quentins:

> The Quentin Compson preparing for Harvard in the South, the deep
> South dead since 1865 and peopled with garrulous outraged baffled
> ghosts, listening, having to listen, to one of the ghosts which had re-
> fused to lie still even longer than most had, telling him about old
> ghost-times; and the Quentin Compson who was still too young to
> deserve yet to be a ghost, but nevertheless having to be one for all
> that, since he was born and bred in the deep South the same as she
> [Miss Rosa Coldfield] was—the two separate Quentin Compsons
> now talking to one another in the long silence of notpeople, in
> notlanguage. . . . [*Absalom!*, p. 9]

Only through the two Quentins could the story of Thomas Sutpen
be told, for it took both the detachment and the passionate involvement, the logic as well as the emotion, the moral conscience as well
as the admiration and anger. It was Faulkner's purpose as historical
novelist to reveal the past of his community, but he knew that understanding what happened in the past is a matter of interpretation,
and that the interpretation, being necessarily performed in the
present, had to exist in a moral as well as analytical relationship to a
history so compelling as that which he proposed to use for his fiction. His genius led him to see that the best way to both chronicle
and judge that history was to let it be discovered and interpreted by
an observer, one who would be near enough to it to be involved
emotionally, yet distant enough from it to view it in moral perspec-

tive. Had he merely selected the conventional point of view, as Margaret Mitchell and most historical novelists have done, the act of his judgment would have to be done anachronistically, from above. This would have forced him to view what for his own time was the most urgent moral issue involved in that past—the racial equation—in a way so different from those of his historical characters that he would falsify the difficulties of their situation through undue emphasis and shallow oversimplification. Either that, or he would have to ignore the dimension of slavery and race altogether, as Margaret Mitchell did, and thus falsify what to him in his time was the essential moral problem of that past epoch. By letting Quentin Compson search out and evaluate the story, as a young Southerner of college age in the year 1909 (or 1910), close enough to the events to hear about them from eyewitnesses and to experience the passions that were still involved four decades afterward, yet far enough removed to be able to see through the passions and not avert his eyes from the central dimension of race, he could tell the story as he wished it told. Writing the story himself a quarter-century after Quentin's involvement in it, he could portray Quentin and Quentin's imagination, as Quentin set out to reconstruct the story. Quentin could do the emphasizing and moralizing; he could show Quentin doing it. He could make his story that of the difficulty of reconstructing the past by showing Quentin trying to do it.

When Malcolm Cowley sent Faulkner the draft of a paragraph from the introduction that he was preparing for *The Portable Faulkner* in 1944, he referred to Faulkner as one who "was writing a story, and one that affected him deeply, but he was also brooding over a social situation." Faulkner was quick to correct him: "I think Quentin, not Faulkner, is the correct yardstick here. I was writing the story, but he not I was brooding over a situation." [11] Precisely. By using Quentin as narrator, Faulkner was able to concentrate as artist on the characterization, to portray Quentin's emotional involvement, without the danger of an unmediated first-hand involvement on his own part inhibiting his ability to explore that "social situation." The result was a triumph of the art of historical fiction: an intensely felt rendition of a historical experience, passionately created yet free of either evasion or falsification. At the close, he could confirm Quentin's divided loyalties—*"I dont hate it. . . . I dont hate it"*—because he had permitted that ambivalence to be used, through the device of the two Quentins, as his method of structure and exploration.

To do this, however, he too had to pay a price. By telling a story about someone telling a story, not merely before and after the main story line as a frame device, but as a structural element throughout, there had to be a loss of surface immediacy. Thus no such lengthy and exciting episode as Margaret Mitchell's description of Scarlett O'Hara during the burning of Atlanta was possible; it could not have been sustained other than through direct, first-hand experience. Nor could he rely on the melodrama that made *Gone with the Wind* so widely popular. No major character could be left importantly unexamined; no character could be presented or considered apart from the attempt to analyze and explain the character's motives. There could be no such dashing, romantic lead as Rhett Butler, for his counterpart in *Absalom, Absalom!,* Charles Bon, had to be interpreted by Quentin (and his alter ego, Shreve) as the victim of the social situation in order to get at the heart of the moral problem. Is Rhett Butler's change from a sardonic, cynical profiteer and rebel against his society's insensitivity into a sentimental seeker after social respectability and conformity really very convincing? The point is that in *Absalom, Absalom!*, so potentially important a question as that could not be left unexplored, because the method of structural narration would immediately focus upon it. Quentin and Shreve could no more have ignored what lay behind Rhett's attitude toward his society than they could have ignored the question of why Charles Bon was drawn toward marrying Judith Sutpen. And if Rhett Butler had been subjected to that sort of psychological and moral exploration, what would that have done to the pathos at the close of *Gone with the Wind*: "My dear, I don't give a damn" (*GWTW,* p. 1035)? It was just this inability to hold back from trying to understand and to judge that made Faulkner into a great novelist, for it also led him into the brilliant technical exploration that would permit him to get at what he wanted. Faulkner's so-called "experimental" technique was never an end in itself; it was always a means toward understanding. Sometimes this made for difficult reading; al-

101

ways it meant that the reader had to get involved in the telling as well as in what was being told. That was no way to write a best-seller.

I don't think that it ever occurred to Margaret Mitchell that she couldn't recreate the past so long as she was faithful enough to her documentation. The result is that she gave us a novel with a very modern heroine in lace and crinoline, whom she felt she had to punish for her emancipated attitudes by taking her lover away. But it is very powerful, for we too are ambivalent about doing what we have to do instead of what we have been taught we should do, and historically quite authentic, for the time and setting were such that decision was demanded in very dramatic and drastic form. The difficulty, which makes *Gone with the Wind* flawed in so many of its parts, is that the author was only intermittently aware of the choice that was being made. William Faulkner, on the other hand, recognized the ambivalence and made it into a technique for the exploration of the relation of the past to the present.

Both these novels were published in the South of the 1930s, a time when, as in the 1860s though less violently, old ways, old attitudes, old standards of conduct were being tested by economic necessity and found in need of adjustment. Another generation of Americans was learning for its time that it takes money to be a lady. Both Margaret Mitchell and William Faulkner were willing to explore the past in terms of what they knew. *Gone with the Wind* found immediate popular readership. *Absalom, Absalom!* did not; we had first to learn how to read it. For Faulkner knew what Margaret Mitchell could not quite face, and to explain why required a new way of telling a story. This was that Melanie Wilkes, the traditionalist, the lady, and Scarlett O'Hara, the opportunist, the woman, were not really two persons, but, like the two Quentins, one and the same flawed human being.

Notes

1. Quoted in Frank Luther Mott, *Golden Multitudes: The Story of Best Sellers in the United States* (New York: Macmillan, 1947), p. 256.

2. Clifton P. Fadiman, "Faulkner, Extra-Special, Double Distilled," *New Yorker,* October 31, 1936, quoted in *Faulkner: A Collection of Critical Essays*, ed. Robert Penn Warren (Englewood Cliffs, N.J.: Prentice-Hall, 1966), p. 290.

3. Quoted in Joseph Blotner, *Faulkner: A Biography* (New York: Random House, 1974), p. 977.

4. Ibid., p. 927.

5. William Faulkner, *Absalom, Absalom!* (New York: Random House, 1936), pp. 16–17 (cited hereafter in text). The quotations in this essay are reprinted with the permission of Random House.

6. Margaret Mitchell, *Gone with the Wind* (New York: Macmillan, 1936), pp. 45–46 (cited hereafter in text).

7. Cleanth Brooks, *William Faulkner: The Yoknapatawpha Country* (New Haven: Yale University Press, 1963), p. 298.

8. Floyd C. Watkins, "*Gone with the Wind* as Vulgar Literature," *Southern Literary Journal* 2 (Spring 1970): 97.

9. E. Merton Coulter, *The South during Reconstruction, 1865–1877* (Baton Rouge: Louisiana State University Press, 1947), p. 153.

10. Thomas Nelson Page, "Marse Chan," *In Old Virginia, or, Marse Chan and Other Stories* (New York: Charles Scribner's Sons, 1887), p. 1.

11. Malcolm Cowley, *The Faulkner-Cowley File, Letters and Memories, 1944– 1962* (New York: Viking Press, 1966), pp. 13–14.

"The Bad Little Girl of the Good Old Days": Gender, Sex, and the Southern Social Order

Anne Jones

Gone with the Wind has often been referred to as "a woman's novel." It is, but not in the way most critics have approached the concept. It is more; it is a novel about men and, more generally, the ways in which social gender roles shape peoples' lives in Southern society.

Although *Gone with the Wind* deals directly and overtly with several themes, one issue that unites them and of which its author appears to be least conscious is precisely the concern for gender. Mitchell herself saw the novel's theme as survival—who makes it through a traumatic, world-destroying event, who doesn't and why. Though her own view of the novel's theme—personal survival— comes close to the heart of her work by emphasizing individual psychology, it is rather imprecise. *Gone with the Wind* itself presents a far more interesting and more complex problem: it questions not only the means but the value of sheer survival, and defines survival quite clearly as psychological and ethical as well as physical. The axes on which Mitchell imagined survival to balance are self-reliance and dependence. Carried to its extreme, self-reliance becomes isolation and even solipsism; dependence, at worst, becomes the loss of selfhood and identity. Because the culture she lived in and the culture she imagined both placed these specific values upon one or the other sex, the novel becomes a study in gender roles, in what it means to be a man or a woman in the South. This essay is an examination of gender roles in the novel and their relationship to the Southern social order.

The first chapter of *Gone with the Wind*, with its famous opening line— "Scarlett O'Hara was not beautiful, but men seldom realized it when caught by her charm as the Tarleton twins were" [1]—was written last, and in that chapter, then, one may reasonably expect to find Margaret Mitchell's final imaginative vision of her novel, those concerns that still—ten years after having begun the work—informed her pen. And central to that chapter is an obsession with gender roles.

Mitchell develops the theme of the memorable first line more

This essay is a version of a chapter in Anne Goodwyn Jones, *"Tomorrow Is Another Day": The Woman Writer in the South* (Baton Rouge: Louisiana State University Press, 1981).

105

fully in the rest of the paragraph with the indication that the concern will be gender and its relationship to action. Thus she continues the description of Scarlett's face as "too sharp" a blend of her mother's feminine face and her father's masculine one. The definition of masculinity in Clayton County soon follows: ". . . raising good cotton, riding well, shooting straight, dancing lightly, squiring the ladies with elegance and carrying one's liquor like a gentleman were the things that mattered" (p. 4). The distinctions continue immediately. True to one ideal of Southern ladyhood, Scarlett rejects any discussion of politics, threatening (in an appropriately feminine symbolic gesture) to "go in the house and shut the door" if the Tarleton twins keep up the talk about war (p. 5). Likewise, while the twins accept the cultural division between masculine and feminine, their own mother bridges the gap by her concern with horses and her ability to control them. That this is perceived as unusual behavior for a woman is clear in their comment that Mrs. Tarleton's daughters won't let her ride her new stallion to the picnic: "They said they were going to have her go to one party at least like a lady . . ." (p. 7). Scarlett reveals her own grounding in gender roles in calling Charles Hamilton a "sissy" (p. 9), yet her deviance from the female type is what attracts the twins to her: she doesn't "hold herself in" or "go around being cold and hateful when she's mad" like most girls (p. 11). Nevertheless, they also fall back on the most conventional gender-based explanation of Scarlett's behavior as she falls silent at the news of Ashley Wilkes's engagement: "Girls set a big store on knowing such things first" (p. 12). Fitting a gender norm is also the basis for their judgment of both Ashley Wilkes and the local poor farmer Abel Wynder. Whereas Wynder is a "real man" because he is the best shot in the Troop and knows all about living outdoors (p. 18), Ashley doesn't fit because he is "kind of queer about music and books and scenery" (p. 16).

Beginning, then, with this jumble of gender distinctions in the first chapter, the novel develops and elaborates these sexual roles and conflicts more thoroughly down to its closing pages. Early on, it presents an exact prescription for Southern ladyhood. It appears most clearly in the observation about Ellen Robillard O'Hara that her

Life was not easy, nor was it happy, but she did not expect life to be easy, and if it was not happy, that was woman's lot. It was a man's world, and she accepted it as such. The man owned the property, and the woman managed it. The man took the credit for the management, and the woman praised his cleverness. The man roared like a bull when a splinter was in his finger, and the woman muffled the moans of childbirth, lest she disturb him. Men were rough of speech and often drunk. Women ignored the lapses of speech and put the drunkards to bed without bitter words. Men were rude and outspoken, women were always kind, gracious and forgiving.

She had been reared in the tradition of great ladies, which had taught her how to carry her burden and still retain her charm, and she intended that her three daughters should be great ladies also.

[p. 58]

Purity, piety, domesticity, and submission are here—but mostly submission to the "weary load." The tone of anger is not Ellen's; it is the narrator's, and it rarely reappears in the novel. Instead, Mitchell created a woman whose ladyhood was only a veneer, and then saw what happened to her. As one might expect, Scarlett successively finds bellehood a trap, marriage a trap and widowhood a trap. There is no female role in which she is happy. So she adopts the male role, as indicated by her looking more and more like Gerald, and by the narrator's insistence that the Gerald in her soul wins over the Ellen. But by the end of the novel, the prescription still remains, consciously still endorsed, in Scarlett's mind:

What would have happened to me, to Wade, to Tara and all of us if I'd been—gentle when that Yankee came to Tara? I should have been—but I don't even want to think of that. And when Jonas Wilkerson was going to take the home place, suppose I'd been—kind and scrupulous? Where would we all be now? And if I'd been sweet and simple-minded and not nagged Frank about bad debts we'd—oh well. Maybe I am a rogue, but I won't be a rogue forever, Rhett. [p. 775]

And it is not by the masculine term "rogue" that her society calls Scarlett; it is "unwomanly" and "unsexed" (p. 947). For that society has carried through the war and into the Reconstruction period its old traditions, including that of the lady:

> The old usages went on, must go on, for the forms were all that were
> left to them . . . the leisured manners, the courtesy, the pleasant casu-
> alness in human contacts, and most of all, the protecting attitude of
> the men towards their women. . . . the men were courteous and
> tender and they almost succeeded in creating an atmosphere of shel-
> tering their women from all that was harsh and unfit for feminine
> eyes. That, thought Scarlett, was the height of absurdity, for there was
> little, now, which even the most cloistered women had not seen and
> known in the last five years. . . . But . . . they remained ladies and
> gentlemen. [p. 608]

It is significant that none of these ladies is a central character in
the novel, with the exception of Ellen. For, if the novel's theme
were truly survival, then the Atlanta women like Mrs. Elsing, Mrs.
Meade, and Mrs. Merriwether, all of whom worked after the war
(sewing, painting china, or making pies for sale) and all of whom
kept up the traditions and survived, would be the heroines. Even
Ellen, at the extreme of ladyhood, and Belle Watling, apparently at
the other extreme, as a madam, stay within the traditional scheme.
Because Ellen dies before the war ends, we do not see what Scarlett's model of the great lady would do after the war, and we are left
only with the prewar vision of sacrificial acceptance. And because
Belle Watling (despite her donations to the Confederacy) knows
her "place" and stays in it, even refusing to permit Melanie to address her on the street, she too endorses traditional definitions of
ladyhood.

The major female characters in the novel, Scarlett and Melanie,
both deviate in important though very different ways from the so-
cietal definitions of ladyhood. Though even before the war Scarlett's ladyhood is only a surface form of behavior, it is possible that
without the war, she would have kept the appearance of fitting the
forms. Yet because the war forces her to become "head of the house
now," the dependence forced on her by her gender role is replaced
by the opportunity to express the "masculine" side of herself, to use
her "sharp intelligence hidden beneath a face as sweet and bland as
a baby's" (p. 59) (an intelligence that, as is repeatedly pointed out,
is masculine because it can figure out dollars but not folks); her
headstrong, impetuous assertiveness (masculine because it came
from Gerald); and her desire to get out into the world (a masculine

108

desire because when she is literally out, she almost gets raped). Although Scarlett's character is complicated—her obstinacy, for instance, cannot be described as gender-specific—it is precisely her stereotypically masculine desires and behavior that form the central conflict within her and within the novel. For these desires and behavior push her towards autonomy and beyond, to the love of power and control of others as well as of the self. Once forced, at Tara, to run a small universe, she later, in Atlanta, enjoys running the sawmill, and still later, cannot stop her obsession with working harder and harder to earn more and more money, and to "bully" and control more and more people.

Yet there is another side to Scarlett, the "feminine" side that does not simply endure but enjoys dependence, the sense that an outer force provides stability. It is evident first consistently in her memories of Ellen, particularly of Ellen's office, the calm functional center of order at Tara. Not by accident did Mitchell describe Scarlett's final dream of Tara—to which she will respond by returning—by saying "she thought of Tara and it was as if a gentle cool hand were stealing over her heart" (p. 1036). That hand, through the novel, is Ellen's; and immediately after thinking of Tara, Scarlett "suddenly . . . wanted Mammy desperately, as she had wanted her when she was a little girl, wanted the broad bosom on which to lay her head: . . . Mammy, the last link with the old days" (p. 1037).

Scarlett's desire for dependence comes through clearly and consistently in her nightmare. In it, she is running through a heavy mist, alone, chased by an unknown presence, and looking for some haven. She repeats the dream several times, describing the "haven" to herself consciously as "Ashley" at one point, and telling Rhett and Melanie both the story of it. By the end of the novel, Mitchell has the dream become real: as Scarlett goes home from Melanie's deathbed, she begins to run through the heavy fog, and sees lights. "In her nightmare, there had never been any lights, only gray fog. Her mind seized on these lights . . . [for] lights meant safety, people, reality" (p. 1020). The lights are those of her home; now, says the narrator, "she knew the haven she had sought in dreams. . . . It was Rhett" (p. 1021). And, of course, it is not Rhett, for he no longer gives a damn about her; hence, her turn to Tara and Mammy.

Scarlett vacillates between these two extremes, never able to reconcile them. Because she has gone so far in the direction of self-reliance, for her sex and her period, she has cut off the fulfillment of her dependency needs, recognizing, for instance, the role Melanie has played to support her only after Melanie dies.

Her conscious independence and less conscious dependence affect centrally Scarlett's attitudes towards children, men and women, and sexuality. Children she cannot abide; some of the narrator's most powerful language is spent in showing her revulsion at Wade's hiccoughs, whining, and clinging to her skirts. It is because they are dependent upon her that Scarlett dislikes children: she does not mind actual responsibility for them, but she does not like being reminded of her own "childish" needs, and, when reminded, she does not like the idea of anyone else's competing with her for a "haven." Some of the vitriol towards blacks (specifically towards Prissy) takes its energy from precisely the same source; Scarlett is repulsed by incompetence and total dependency because she has had to fight to repress those very desires in herself. Women she dislikes too, as a group, because she thinks they are spineless and weak, dependent. Only when Melanie appears at the top of the stairs prepared to kill the Yankee marauder with a sword does Scarlett begin to have respect for her; eventually she learns that Melanie's courage, though differently expressed, is quite as real as her own, and Melanie becomes perhaps the only character in the novel with whom Scarlett begins to have an interdependent relationship. Other women are either, like Ellen and Mammy, perceived as totally powerful, or, like her sisters and the Atlanta women, boring because they continue the old forms.

It is with men, and specifically with her sexual relationships with them, that the conflict between control and dependence comes most clear and affects most centrally Scarlett's behavior. Ashley and Rhett, the two men she feels physical desire for, are the two men she cannot control. Immediately after losing Ashley, she marries the boy Charles Hamilton with his "calf" eyes; immediately after Rhett tells her he has no money for Tara, she turns to the "sissy" Frank Kennedy. Rhett calls her, at one point, a "bully" who will run all over anyone she can; this includes her own children—and two of her husbands for neither of whom she feels any physical attraction.

110

Yet Scarlett is by no means "frigid," as her author once said. Certainly the scene when she and Ashley meet in the orchard at Tara is one of mutual passion: when he kisses her, he feels "her change within his grip and there was madness and magic in the slim body he held and a hot soft glow in the green eyes . . . the lips were red and trembling" (p. 533). Until now, Scarlett has consistently viewed Ashley as her Perfect Knight, the living embodiment of stability who is also, fortunately, male: hence she can have both erotic and dependency fantasies about this blond, beautiful man. When he is home for furlough during the war, Scarlett crams the weeks with "incidents to remember . . . from which she could extract every morsel of comfort." Here are those events: "dance, sing, laugh, fetch and carry for Ashley; anticipate his wants, smile when he smiles, be silent when he talks, follow him with your eyes so that each line of his erect body . . . will be indelibly printed on your mind . . ." (p. 271).

Does this sound like a happy slave? It should, for Scarlett's erotic fantasies are inextricably linked with her desire for a benevolent paternalism. Hence it is no surprise that, in the famous scene with Rhett which is so much like rape, Scarlett feels the "wild thrill" of "joy, fear, madness, excitement, surrender to arms that were too strong, lips too bruising, fate that moved too fast" (p. 940), that she feels the "ecstasy of surrender" to someone "who was bullying and breaking her" (p. 941).

Not only is Rhett the tower of strength she wants in Ashley; in his brutality, he is paying her back, punishing her, for her own bullying and breaking of others. For certainly it is not a traditionally erotic scene: a "terrifying faceless black bulk" (p. 933) speaks with "violence as cruel as the crack of a whip," his eyes glowing "redly like twin coals" (p. 935), and threatens to tear her to pieces and to smash her head like the shell of a walnut (p. 937). Furious about Ashley, Rhett carries her upstairs, claiming that "By God, this is one night when there are only going to be two in my bed" (p. 939). The way is accomplished by force.

Elsewhere in her relationship with Rhett, each time Scarlett feels physical desire it is precisely because Rhett has shown he can overpower her. And the animal imagery that pervades the novel supports this connection: men are associated either with dogs and calves and asexuality, or with horses, panthers, and leopards—sexuality.

Scarlett then can find no satisfactory reconciliation between the felt need for autonomy and that for dependence. As the one becomes more extreme, so does the other, until finally she finds it equally exciting to rule like a dictator and to be raped.

Like Scarlett, Melanie rebels against conventional mores that define the lady. Yet unlike Scarlett, her revolt takes the form not of defying but of transcending those mores. Melanie defends Scarlett against the opprobrium of Atlanta, saying that people simply don't like a smart woman. She, too, works in the fields until she drops; she is ready to kill the soldier; puts out the fire in the kitchen and saves Scarlett from burning to death. Each time she goes against her culture, though, she does it for a "higher" ideal; Scarlett rebels for "selfish" reasons. Moreover, Melanie's differences concerning the definition of a lady depend on her special vision, a view of reality that finds and believes only the good about those she loves. Her goodness depends on ignorance; it is prelapsarian in nature—also prepubescent. Melanie's body is consistently described as that of a child, a girl; she dies because her pelvis is too narrow to deliver children. When her sexual "ignorance" is tested, when she is alone with Rhett after Scarlett's miscarriage, she is repulsed: Rhett's body, hairy and muscular, frightens her and turns her away. The novel implies, not just by her death in the larger plot, but also by her physical and emotional description, that Melanie's sort of goodness and strength, real though they are, are limited to a world that is neither virile nor evil.

Yet the world, as Mitchell envisions it, is both virile and evil. In fact, the two are virtually equated. For example, the one activity which gives Frank Kennedy a sense of masculinity and hence dignity—and the one activity from which Scarlett feels herself utterly excluded—is violence, the violence of the Ku Klux Klan. More importantly, the characterization of Rhett Butler has a dose of the devil in it. He is described physically as a devil: his eyes glint, he watches Scarlett like a cat watching a mouse hole, he prowls with a contained ferocity—and he has an uncanny ability to read other people's minds. Most striking of all is Rhett's astonishing ability to appear on, and to leave, the scene at exactly the right moment. To choose only a few examples, he manages to appear just as Scarlett is sobbing over Ashley during the war; just as the family appear at the train station to find out the casualties; just as they prepare to evacuate the city; just as the last of Aunt Pittypat's chickens is cooked.

Margaret Mitchell endows this character with such remarkable powers of knowledge that it is easy to make the mistake of thinking that he is her authorial point-of-view character; indeed, the narrator herself often agrees with his perceptions when they conflict with others', and enhances our sense of his omniscience by never directly entering his mind, as she does with almost every other character. And, in various contexts in the novel, it becomes clear that such "cold" objective knowledge and concern with larger issues are exclusively the province of males, while personal, psychological knowledge and concern with personal issues are that of females. Hence, in his constant ratiocination, in his near-telepathy, and in his large, very male body (with the odd exception of lips and feet like a girl's), Rhett Butler is the principle of masculinity. And in his hidden emotions, his violent nature, and his grasping opportunism, he is simultaneously the figure of evil. Although his "mainspring is broken," like the other "non-survivors" Mitchell planned to write about—though he is, as Scarlett finally perceives, a child like herself—he is also an adult in his knowledge. And it is knowledge of a specific sort that the novel finds to be the link between Ashley and Rhett and the distinction between men and women. Although Scarlett has the "male" head for business, although Rhett has the "female" mind for character, no women in the novel can see—as can Rhett and Ashley—the larger implications of history and of their actions. No woman can, in a word, think abstractly. This is surprising to find in a novel written by a woman (who of course imagines the abstract thinking of Rhett and Ashley), and reinforces once again the suspicion that Mitchell sees her voice as essentially masculine, just as she has Scarlett wanting not just to have or to love but to *be* Ashley and Rhett.

But Mitchell seems to do an about-face. Though she identifies the forces of knowledge and power and truth with Rhett and Ashley, both these men, like Gerald, are finally brought to their knees by females: Ashley by Melanie's death, Rhett by Bonnie's. The other

113

side of the definition of the Southern lady is that of the Southern gentleman. If the woman must be protected, the man needs someone to depend upon him. Mitchell is quite explicit about this. For instance, she has Melanie and Scarlett plot together—at Melanie's death—to protect Ashley and simultaneously to keep him ignorant of the protection, for the sake of his "masculine pride." We have already seen Frank become "manly" when he has the chance to protect, by force, his family; more important is the revealing speech Rhett makes when he tells Scarlett why he turned to Bonnie Blue:

> I wanted to take care of you, to pet you, to give you everything you wanted. I wanted to marry you and protect you and give you a free rein in anything that would make you happy—just as I did Bonnie. . . . I wanted you to stop fighting and let me fight for you. I wanted you to play, like a child—for you were a child, a brave, frightened, bull-headed child. I think you are still a child. . . . I liked to think that Bonnie was you, a little girl again, before the war and poverty had done things to you. She was so like you . . . and I could pet her and spoil her—just as I wanted to pet you. . . . [pp. 1030–31]

Genuine and tender though his feeling is—Scarlett feels honestly sorry for him, without contempt—it is a desire that, the reader knows, could never come true: for Scarlett has come through the war and through poverty, and has emerged, not a child, but "a woman" (p. 430). Because the code insists that manliness is a function of woman's weakness, men are excruciatingly vulnerable to women who are strong. And thus the limiting definitions of each sex end up hurting both.

Mitchell's real concern in *GWTW* is to see whether the traditional South can absorb new modes of behavior, especially but not only new gender roles. That it, ultimately, cannot is clear in the conclusion. The two who rebel most overtly against their society turn finally back to it, Scarlett in her return to the "old days," at Tara, and Rhett in his return to Charleston, where he wants ". . . the outer semblance of the things I used to know, the utter boredom of respectability—other people's respectability, my pet, not my own— the calm dignity life can have when it's lived by gentle folks, the genial grace of days that are gone. When I lived those days I didn't realize the slow charm of them—" (p. 1034).

So if there is a winner in *GWTW,* it is the "old days." Fight as the four major characters do to find a way to live in the new, and different though their tactics may be, all are finally defeated. Scarlett and Rhett, of course, come closest to inventing a new pattern of life; but they so deeply incorporate contradictory elements of the old, particularly those which defined men and women, that they both are doomed to failure. Perhaps this is what makes the novel both peculiarly southern and internationally popular. It articulates, challenges, and finally confirms the traditional view of the nature and roles of the sexes. Perhaps that is the price Mitchell felt she had to pay to stay in the South. She believed that she "couldn't live anywhere else in the world except in the South. I suppose, being adaptable, I *could* live elsewhere, but I probably would not be very happy. I believe, however, that I see more clearly than most people just what living in the South means. There are more rules to be followed here than any place in the world if one is to live in any peace and happiness. Having always been a person who was perfectly willing to pay for anything I got, I am more than willing to pay for the happiness I get from my residence in Georgia."[2]

Notes

1. Margaret Mitchell, *Gone with the Wind* (New York: Macmillan, 1936), p. 3 (cited hereafter in text).

2. Richard B. Harwell, ed., *Margaret Mitchell's "Gone with the Wind" Letters, 1936–1949* (New York: Macmillan, 1976), pp. 222–23.

In 1962 Edmund Wilson published his brilliant survey of Civil War literature, *Patriotic Gore.* As much American intellectual history as it is literary criticism, his study uses Harriet Beecher Stowe's *Uncle Tom's Cabin* as the central organizing device for the book and as a microcosm of the values of the Civil War era. He treats Stowe's work itself with high seriousness, so that this Yankee melodrama becomes a means of understanding an important slice of American history. While he limits his study to the generation that experienced the war, he does at one point suggest that *Gone with the Wind* is the perfect twentieth-century counterpart to Stowe's work. *Patriotic Gore* is a model for integrating high and popular culture, literature, and history, and Wilson's suggestive insight into the relationship between *Uncle Tom's Cabin* and *Gone with the Wind* is the starting point of this section.

The first two essays are concerned primarily with *Gone with the Wind,* both film and novel, as an artifact of national history and national culture. The last three essays of the section deal exclusively with the novel as a document in Southern history and culture.

If Edmund Wilson's study of the Civil War traces the triumph of Puritan and New England values in nineteenth-century America, what comparable meaning does *Gone with the Wind* have for the United States in the twentieth century? Gerald Wood's essay focuses on this question. Like Wilson, Wood approaches *Gone with the Wind* as a document in American intellectual history; also like Wilson, he compares the literary and the cinematic versions of the work. He establishes still another framework for considering the Mitchell-Selznick phenomenon: Thomas Dixon's 1905 Southern melodrama, *The Clansman*, and its cinematic avatar, D. W. Griffith's notorious *Birth of a Nation.* The comparison is logical: two commercially successful tales by Southern writers about the war and Reconstruction, which were translated into landmark popular movies. The similarities are obvious, and most critics have tended to link them in all respects, focusing especially on melodrama, sentimentality, nostalgia—and most of all on racism.

Wood finds still more compelling common themes. After examining the basic fabric of all four works (with particular regard to the technical innovations of the two films), he argues that the "primal appeal" of all four lies in their reliance upon what he calls the "do-

117

mestic melodrama." Developing this idea, he suggests that all of
these works confirm that the American past can best be understood
within the framework of domesticity and the home. By this measure, our history is really the record of individual American
families.

Yet Wood is concerned with intellectual contrasts as well as common themes. Particularly between the two versions of *Gone with
the Wind* he sees significant value shifts. Thus he finds Mitchell's
book much more pessimistic and fatalistic than the bright romanc-
ing of the film. These differences are minor, however, compared to
the grand alteration of values in *Gone with the Wind* from those in
Dixon and Griffith. And this is the key to his essay.

For all the violence, rape, and murder in Dixon and Griffith, their
works are fundamentally optimistic and progressive. The suffering
and violence they describe have meaning and significance within a
cosmic or divine plan; they are redemptive. In Dixon and Griffith,
the past becomes the source of a brighter future. *Gone with the
Wind*—from Hollywood and Atlanta—teaches very different lessons. Social or political redemption has no place in the ruthless
struggle for survival in Mitchell's novel; happiness and optimism are
chimera. Although Selznick avoids this moral bleakness, his vision
reinforces similar values in a new age. The past has no redemptive
quality in Mitchell's novel; it is a burden to be borne. It is no more
redemptive in Selznick; it becomes instead an artificial construction
in whose perfection one may escape the confusions and dilemmas
of the future and the present.

In the broad contrast between these two sets of artworks, Wood
discovers a critical shift in American social and intellectual values,
the product of growing "anxiety over America's unique place in history, the complexities of modern life, the tenuousness of material
well-being and uncertainties about the future." By this measure,
both Mitchell's and Selznick's works mark the "loss of American innocence" and in their own ways record the effects of Modernism
upon the generation of the Great War and the Depression.

As suggested earlier, the most common point of comparison
among the four works is their ostensible Negrophobia. Both Mitchell and Selznick are seen as perpetuators of the violent racism of
Dixon and Griffith. Thomas Cripps begins on this note with a quota-

tion from Malcolm X recalling his mortification on viewing Selznick's film; yet the purpose of his essay is to revise the bleakly racist interpretation of *Gone with the Wind.*

With the New Deal and changing racial demography in the United States, the 1930s witnessed a significant departure from the violent racism of the turn of the century. Even in the rock-ribbed racist South, lynching, that ultimate expression of regional mores, had virtually vanished by 1930. Cripps argues that David Selznick, and even Margaret Mitchell, reflected this lessening of antiblack attitudes. One part of his essay is a study of *Gone with the Wind* as a measure of these racial changes. Another is an examination of the film as a watershed among black Americans themselves. The film symbolized a new level of social and political engagement by American blacks; the cast and crew members asserted themselves in ways unthinkable twenty-five years before. Likewise, Hattie McDaniel's Academy Award was seen as a vicarious triumph for all black America.

Although he revises the general Negrophobic interpretation of *Gone with the Wind*, Cripps also catalogues the ways in which it perpetuated racial biases and stereotypes. Indeed, the dilemma of *Gone with the Wind* as it represents both racial progress and reaction is the heart of Cripps's essay, and he treats it as a metaphor in black social and intellectual history. Black victories in the film tended to undercut a more radical critique of American society that had begun among black intellectuals; the problem was particularly apparent within the American Communist party and its relationship to the black community. By legitimizing a liberal, centrist position—the idea of victories within the system—*Gone with the Wind* signaled a new conservatism among blacks, especially a turning away from radical solutions. One effect was stagnation among the black leadership that would not be thoroughly redressed until the appearance of Martin Luther King and the urban riots of the sixties.

Like Wood and Cripps, Kenneth O'Brien also examines the racial aspects of the film/novel phenomenon of *Gone with the Wind*. His method is similar, comparing *Gone with the Wind* to turn-of-the-century Southern romances of the Civil War and Reconstruction, specifically Thomas Nelson Page's *Red Rock,* a classic expression of the genre published in 1895. O'Brien's objective is to test the assumption, expressed most succinctly by Malcolm Cowley, that *Gone with the Wind* is no more than "an encyclopedia of the plantation legend." On the surface, O'Brien confirms the critics' objections: the novel does contain all the stereotypical scenes and people of the Reconstruction romance—bad Yankees, loyal and submissive slaves, kindly plantation owners, misguided freedmen, violent blacks, interracial rape, and so on. Mitchell clearly worked within the traditions of the postwar Southern romance, but O'Brien argues that to stop here distorts the real meaning of her work (if not of the racist romances themselves). What holds these earlier novels together is simply missing from Mitchell's work: the theme of white political redemption over violent black insurrection. Those earlier works are political morality tales, as Gerald Wood implies in his essay; in *Gone with the Wind* race and politics and their Reconstruction moral are quite irrelevant, constituting no more than a backdrop for the real story—Scarlett O'Hara's struggle against the confines of Southern womanhood. What Mitchell attempted was to take the forms and conventions of the earlier genre and to fuse them with the alien themes of individual and sexual liberation. Her inability to synthesize these two themes, according to O'Brien, muddled both her social and her artistic vision, but this very lack of clarity is significant in itself. Readers might end the novel however they wish, and this is one source of *Gone with the Wind*'s enduring popularity. Is Scarlett punished for her violation of social conventions or does she find fulfillment in an affirmation of tradition? The work is able to absorb both interpretations. In the final analysis, however, Mitchell's ambivalence should not obscure the significance of her attempt at innovation—nor, indeed, its meaning for national and regional social history.

Mitchell's ambivalence about Southern history is the theme of both of the two final essays. Like Wood, Richard King is interested in domestic values in *Gone with the Wind*; but he analyzes them within a specific Southern context and in comparison with other monuments of the Southern literary Renaissance of the interwar years. He finds that the "Southern family romance" was crucial to most of the Southern intellectuals of the period, but argues that Mitchell refused to fit the model and that *Gone with the Wind* is a kind of bastard child of the family tradition. For King, however, this

120

bastardy has its own symbolic legitimacy in another regional value or tradition: the novel's ambivalence represents the peculiarities of a particular capitalist ideology that dominated the South between Reconstruction and World War I, a kind of quasi-religion discussed by W. J. Cash and called by Paul Gaston the "New South Creed."

This peculiar form of regional capitalism advocated progress, industrialization, and urbanization, yet it employed the rhetoric of "The Lost Cause," the agrarian community, and the plantation past to support its antitraditional alteration of Southern society. While recalling a universal bourgeois inclination to glorify the olden days (as suggested by Louis Rubin), this contradiction was especially profound within a Southern context. Unable to commit itself totally to a capitalistic order or to a traditional one, the New South ideology was false by its very nature. It produced, according to King, an unstable, immature, or even infantile desire "to have it both ways." This ideological inconsistency is the source of the novel's ambiguity and contradiction and makes *Gone with the Wind* the representation, par excellence, of the New South creed.

The final essay of the collection, "The Inner War of Southern History," begins with the idea stressed by King and also by Commager that ambivalence lies at the heart of the novel and, further, that this divided mentality is itself a significant reflection of distinctive regional intellectual or social norms. But where those two essays, and likewise O'Brien's, associate this division with a particular moment in Southern history after the Civil War, the last essay contends that this inner divisiveness represents a fundamental problem within the three-hundred-year record of Southern tradition. This divisiveness is both cause and effect of an intellectual dualism that is the chief characteristic of the Southern mind, a characteristic that is at sharp variance with the dominant Lockean values of mainstream American history.

The core of the division in the Southern tradition is geographical: a distinction between the coast or "low country" and the interior or "backcountry." As indicated in her self-conscious setting of the action in Atlanta and on the plantations of the interior frontier—in specific contrast to the plantation country of the coast—Mitchell played on this internal division. She was also sensitive to the ways in which these geographical identities became enmeshed in a complex web of other distinctions—economic, social, racial, cultural, and even sexual. In the novel, as well as in the Southern tradition, the coast represents the past: tradition, culture, civilization, aristocracy, femininity, and ultimately death. Conversely, the interior stands for the future: progress, innovation, change, individualism, masculinity, and vitality. Aware of these distinctions, Mitchell was equally keen to show how these halves of the Southern experience ran together and became a part of the dualistic regional whole, which she expresses realistically in the interregional "mésalliance" of the backcountryman Gerald O'Hara and his coastal antithesis, Ellen Robillard. If marriage represents, both realistically and symbolically, a formal, institutional means of recombining the explosively centrifugal components of the Southern experience, the existence of a rigidly defined social system of roles, manners, and prescribed behavior serves much the same function when the dualism of the Southern experience is internalized in individual Southerners. In this regard, the author suggests that Scarlett's energetic mindlessness, Melanie's or Ellen's iron will, Rhett's obscuring irony, and Ashley's fainting irresolution are classic Southern responses to a Southern cultural dualism that approaches a kind of social schizophrenia. By this definition the novel becomes a more realistic rendering of regional society than even Mitchell might have suspected.

From *The Clansman* and *Birth of a Nation* to *Gone with the Wind*: The Loss of American Innocence

Gerald Wood

In the summer of 1936, thirty-one years after the publication of *The Clansman*, his own successful Civil War romance, Thomas Dixon wrote Margaret Mitchell an enthusiastic letter of praise for *Gone with the Wind*. He said she had "not only written the greatest story of the South ever put down on paper, you have given the world THE GREAT AMERICAN NOVEL." He then expressed his pleasure at seeing Yankees lined up at bookstores to purchase what he considered to be a novel based, like his own, on authentic Southern history: "It certainly warms the cockles of my heart to see these good old damyankees flocking into the bookstores and joyfully paying $3. per copy for the record of their mean deeds."[1] Although Mitchell's response was more restrained, avoiding references to sales in the North or anywhere else, she was obviously pleased: "Your letter of praise about "Gone With the Wind" was very exciting. . . . I was practically raised on your books and love them very much."[2]

These letters reveal the respect the novelists had for one another and suggest their mutual regard for their Southern heritage; however, their correspondence barely hints at the important role their stories have played in American cultural history, first as novels, then as movies. Dixon's novel was a best-seller, and Margaret Mitchell's of course has become internationally famous; but as films—D. W. Griffith's *Birth of a Nation* (1915) and David O. Selznick's *Gone with the Wind* (1939)—the stories have reached even wider audiences and generated greater controversy. Both films involved major technical achievements in their making and were significant expressions of the film styles of their eras; this essay is in part an examination of these artistic and technical achievements. But their unusual power to seize the imagination of American audiences and stimulate strong reaction suggests that there is more than aesthetic appeal behind their popularity. The larger purpose of this essay is to analyze the social appeal of the two phenomena: their common reliance on domestic melodrama that seeks to reaffirm social values about love, marriage, and the home and their integration of these domestic values with actual historical events so that our history becomes, in effect, the collective record of private American families.

Finally, while all four works reflect common themes about the domestic melodrama in American history, they differ significantly in their treatment of those themes. Mitchell's world view is far bleaker

123

than Selznick's rosy vision, but the greatest contrast is between their similar social assumptions over against Dixon's and Griffith's. *The Clansman* and *Birth of a Nation* represent a positive, progressive, and moral vision of the world and of American destiny. In different ways, both versions of *Gone with the Wind* record the loss of this late Victorian innocence. From Atlanta and Hollywood, *Gone with the Wind* becomes a document in American intellectual history and a landmark in the twentieth-century skepticism, pessimism, and demoralization that followed World War I.

The making of *Gone with the Wind* is probably the better-known story of the two, but the influence of *Birth of a Nation* on film production, race relations, and politics has been even greater than that of Selznick's film.[3] Technically, *Birth of a Nation* exhibited a major advance in the style and structure of motion pictures; its release was also a crucial event in the legitimation of movies as an art form—the advance from the nickelodeon and vaudeville circuit to the luxurious stage of the feature film theater.[4] The financial rewards from this move toward theatrical respectability underscored the significance of artistic innovation. Recent estimates are that during 1915 alone over five million people (825,000 in New York) saw *Birth of a Nation,* and, while figures vary widely, the film has made gross profits in excess of fifteen, maybe more than sixty, million dollars.[5] In any case, as Daniel Leab has clarified, "Although the precise financial details are hazy, it surely ranks as the all-time box office champion among American silent films."[6] Among its many devotees—North and South, liberal and conservative—was President Woodrow Wilson, who is reported to have said, "It is like writing history with lightning. And my only regret is that it is all so terribly true."[7]

At the same time, because of its obvious racist and reactionary content, opposition from many blacks and liberal whites to the screening of *Birth of a Nation* was vociferous and, at times, politically effective. There were riots and public demonstrations in Boston and New York and protests in major cities like San Francisco, Los Angeles, and Philadelphia, as well as in many smaller places, especially in the Midwest and East.[8] Among those joining the opposition to the film were Harvard President Charles Eliot and social worker Jane Addams, and even President Wilson later felt the need to "leak" a statement reversing his early enthusiasm, to the effect that *Birth of a Nation* was an "unfortunate production."[9] Though the right to freedom of expression eventually undermined liberal opposition to the film, the attacks on *Birth of a Nation* are credited with raising black awareness in many cities and helping particularly the NAACP to consolidate black and liberal support for its causes.[10] Although during the years from *Birth of a Nation* to the sound era there were actually fewer black roles and less attention to all-black productions, the black film *The Birth of a Race* (1919) and those of the Frederick Douglass Film Company were made specifically in reaction to *Birth of a Nation*.[11]

But it is probably *Gone with the Wind*, not *Birth of a Nation*, that has been, if not the most influential, at least the most popular American film. Margaret Mitchell's story, published in 1936, had been phenomenally successful as a novel, and the public's interest in the film version of her story was raised to even greater heights by the unprecedented cost of $50,000 for the film rights. Partly because it was calculated to do so, the search for the actors to play Rhett, Scarlett, and the others became a national project. Subsequently the film broke all records as a money-maker, reportedly making $75 million by 1967 and $120 million before rights were sold to television.[12] Further attention was given to the film's view of blacks, but, as in the case of *Birth of a Nation*, the opposition from the left was divided, this time because blacks had dignified (if subservient) roles and because Hattie McDaniel's performance as Mammy won an Academy Award for best supporting actress.[13] Moreover, black and white filmgoers alike found much to admire in the film; as Russell Merritt and Thomas Pauly have shown, survival, nostalgia, romantic love, and the family were attractive themes for all audiences.[14]

Indeed, in all four works the centrality of family and of domestic values in times of social upheaval is a major source of their almost primal appeal for American audiences. In the Dixon-Griffith story, Abraham Lincoln provides the "fostering hand" of a "Christian father"; in *Gone with the Wind* Gerald O'Hara serves a related function, as does Rhett Butler with his "strong arms . . . broad chest . . . and complete understanding. . . ."[15] Complementing this fatherly support is the "mother's heart" of Mrs. Cameron in *The Clansman*,

125

and of Ellen O'Hara in *Gone with the Wind*, who "represented the utter security that only Heaven or a mother can give . . . the embodiment of justice, truth, loving tenderness and profound wisdom" (p. 60). Mammy and Tara likewise fill the need for a surrogate mother; Scarlett is comforted by her thoughts of home, which recall her "mother's face under the lamp at prayer time" (p. 28).

In treating traditional roles within the family and conventional relations between the sexes, Griffith maintained Dixon's idealized conceptions. In *The Clansman,* love is a mystical experience in which a man "leads, charms, dominates, and yet eludes," needing finally a "woman's hand to lead [him] into the ways of peace and life."[16] In *Birth of a Nation,* this idea of peace and light, or reconciliation, is extended from one man to the whole nation. Thus the emotion engendered by one man's glimpsing the picture of a beautiful woman binds families together, obviates ideological and regional divisions, and potentially gives birth to a new age of peace and harmony.

Likewise, Margaret Mitchell builds a major subplot around conventional romantic love: Scarlett's attachment to Ashley and Rhett's to Scarlett. Mitchell's novel, like the previous works by Dixon and Griffith, is steeped in romantic conventions; it is concerned with Scarlett's refusal of, then inability to achieve, conventional love and family life. But *Gone with the Wind* is more complex psychologically than either Dixon's novel or Griffith's film; in Margaret Mitchell's story the heroine is so willfully self-involved that she is incapable of the mutuality out of which love grows.[17] Consequently, Scarlett's repeated calls for "tomorrow" are characterized as irresponsible denials of her own past.

David Selznick simplifies these psychological implications largely by ignoring them—as had the majority of the readers of Margaret Mitchell's novel. In Selznick's version Scarlett's belief in "tomorrow" merely demonstrates her resilience, her belief in the future, and her hope that she might yet regain Rhett's love. Thus, romantic love and the need for ties to a loving family are central in all four Civil War stories; but while Dixon and Griffith thought that romance was capable even of ordering history into some divine loving plan, Selznick transformed Margaret Mitchell's complex struggle between survival and tradition into what Michael Wood calls "one of the great American celebrations of self." [18]

These essentially domestic dramas take on epic proportions and appeal because they are surrounded by an aura of historical moment. The "primal attraction" of the love stories is intensified by the claims to authenticity made by their narratives and images. Consequently, there is an ennobling fusion of the love interest and the Civil War, recognized as the definitive crisis of American history. [19] For example, in his preface to *The Clansman*, Thomas Dixon assures the reader that "I have sought to preserve in this romance both the letter and the spirit of this remarkable period. The men who enact the drama of fierce revenge into which I have woven a double love-story are historical figures. I have merely changed their names without taking a liberty with any essential historical fact." Dixon believed that history itself, in times like the Civil War, is inherently dramatic. His "romance" is not genuinely fictional, for he merely preserves for the reader the "letter and spirit" of history's drama. Following Dixon's lead, D. W. Griffith insisted that in *Birth of a Nation* he was telling the "truth about the South, touched by its eternal romance which I had learned to know so well." He underlines the historical verisimilitude by emphasizing in the film that such scenes as Lee's surrender and Lincoln's assassination are "facsimiles" made from photographs and paintings of the actual events. [20] In the same vein, Margaret Mitchell prided herself on the historical authenticity of *Gone with the Wind*; the history of her tale "was as water proof and air tight as ten years of study and a lifetime of listening to participants would make it." [21] And, while Selznick's reliance on Hollywood stereotypes of the Southern belle and plantation at times amused the novelist, the movie makes elaborate and detailed attempts to replicate, for example, the destruction of Atlanta and even the red clay of the Georgia piedmont. [22]

By grounding their domestic romances in what are portrayed as the essential, dramatic events of history, the films integrate the two themes and express the popular notion that the meaning of American history can be read best, or even exclusively, through domestic themes. By giving Dixon's story of love and revenge the look of history that he and Dixon valued so highly, D. W. Griffith suggests that the Civil War was, in the final analysis, about the preservation of innocence, the victory of harmony, love, and marriage over violence, and the conversion of the United States to brotherhood. More concerned with private domestic virtues than with the public drama of *Birth of a Nation, Gone with the Wind* suggests that national crises demand the reaffirmation of love and courage, the traditional foundations of family life. The hope expressed at the end of Selznick's film is that, despite the problems of love and the tenuousness of a happy family life, the most valuable goals of human history are still personal, individual virtues—strength in adversity, resilience, and the struggle to find satisfying love.

But, while the two films share a common respect for the drama of American history and a belief that romantic love and the institution of the family play key roles in that drama, *Birth of a Nation* and *Gone with the Wind* make substantially different uses of the past. Griffith's film, like Dixon's novel, is based on the belief that the future can redeem and improve upon the past. *The Clansman* relies on Thomas Dixon's fundamental belief in the potential for improvement in American life.[23] Although it is a tale of the corruption of Southern purity by the carpetbagging North, leading to rape, murder, and revenge, this violent, ugly story is still basically optimistic; Phil Stoneman can still prophesy confidently that the South "will yet rise to a nobler life than she has ever lived in the past" (p. 66), and Lincoln declares serenely that the nation "will yet swell the chorus of the Union" from the "mystic chords of memory" (p. 53). The sufferings of the past, as wicked as they appear, actually serve a better future. Thus Mrs. Cameron is able to face the imprisonment of her husband because "The heritage of centuries of heroic blood from the martyrs of old Scotland began to flash its inspiration from the past" (p. 101), and Elsie Stoneman learns that the apparently "wicked, cruel, and causeless" war will serve a higher purpose: "She began to understand why the war, which had seemed to her a wicked, cruel, and causeless rebellion, was the one inevitable thing in our growth from a loose group of sovereign states to a United Nation" (p. 149). While Dixon's social concerns are for the purity of the white race and Southern womanhood, his hope for national improvement and faith in the providential order of history demand that the future of his characters be rescued by the strength of their past.[24]

D. W. Griffith's view of history in *Birth of a Nation* is essentially the same as Dixon's. Like Dixon, Griffith envisions the United States as a "once happy land" before slavery and the Civil War disrupted its pristine harmony. The film records, then, the process by which America recovers its unity, symbolized in the marriage of the Camerons and Stonemans at the end of the film. As in *The Clansman*, the end of state sovereignty and the war are necessary stages in the fulfillment of Daniel Webster's dream of national unity that would last through eternity; in *Birth of a Nation* the country is seen as becoming "one and inseparable, now and forever." And, like Dixon, Griffith sees this whole process as being under the divine providence of the historical Christian God, who, in his apocalyptic way, is bringing about the better future not only of American unity but of universal brotherhood and global democracy. The epilogue to *Birth of a Nation* is thus written in terms of newness, "hope," and "the world-millennium": "The establishment of the South in its rightful place is the birth of a new nation. . . . The new nation, the real United States, as the years glided by, turned away forever from the blood-lust of War and anticipated with hope the world-millennium in which a brotherhood of love should bind all the nations."[25] American history in Griffith's film, like that in Dixon's *Clansman*, puts a disorderly but heroic past in the service of an even greater and nobler future.

Griffith shared Dixon's desire to improve on history, but Selznick met ambiguity in Mitchell's treatment of the past. On the one hand, the novel is pervaded by the feeling that the present and future always need to be evaluated against a more stable and heroic past. The O'Hara family, for example, is haunted by the almost genetic anxiety of having been reduced, long before the Civil War, to tenancy on their land in Ireland and by "the family tradition of past glories, lost forever" (p. 43). Ashley best articulates this fearful nostalgia when, in his letter to Melanie, he confides, "I do not know what the future will bring, but it cannot be as beautiful or as satisfying as the past" (p. 212). Even Rhett, who early on betrays the South in the name of survival and wealth, says at the close of the novel that he is beginning "to value the clannishness of families, honor and security, roots that go deep" and so is "going to hunt in the old towns and old countries where some of the old times still must linger" (pp. 1034–35).

Scarlett appears to be the most future-loving of the characters; throughout the postwar years she convinces herself that "these proud fools weren't looking forward as she was doing. . . . They drew their courage from the past. She was drawing hers from the future" (p. 610). But while she tries to deny it, Scarlett, too, is drawn to the past: she respects the morality of her mother and Melanie, and her father's words about Tara bring her back to the land and her family traditions. Late in the novel, when Ashley reminds her of the pain and loss they have suffered, Scarlett reveals that her obsession with the future is actually an attempt to avoid the pain and insecurity involved in accepting the burden of the past: ". . . no matter what beauty lay behind, it must remain there. . . . It hurts too much, it drags at your heart till you can't ever do anything else except look back. . . . This is what happens when you look back to happiness, this pain, this heartbreak, this discontent" (pp. 924–25).

At the same time, however, Mitchell qualifies this idealization of a more substantial past by insisting on the need for a realistic appraisal of the present and the gumption to survive in the future. Ashley's ancient codes of honor are useless in dealing with the anxieties and brutal realities of the postwar South, just as Melanie's death indicates that the purity of her selflessness and altruism cannot survive in the New South. Furthermore, it is not clear that Rhett's return to older ways will be successful, and his late preference for the past has to be placed alongside his early opportunism and desire to survive at all costs. But most characteristic of the novel's ambiguity is the inconclusive ending in which Scarlett claims to be moving homeward while she calls for "tomorrow." Scarlett does achieve a partial conversion to the past when, near the end of the novel, she claims an identification with her fellow Confederates and with their common history. She does turn at last to "Home! That was where she wanted to go. . . . At this realization it was as though chains fell away from her and with them the fear which had haunted her dreams since the night she stumbled to Tara to find the world ended. . . . And, though she had won material safety since that night, in her dreams she was still a frightened child, searching for the lost security of that lost world" (p. 1021). The ending, however, is indefinite. Scarlett is returning to Tara and "Mammy, the last link with the old days" (p. 1037), but her commitment to her roots is untested and her call for tomorrow echoes the evasion and denial that have characterized her life. Mitchell was aware of the sense of regret and loss that goes with having a secure and beautiful past, but she also respected the courage and resilience that it takes to live for the future. *Gone with the Wind* is consequently ambiguous to the end; it values both recognition of the past and strength for the future.

David Selznick purged *Gone with the Wind* of Mitchell's ambiguity. His nostalgia contrasts sharply not only with Mitchell's ambivalent vision but with Dixon's and Griffith's religious progressivism. Rather than dramatize, as Mitchell does, an inconclusive conflict between aristocratic idealism and lumpish realism, the filmmaker makes a clear preference for days-gone-by when, in the prologue, he describes the prewar South as a chivalric and orderly world that has tragically been lost, "a dream remembered." [26] The present and the future, the film implies, are no match for the past portrayed in the story about to be told. Consequently, Scarlett's problem is not as Mitchell depicts it—an internal struggle between traditional morality and opportunism; rather, it is external—how to return to the "charm and grace" of her past. While Scarlett's uncertainty and fickleness come through in both the novel and the film, Selznick's Scarlett is the more attractive one because the film emphasizes her passion and willfulness without giving attention, as Mitchell does, to the evasion and denial in her personality. In the book, despite the need of many readers to find differently, Scarlett's final speech about tomorrow is two-sided: it shows her desire to persevere, but it also reminds the reader of her persistent need to procrastinate and avoid situations potentially damaging to her ego. The conclusion to the film, on the other hand, holds out the hope that Scarlett can yet—through one more act of assertiveness— recover a "safe and warm" past by following her father's call back to

Tara.[27] Thus, while the outcome is still in doubt, Selznick's Scarlett makes an unequivocal and heroic return to the security of her home and her past.

The two films—*Birth of a Nation* and *Gone with the Wind*— thus reflect an important shift in popular concepts of history after World War I. *Birth of a Nation* echoes the optimistic progressivism of turn-of-the-century America. In the early twentieth century the consensus was that America had endured the economic downturns after the Civil War, the labor unrest of the 1870s, and the agrarian discontent of the 1890s in order to usher in a new era of industrial expansion and plenty. Intervention in the Philippines, China, and Cuba (and later in Mexico and Europe) was, justifiably, the inevitable extension of American democratic institutions to the rest of the world. New evolutionary theories in biology and programs of social improvement embodied in the Social Gospel movement or in political progressivism seemed the natural result of America's advances. Despite growing economic interdependence with other countries, America still saw itself as special, isolated, and privileged—a people defined by the nineteenth-century rural virtues of hard work, individualism, voluntary cooperation, optimism, and the mission God had apparently given to those living under democracy. Henry May summarizes these feelings in *The End of American Innocence*:

> Far more than most periods of American history, more than any since the Civil War, the early twentieth century was a time of sureness and unity, at least on the surface of American life. Even the past had begun to change for the better. People looking back on the nineteenth century tended to forget the labor wars and agrarian rebellions. Radicalism, like religious doubt, had been converted into progress. Looking back, the *Outlook* in 1912 said of the nineteenth century that "our electric lights do not dim its glorious sunburst of genius, and most of our legislation and organization for social justice are experiments in pursuit of its ideals." [28]

Birth of a Nation captures this prewar sense of hope and progress; the Civil War was viewed by Griffith, as it had been by Dixon, as a means of recovering America's natural unity in order to create a better future, a future still believed in by filmgoers in 1915.

In contrast, the nostalgia of *Gone with the Wind* reflects a sense of disillusionment and introversion that characterized much of American life after World War I, when anxiety, cynicism, and a skepticism regarding the present undercut even the prosperity of the twenties. Following the war, the progressive faith in Woodrow Wilson's moral idealism was replaced by a retreat into diplomatic isolationism and nationalism. Moreover, the new affluence was threatened by the 1920–21 recession, the plight of the farmers throughout the decade, and the shallowness of prosperity. The restriction of immigration and the resurgence of the Ku Klux Klan indicated a fear of the future, a fear compounded by a new cynicism toward middle-class life as it had been popularized by H. L. Mencken, Ernest Hemingway, F. Scott Fitzgerald, and Sinclair Lewis. The 1929 crash exacerbated these anxieties about the quality of American life and stimulated a subliminal desire to restore traditional authority. Behind the attempt to recapture the integrity of the American experience in the regional and national art of the thirties lay the rural violence of 1932, the 1937 recession, and the inevitable strain the depression put on family ties—all of which undermined much of the public recovery of hope. Even the emphasis on social action (in the works of John Steinbeck and Clifford Odets, for example) and the affirmation of poets like Carl Sandburg betrayed a desperate need to reestablish native American values and purposes, especially in the face of rising Fascism in Europe. Thus, when *Gone with the Wind* finds the pre–Civil War past more attractive than the future, the film's nostalgia reflects the post–World War I anxiety over America's unique place in history, the complexities of modern life, material well-being, and uncertainty about the future.[29]

Birth of a Nation and *Gone with the Wind* are domestic melodramas which express popular myths of history in their respective times—the progress myth and the Eden myth. *Birth of a Nation* depicts history as the record of the growth of good men within God's design for human events. It teaches that man's primary task is to recover pristine innocence in order to gain a radical improvement in the future. Blessed by God's special providence, America retains a purity no longer available to decadent European civilization and is destined to remake the world in its own image for the glory of God. *Gone with the Wind*, on the other hand, sees American history as a fall from innocence and imagination into experience and reality. In this view, the European culture (which the name Tara recalls) is better than ours, and we must bear the national guilt associated with corrupting the natural order of the New World. Both stories imagine a meaning and purpose for American history. But while *Birth of a Nation* would have an insufficient past serve a glorious future, *Gone with the Wind* offers the past as a refuge from a hopeless present.

Notes

1. This letter was dated August 5, 1936. On August 27 in the same year, Dixon wrote another letter to "Peggy Mitchell" in which he showed satisaction that *Gone with the Wind* was selling so well, since "oh boy, a lovely SOUTHERN girl has done it! The high brows up here [New York] are calling it the new REBEL YELL. And thank God for it in these days of renewed slander of the South on the stage and in books." These letters are in the Margaret Mitchell Marsh Papers, University of Georgia Libraries, Athens.

2. Richard Harwell, ed., *Margaret Mitchell's "Gone with the Wind" Letters, 1936–1949* (New York: Macmillan, 1976), pp. 52–53.

3. Edward Wagenknecht, *The Movies in the Age of Innocence* (New York: Ballantine, 1971; first published by University of Oklahoma, 1962), p. 89.

4. See, for example, Edward Wagenknecht, in *The Films of D. W. Griffith*, ed. Edward Wagenknecht and Anthony Slide (New York: Crown, 1975), p. 59; Lewis Jacobs, *The Rise of the American Film: A Critical History* (New York: Harcourt, Brace, and Co., 1939), p. 171; Wagenknecht, *Movies in the Age of Innocence*, p. 89n.

5. See Daniel J. Leab, *From Sambo to Superspade: The Black Experience in Motion Pictures* (Boston: Houghton Mifflin, 1975), p. 34; Robert M. Henderson, *D. W. Griffith: His Life and Work* (New York: Oxford University Press, 1972), pp. 160–61; Wagenknecht, *Movies in the Age of Innocence*, p. 88; Roy E. Aitken and Al P. Nelson, *The Birth of a Nation Story* (Middleburg, Va.: William W. Denlinger, 1965), p. 5.

6. Leab, p. 34.

7. Thomas Cripps, *Slow Fade to Black: The Negro in American Film, 1900–1942* (New York: Oxford University Press, 1977), p. 52. See also Leab, p. 37; Jacobs, p. 175; Aitken and Nelson, p. 6.

8. Cripps, pp. 53, 58–60, 63; Peter Noble, *The Negro in Films* (Port Washington, N.Y.: Kennikat, 1963; first published in 1948), p. 39; Henderson, p. 158; Jacobs, p. 178; Wagenknecht, *Movies in the Age of Innocence*, p. 89.

9. Cripps, pp. 62–63; Leab, p. 37; Henderson, p. 160.

10. Cripps, pp. 53, 58.

11. Cripps, pp. 61, 64, 74–76, 79; Leab, pp. 39, 60–64, 70–71.

12. See Gavin Lambert, *GWTW: The Making of Gone with the Wind* (Boston: Little, Brown, 1973); Roland Flamini, *Scarlett, Rhett, and a Cast of Thousands: The Filming of Gone with the Wind* (New York: Macmillan, 1975).

13. Cripps, pp. 361–366; Nobel, pp. 75, 79–80; Leab, p. 99.

14. Russell Merritt, "Dixon, Griffith, and the Southern Legend," *Cinema Journal* 12, no. 1 (1972): 31–35; Thomas H. Pauly, "*Gone with the Wind* and *The Grapes of Wrath* as Hollywood Histories of the Depression," *Journal of Popular Film* 3 (Summer 1974): 204–5, 213–15.

15. Margaret Mitchell, *Gone with the Wind* (New York: Macmillan, 1936), p. 1021 (cited hereafter in text).

16. Thomas Dixon, Jr., *The Clansman* (New York: Doubleday, Page and Co., 1905), p. 129 (cited hereafter in text).

17. See Margaret Mitchell's letter to Dr. Hervey Cleckley, quoted in Finis Farr, *Margaret Mitchell of Atlanta* (New York: William Morrow, 1965), p. 163: "I set out to depict a far-from-admirable woman about whom little that was good could be said. . . . I thought it would be obvious to anyone that Scarlett was a frigid woman, loving attention and adulation for their own sake but having little or no comprehension of actual deep feelings and no reactions to the love and attention of others." On the psychological aspects of Scarlett's obsession with "tomorrow," see, for example, *GWTW*, p. 210.

18. Michael Wood, *America in the Movies* (New York: Basic Books, 1975), p. 35.

19. In *The Immoderate Past: The Southern Writer and History* (Athens: University of Georgia Press, 1977), C. Hugh Holman demonstrates that a sense of history has been an integral part of the Southern literary tradition, the tradition out of which the two films grew.

20. Wagenknecht, *Movies in the Age of Innocence,* p. 71; Henderson, pp. 146, 151; Leab, pp. 36, 24. Cf. Noble, pp. 34–35, 37. Because of his steadfast belief in the truthfulness of his tale, Griffith offered $10,000 to charity if Moorfield Storey, head of the Boston NAACP, could "find a single incident in the play that was not historic." The best discussion of D. W. Griffith's use of history is by Russell Merritt in "Dixon, Griffith, and the Southern Legend": "Much of what Griffith filmed is historically accurate, but the illusion of general historical truth and perspective is largely the product of Griffith's art. . . . Whether Griffith knew it or not, the initial and determining impulse behind his film was not historic truth, but the dramatization of a familiar legend" (p. 29). See also Henderson, p. 151; Wagenknecht, *Films of D. W. Griffith,* p. 60; Everett Carter, "Cultural History Written with Lightning: The Significance of *The Birth of a Nation,*" *American Quarterly* 12, no. 3 (Fall 1960): 347–57.

21. Harwell, p. 39. See also Harwell, p. 310; and see Farr, p. 104: ". . . she dreaded

being caught in an historical error more than she feared criticism of plot and style."

22. It was his reliance on historical fact that led David Selznick to respond to criticisms of the movie's portrait of Northern troops: "We have not only followed Miss Mitchell, but we have also been careful to have each of our historical facts checked thoroughly by a historian, Mr. Kurtz": *Memo from David O. Selznick*, ed. Rudy Behlmer (New York: Viking, 1972), p. 227.

23. For Dixon's interest in progress and history, see Raymond Allen Cook's studies, *Fire from the Flint* (Winston-Salem, N.C.: John Blair, 1968), p. 181, and *Thomas Dixon* (New York: Twayne, 1974), pp. 52–53.

24. See the study by F. Garvin Davenport, Jr., of Dixon's role in the Southern interpretation of history in *The Myth of Southern History: Historical Consciousness in Twentieth-Century Southern Literature* (Nashville: Vanderbilt, 1967): ". . . What Southerners needed, and what such a motion picture as *The Birth of a Nation* could in part provide, was a way to reconcile regional knowledge and suffering with the concept of national innocence, violence with harmony, and an inescapable past with a faith in unhampered progress. Finally, it could provide a sense of mission—a belief that the violence, suffering, and injustice so much a part of Southern life before and after 1865 had been the means to a much greater, more significant national destiny."

25. Quoted in Jacobs, p. 177.

26. Quoted in William Pratt, *Scarlett Fever* (New York: Macmillan, 1977), p. 218.

27. In analyzing the plantation in Southern writing, Davenport explains that "The image of the house and its surrounding grounds symbolizes among other things order, innocence, and white supremacy as well as the important concept of stability and permanence unaffected by history. Such associations have the same appeal to the national imagination as they do for Southerners, evoking that nostalgic sense of Southern uniqueness and a vanished simple and good life . . . (p. 85). See also *Memo from Selznick*, pp. 212–13.

28. Henry F. May, *The End of American Innocence* (New York: Knopf, 1959), p. 18.

29. See Davenport, pp. 91–92, and Lambert, p. 159. For a more complete discussion of this search for identity in America in the second half of the 1930s, see Warren I. Susman, "The Thirties," in *The Development of an American Culture*, ed. Stanley Coben and Lorman Ratner (Englewood Cliffs, N.J.: Prentice-Hall, 1970), pp. 188–89; Charles J. Maland, *American Visions: The Films of Chaplin, Ford, Capra, and Welles, 1936–1941* (New York: Arno Press, 1977), pp. 2, 8, 17; Richard Pells, *Radical Visions and American Dreams* (New York: Harper & Row, 1973), pp. 117, 200, 314–15, 360.

Winds of Change: *Gone with the Wind* and Racism as a National Issue

Malcolm X grew into manhood with a vivid memory of *Gone with the Wind*. As a teenager, he went to see the film in his Michigan hometown: "I remember one thing that marred that time for me. . . . I was the only Negro in the theatre, and when Butterfly Mc-Queen went into her act, I felt like crawling under the rug."[1] In December 1939, a few weeks earlier, 300,000 Atlantans, most of them white, had filled the streets for the premiere that simultaneously celebrated the release of the movie and a revival of Southern consciousness. Wherever Margaret Mitchell's 1,000-page novel was sold and wherever the movie version played, the story was the same: audiences were divided along racial lines.

But to see *Gone with the Wind* only as the center of a racial debate is to miss much. In addition to its obvious socially divisive ingredients of sectionalism and racism, it contained elements calculated by its makers, Mitchell and producer David O. Selznick, to temper and modulate high-running racial feelings. Indeed, their half-formed liberal assumptions that contributed to the political texture of the film anticipated the more sharply focused racial liberalism of World War II.

In this sense, *Gone with the Wind* signaled a revival of an old abolitionist quest to make racism a national issue. By standing astride a moment between the Great Depression and a world war during which American social attitudes changed, in part prodded by forces released by wartime propaganda calling for national unity across ethnic lines, the movie provided a punctuation mark between the last era in which racial matters were considered to be purely local and a new era when they resumed a role in national public policy.

Moreover, this halting step toward more liberal racial politics, made urgent by the coming of war, was not unnoticed by Afro-Americans. As the need to solve racial problems emerged, black critics debated the merits of the novel, made hopeful gestures to change the movie during production, and scrutinized the product as a reflection of changing American social attitudes. Selznick, for his part, excised all references to the Ku Klux Klan, renegade Negroes, and other Southern legends, as though weeding out prickly points in order to allow the movie to speak, however softly, to a generation of Americans who faced a tense and unstable racial future.[2]

During the depression, President Franklin Roosevelt's New Deal programs brought increasing numbers of blacks into government: judges, senior officials, the first black governor-general of the Virgin Islands, and an informal "Black Cabinet" composed of federal officeholders. Mrs. Roosevelt acted unofficially as the administration's conscience in racial matters by calling public attention to incidents of racial injustice. Although some federal programs designed to alleviate the burdens of the depression were discriminatory and segregated, others, such as the Federal Theatre Project, had black participants.

Similar changes could be seen in the movies. After a flurry of activity between 1934 and 1936, Stepin Fetchit and Bill Robinson, the bugbears of organized black advocates of broader opportunity in Hollywood, failed to have their options picked up. At 20th Century Fox, Darryl F. Zanuck supported the efforts of black activists, and his two liberal Southern writers, Lamar Trotti and Nunnally Johnson, wrote a variety of strong black roles into their scripts. A new generation of black actors, exemplified by Rex Ingram and his three roles in Warner Brothers' *The Green Pastures* (1936), challenged studio regulars. Paul Robeson returned from Europe for Universal's remake of *Show Boat*. The era ended with two barbed social dramas about the South: William Wellman's *Jezebel* (1938) and William Wyler's *The Little Foxes* (1941).

When war came in 1941, the liberal trend was absorbed by Allied war aims in the form of Roosevelt's "four freedoms" speech, the anticolonial portions of the Atlantic Charter, and other documents. The war that unified the Western democracies encouraged Negroes to extend and codify their social gains. The National Association for the Advancement of Colored People held its national convention in 1942 in Los Angeles, hoping to influence movies at their source, a tactic that resulted in a loose agreement by the studios to broaden opportunities for blacks. Black picket lines formed whenever a specific film-maker seemed to ignore or evade the agreement. NAACP Executive Secretary Walter White briefly considered making a film of his own.[3] Several war movies integrated black soldiers into their combat units. The army itself took up the issue with its training film, *The Negro Soldier*, which traced the history of blacks in American wars, a theme so popular that the Office of War Information released a version to civilian theaters. On at least one occasion, the direct intervention of the NAACP and its allies affected a film at the studio level: Metro-Goldwyn-Mayer softened in *Tennessee Johnson* its intended harsh portrait of Reconstruction Congressman Thaddeus Stevens, a hero among blacks.[4]

Released in 1939, *Gone with the Wind* arrived exactly on the eve of this wartime liberal campaign. And for all of Malcolm X's aversion and the hostility of those black critics who saw it as the sum of a long tradition of Hollywood Civil War movies, the film had been stirred by these winds of racial change.

The book itself reflected the growing national ambiguity in racial attitudes. Its author was neither a liberal nor a mossback. Born in 1900, Mitchell broke one pattern of Southern women by going to college in the North, then taking a job with the *Atlanta Journal*. Yet she grew up amidst tales of Sherman burning Atlanta, of refugees walking the road to Macon, of Confederate soldiers suffering and Southern women sacrificing. Her visits to the Stone Mountain Cyclorama, hikes along the old Confederate earthworks, and knowledge of "Sherman's sentinels"—the blackened ruins that dotted the countryside— all reinforced a legendary sense of the past.[5]

But Mitchell had more than memories of "the lost cause." Her job on the *Journal* thrust her into the present. "Professional Southerners" annoyed her, and she admired W. J. Cash's incisive dissection of *The Mind of the South* (1941). In her twenties, she attempted a novella of "flaming youth" about a liaison between a mulatto and a white woman. She came to hate the Southern exploiters who came forward as her book grew into a film. Of one of them she wrote to Katharine Brown of Selznick-International: "I wish to God you could have seen the white woman who turned up last week with a can of blacking in her pocketbook and the determination of playing Mammy."[6]

In the novel, Mitchell had wavered between realism and romance, even as her art and politics straddled racial issues. As she told her editor, she would be "upset and mortified if Left Wingers like the book," but, on the other hand, "I sweat blood to keep it from being like Uncle Remus." She read Southern regionalists like Rebecca Yancey Williams as well as Southern critics like Cash. Of Henry Steele Commager's biography of Theodore Parker she could

139

say, "The parts about the fugitive slaves I liked best and reread," while in the same summer she wrote to the racist Thomas Dixon that "I was practically raised on your books and love them very much."[7] And, like many white Southerners, she loved her black servants but, at the same time, believed the Ku Klux Klan to be a historic necessity. She remained ever Southern and, despite her literary celebrity, yearned to be accepted by Southern readers. As one of her characters says: "Miss Scarlett, tain' gwine to do you no good to stan' high wid de Yankees ef yo' own folks doan' 'prove of you."[8]

The book's reception by the American public and critics pointed toward its eventual success as a film but also toward the problems Selznick faced in producing it. Sales ran into millions, as friendly critics praised it as a vast tapestry of antebellum Southern life. And yet on the flanks of the great audience were critics for whom *Gone with the Wind* was a failure: on the right, doctrinaire Southerners expecting a reflowering of the old myths; on the left, critics joining in Malcolm Cowley's blast at the refurbishing of "the plantation legend."[9] Selznick's job as producer necessarily included taking into account the spectrum of criticism with a view to bringing a Southern novel into the center of American popular opinion.

For Selznick and the first of his scriptwriters, Pulitzer Prize—winning playwright Sidney Howard, the initial task was to shift the perspective of the film toward their own liberal politics. As Selznick wrote in a memorandum, "I, for one, have no desire to produce an anti-Negro film either. In our picture I think we have to be awfully careful that the Negroes come out decidedly on the right side of the ledger." Such liberalism helped eliminate a Ku Klux Klan episode. "I personally feel quite strongly that we should cut out the Klan entirely," wrote Selznick; otherwise, the film "might come out as an unintentional advertisement for intolerant societies in these fascist-ridden times."[10]

Their best liberal intentions lacked consistency, however. Howard, for example, as a way of praising Mitchell's honesty, used an old Southern term that was insultingly nettlesome to blacks: her blacks were "the best written darkies, I believe, in all literature . . . the only ones I have ever read which seem to come through uncolored by white patronizing." In another instance, Selznick insisted that "the picture must not emerge as anything offensive to negroes" or **140** throw "too bad a light on even the negroes of the reconstruction period." A typical solution was to reconstruct a rape scene by making "the negro little more than a spectator," which put aside rather than solved the problem of how to depict the free and politically and socially assertive blacks of Reconstruction.[11]

Selznick and Howard also shared an ignorance of the details of plantation life and the slavery system, which they hoped to correct by hiring a consultant. At first, they sought Mitchell herself as a historical adviser but, failing that, turned to two white Southerners whom Mitchell had recommended: Wilbur Kurtz, an Atlanta architect, and Susan Myrick, a reporter for the *Macon Telegraph*.[12] Earlier, Selznick had approached Walter White of the NAACP to join them as adviser but without success.

Kurtz, a Northerner by birth and an avid Civil War buff, counseled on manners, dress, architecture, weaponry, and ambience—and eventually on black accents, garments, and society. His carefully worked memoranda, augmented by his reading of black historian William Still's *Underground Railroad*, provided details of plantation activity, equipage, and personnel that black critics could not effectively challenge. In Tara's washyard, for example, he missed nothing: the little Negro girl who swept it; the old pipe-smoking woman who presided over the boiling clothes in the iron washpot; the black boy who stoked the fire and fetched the water. Every black resident of Tara was the subject of a sketch. Not only Mammy, Pork, Dilcey, and Prissy, but also the cobblers, wheelwrights, barbers, drivers, herders, flyswishers, and black foremen received at least a line of type. As the Civil War came to Atlanta, drying up the labor pool, Kurtz's memoranda caught the motley black labor gangs marching in their tatters through the city, pickaxes on their shoulders, under the eyes of the old men of the Home Guard. Yet Kurtz's point of view, like that of Mitchell and Selznick, was of a narrow gauge that missed details such as whips and chains—no surviving memorandum recorded them.[13]

Although Susan Myrick, the other adviser, was a native Georgian, the grandchild of a Confederate general, and a member of an old family, her strength, according to Mitchell, was her "utter lack of sentimentality about what is tearfully known as 'The Old South'." As a reporter for the *Macon Telegraph*, she gave frequent and sympathetic coverage to Negro events; she often spoke at black gatherings and was seen by the black community as an advocate. When she recommended Myrick, Mitchell repeated a black tribute: "De race got two friends in dis county, sweet Jesus and de Macon Telegraph."[14]

In Hollywood, Myrick spent her days viewing older Southern movies, advising director George Cukor and his successor, Victor Fleming, on accents, costuming, manners, "talk[ing] Southern" to the English actors, and scouting local productions, such as the Federal Theatre's *Run Little Chillun,* in search of "any good negro actors."[15] Thus she became the most active liaison between Hollywood and Atlanta, reporting back to Mitchell that she had often prevented gross errors and misstatements of Southern lore.[16]

As production reached full tilt in mid-1939, Mitchell maintained her distance from the project, hoping that the advisers would head off both the triteness that rankled white Southerners and the stereotypes that spoiled movies for blacks. "Even more wearying than the choral effects are the inevitable wavings in the air of several hundred pairs of hands with Rouben Mamoulian shadows leaping on the walls," she wrote to Katharine Brown of her recollections of Broadway's excesses. "This was fine and fitting in 'Porgy' but pretty awful in other shows where it had no place. I feared greatly that three hundred massed Negro singers might be standing on Miss Pittypat's lawn waving their arms and singing 'Swing low, sweet chariot, Comin' for to carry me home' while Rhett drives up with the wagon."[17]

During production, black critics watched and waited, unable or unwilling to mount a cohesive campaign that might have permitted them to provide a third force between Selznick and his white Southern advisers. Leftist revisions of Reconstruction history, such as W. E. B. DuBois's *Black Reconstruction* (1935) and James S. Allen's *Reconstruction: The Battle for Democracy* (1937), reached only small Marxist and academic audiences, thereby leaving unchallenged the popular notion of the period as a nightmare of corruption and black domination of the ballot box. As a consequence, the black press could take Mitchell to task primarily for her use of the epithets "nigger" and "darkie." Even this campaign was short-circuited long before it began. Months before February 1939, when Ruby Berkeley Goodwin's Associated Negro Press column reported the excising of "nigger" from the script, Selznick had already written Howard that, although blacks refer to each other as "nigger," "the word should *not* be put in the mouths of white people."[18]

The NAACP mustered only a low-voltage force, in no way equal to the intensity and focus that developed during the world war. Walter White expressed almost apologetically his apprehension over the forthcoming movie. "I want to emphasize again that I do not by this mean to stress racial chauvinism or hypersensitiveness," he wrote to Selznick. "Our interest is solely that of accuracy." After an inconclusive exchange of letters with Howard, he departed for two months to the Virgin Islands, leaving a void to be filled by local branches, if at all. For a black adviser on the set he recommended Hall Johnson, a veteran Hollywood choir director whose livelihood depended upon getting along with studio bosses. Indeed, Johnson confessed to Myrick that he was "unhappy that some of his race failed so miserably to understand" *Gone with the Wind*. Consequently, the producers worried less about Negro opinion and more about appeasing conservative watchdogs of historical trivia, such as the United Daughters of the Confederacy and the Society for Correct Civil War Information. At the same time the Christmas issue of *Crisis,* the house organ of the NAACP, symbolically reduced the matter to a lower priority by running a casual snapshot of editor Roy Wilkins in a group of black visitors to a movie set, thereby, on the eve of the premiere, implying black tolerance of Hollywood's activities.[19]

Within the limits set by their roles, black actors had an effect on the shaping of the movie. Early on, Selznick rejected fanciful notions such as casting Mrs. Roosevelt's maid as Mammy, preferring to audition experienced actors such as Hattie McDaniel, Louise Beavers, and Hattie Noel. Eventually he chose McDaniel, who had built a six-year career playing preternaturally wise maids in such movies as George Stevens's film of Booth Tarkington's *Alice Adams.* For Prissy he picked Butterfly McQueen, a veteran of Broadway revues with a fey persona that concealed a stubborn resistance to stereotyping. Eddie Anderson came from vaudeville, radio, and a stint as Jack Benny's comic valet to play an old servant. Others were Hollywood hands, including Oscar Polk as Pork, the Geechee butler, and Everett Brown as Big Sam, the black foreman.

On the set, blacks presented a wide range of behavior that no one mistook for humble Southern demeanor. Early in the filming, a delegation of them threatened to walk off the set unless racial designations were removed from the lavatories. The craftsmanlike McDaniel dutifully learned to drawl, soaked up "fundamental Southern philosophy" from Myrick, and polished her role. McQueen confounded white observers, sometimes playing the "'nigger' through and through," as Cukor playfully threatened to "use a Simon Legree whip," but driving him to snappishness when she paused to concentrate on capturing a mood. On one occasion, after "Scarlett" slapped her too smartly, she indignantly stepped out of character, crying "I can't do it, she's hurting me. . . . I'm no stunt man, I'm an actress." Despite Cukor's anger at her stopping the action, she refused to resume until Vivien Leigh apologized. Off-camera she intrigued witnesses by reading George Jean Nathan's column in *Esquire* and Alexander Woollcott's essays. Of all the blacks, only Polk played a drawling "house hand" that whites found familiar, yet with enough exaggeration to have drawn perhaps a wink from the other blacks. The extras played black games, strutted about in "Central Avenue overcoats," and applauded the work of the featured black actors.[20]

The black press plugged their work, as yet unseen, especially McDaniel's "coveted" role of Mammy, to which she brought the "dignity and earnestness" that made her "more than a servant." She became "confidante, counselor, and manager of the O'Hara household," said the *Amsterdam News* in an early blurb.[21]

Although Selznick-International turned out one of the great events of film history, for blacks *Gone with the Wind* remained an ambiguity caught between old dying black images and as yet unformed new images. While no Klansmen appeared, neither did a single rebellious slave or black soldier. No black characters shared any emotional bonds, except those of loyalty to whites, and those few who left the plantation in favor of freedom were depicted as shantytown renegades. Yet Mammy grew from her stolid presence on Mitchell's pages into a heroic, rocklike figure on whom the defeated whites relied. Other blacks, though lacking depth, conveyed a plodding resilience and warmth. Thus, if McQueen's comic bits caused blacks to wince, other actors maintained a studied dignity that pleased black audiences and confounded black critics.

Predictably, leftists branded such accomplishments as no more than bourgeois opportunism and damned the entire production as a racist tract. Throughout the winter of 1939–40 the *Daily Worker,* led by its critic, David Platt, nagged at the movie. The organ of the American Communist Party deviated only once from its persistent campaign, when Howard Rushmore gave it a mixed review flecked with a few admissions of merit. The centerpiece of the campaign was Carlton Moss's "open letter" to Selznick, a systematic attack on the producer's vaunted historicity. A flavorful sample of the critics can be found in Peter Noble's *The Negro in Films* (1948). The *Socialist Appeal* saw the film as only "a distorted glorification of the Old South." "It revives every foul slander against the Negro people . . . in a slick package of sentimentality," said the New York state committee of the Communist Party, adding that "This movie is a rabid incitement against the Negro people. The historical struggle for democracy in this country which we have come to cherish so dearly is vilified and condemned. The great liberator, Abraham Lincoln, is pictured as a tyrant and a coward." The intention of the producers seemed clear: "to provoke race riots," which would undermine the unity of workers. Black Communist William L. Patterson, in a *Chicago Defender* review, saw the film as a challenge to those "seeking to advance democracy today" and backed his argument by leading a picket line in Chicago.[22]

The broad center of Negro opinion represented in the monthlies either generally admired the film for its modest revisions of ancient stereotypes or considered it an irrelevancy. DuBois, for example, dismissed it as a "conventional provincialism about which Negroes need not get excited." *Crisis* shared his view, pointing out that the film "eliminated practically all the offensive scenes and dialogue so that there is little material, directly affecting Negroes as a race, to which objection can be entered." The Urban League's *Opportunity* made no direct reference to the movie. A trade paper, *Negro Actor,* ran Edward G. Perry's review in which he admitted he "was not offended or annoyed." This sentiment was echoed in the white liberal press; thus Lincoln Kirstin complained that the movie failed as art and social history but said that it was not a racist tract.[23]

Negro newspapers, weighing internal evidence and external effect without reference to a holistic political ideology, judged *Gone with the Wind* as a tolerably salubrious event. Taking the actors' point of view, the *Amsterdam News* reckoned that acting jobs generated by the film brought "economic joy and artistic aplomb to the local colony of sepia screen players." The Washington *Afro-American* played the same angle, saluting McQueen's meteoric career and 12,000 days of work by black extras as evidence of the benefits of *Gone with the Wind*.[24]

Newspaper critics dismissed the servile roles as predictable elements of a period film and hailed each break with old convention as a triumph. The *Norfolk Journal and Guide,* for example, admired the modernity of the relationship between Rhett and Mammy. Several critics agreed that "there was no reason for Negroes to feel indignant over the film." A few, like Lillian Johnson in the Baltimore *Afro-American*, even found it "magnificently done" and "truly the greatest picture ever made."[25]

Thus, at the height of national excitement over *Gone with the Wind*, organized blacks spoke with many voices, ranging from the temperate responses of the NAACP and the black press to the barely controlled rage of the black left that spoke through the *Daily Worker* and the National Negro Congress. As though accommodating the breadth of the spectrum, the black press sometimes balanced hostile critics by running their columns in tandem with friendlier observers or by printing readers' letters that reflected the range of praise and calumny or by running "boilerplate" generated by wire services and studio press agents as counterweights to negative stories filed by staff writers.

Almost always, this evenhandedness extended to balancing rave reviews against equally kind words for the black protesters and pickets who sometimes marked local premieres. In Washington, Cleveland, Richmond, Norfolk, and other cities, local theaters held dressy premieres that attracted opposites—formally dressed black bourgeoisie and the black protesters whose picket lines they crossed, sometimes guiltily. In Washington, for example, the moviegoers were obliged to pass under signs proclaiming "You'd

146

Be Sweet Too Under A Whip!" Most black papers took the line adopted by the *Gary American*, which covered both angles, head-lining that "Protest Fails to Stop Film Showing" while reporting that "all" inside the theater applauded the movie. Or as Lillian Johnson analyzed her own reaction to breaking the ranks by going inside to see the film: "I crossed a picket line. I wasn't sorry." [26]

More than a mere surface division of black circles over some ephemeral event, the black reaction to *Gone with the Wind* fore-shadowed a shift in black political and aesthetic attitudes toward a more solid, acute collective attention directed at motion pictures and their impact on black life and white prejudices. This emerging awareness of the social impact of Hollywood's products could be seen in two episodes that occurred after the release of the movie. The first was a black-led victory against a feckless attempt to re-make *The Birth of a Nation* (1915), D. W. Griffith's silent movie that combined art and racism with celebrated effect. In black circles, the collapse of the project signaled a political victory that diverted some of the limelight from *Gone with the Wind* but confirmed a sense of black cohesiveness and underlined a rising commitment to an alliance with liberal white activists. [27]

The second event was Hattie McDaniel's Oscar for her portrayal of Mammy. Her day in the Hollywood spotlight, followed by a tour of black theaters, gave a priceless boost to black morale. The black press treated her as a hero, *Opportunity* and *Crisis* both giving her cover stories celebrating "the first time a colored film actor or actress has ever been given this honor." If a few black pickets turned out, the evening of the awards presentation was still grandly hers. After Fay Bainter presented the statuette, McDaniel offered a homily to black youth, whom she urged to "aim high and work hard" in the better times ahead. In true Hollywood fashion, she ar-rived late, wrapped in furs against the rigors of Southern California springtime, sat at Selznick's table, and later received a kiss from Viv-ien Leigh and a handshake from Clark Gable. [28]

What did all this mean to blacks? What social forces were re-leased and symbolized by *Gone with the Wind*? Most significantly, the film clearly was not a revival of the mystical, repellent, *Kultur-kampf* image conjured among blacks by *Birth of a Nation*. On the contrary, it foreshadowed a decline in racism of that sort, a decline seen in the integrity of the film's black actors, their recognition by the white community, and the related black-led victory over the *Birth of a Nation* remake project. Their successes further affected the blacks' political alliances, in that the film also encouraged the liberal expectation that individual blacks might also find their place alongside whites in the American dream of success and self-fulfillment. Moreover, for many years previously, organized blacks in the Urban League and NAACP had enjoyed the cooperation of Communists and other radicals, accepting their support without subscribing to Marxist ideology or allowing infiltration of black groups; but Selznick's movie opened the way to an opportunity to seek allies closer to the liberal center of social activism rather than along its radical fringe.

Eventually, *Gone with the Wind* became a template against which to measure social change. The title itself became a rhetorical device among black journalists. *Opportunity*, for example, in its editorial congratulation to Hattie McDaniel, used *Gone with the Wind* as a reminder of the "limit" put upon black aspiration by old prejudices. When the *Cleveland Call & Post* attacked journalistic racism, its bannerline was "All Did Not Go with the Wind," while black Communist Ben Davis used the financiers of the movie as evidence of his conviction that capitalists and the Ku Klux Klan were two sides of the same equation. Charles Rowan in *Crisis* blasted vestiges of peonage under the title "Has Slavery Gone with the Wind in Georgia?" Songwriter Andy Razaf's ironic poem in *Crisis* used the title to capture a sense of imprisonment between the past and future:

> What of the black man's liberty?
> Today, he is half slave, half free,
> Denied his rights on every side,
> Jim Crowed, lynched and crucified,
> He's even barred in Washington—.
> Gone with the Wind? You're wrong, my son.[29]

The muted and ambiguous signals of shifting racial attitudes sent out by *Gone with the Wind* echoed not only in circles of black critics but in Hollywood itself. Dozens of movies made small gestures of recognition of the trend. Among the most significant in contributing to the changed mood in Hollywood was Sol Lesser's *Way Down South* (1939), a treatment of the plantation tradition that itself broke tradition by employing black writers Langston Hughes and Clarence Muse. Far more boldly than Selznick had, they intended to use a movie about the plantation tradition as a voice of a modern temper. As Lesser told his staff, "Messrs. Muse and Hughes are to be given the utmost liberty in developing the Second Draft Screenplay, so that it will contain every element of their conception of the story." Although the completed film fell far short of the writers' expectations, at a B-movie level *Way Down South* retained a few vestiges of their social consciousness. Thereafter, throughout the war and beyond, Hughes kept up a personal interest in the political potential of movies, and Muse placed the name of the film on the masthead of his personal stationery.[30]

Like *Gone with the Wind*, Lesser's *Way Down South* signaled no revolution, yet it too supplied the end punctuation to an era when racism had been considered a regional issue that had no national importance. Only a few weeks after *Gone with the Wind* and *Way Down South* had completed their first runs, a story editor at Warner Brothers composed a memorandum about *Mississippi Belle*, a script that promised a regression to the worst traits of the plantation tradition. Her note to Walter Wanger reflected what black moviegoers had seen in *Gone with the Wind*: that by having departed from the worst excesses of Southern plantation movies, it had rendered the genre so obsolete as to be unproducible. "I confess I am a bit puzzled to know why such a story should be made," she wrote. "I just can't believe that anybody would be interested. . . . It all seems so old-fashioned and remote."[31]

Notes

1. Malcolm X, with Alex Haley, *The Autobiography of Malcolm X* (New York: Grove Press, 1965), p. 42; Frank Daniel, "Cinderella City: Atlanta Sees 'Gone with the Wind'," *Saturday Review of Literature*, December 23, 1939, p. 9.

2. See Richard Harwell, ed., *Margaret Mitchell's "Gone with the Wind" Letters,*

149

1936–1949 (New York: Macmillan, 1976), p. 61. On the economic and social meaning of *Gone with the Wind* see Thomas H. Pauly, *"Gone with the Wind* and *The Grapes of Wrath* as Hollywood Histories of the Great Depression," *Journal of Popular Film* 3 (Summer 1974): 203–18.

3. For a detailed account of the period, see Thomas Cripps, *Slow Fade to Black: The Negro in American Film, 1900–1942* (New York: Oxford University Press, 1977), chap. 13. See also Walter White to Virginius Dabney, April 8, 1940, copy, NAACP Records, Library of Congress.

4. Thomas Cripps and David Culbert, *"The Negro Soldier* (1944): Film Propaganda in Black and White," *American Quarterly* 21 (Winter 1979): 616–40.

5. Finis Farr, *Margaret Mitchell of Atlanta* (New York: William Morrow, 1965), pp. 26, 28, 30, 39, 43–44, 47, 50, 76, 90–93.

6. Mitchell to Katharine Brown, March 8, 1937, Margaret Mitchell Marsh Papers, University of Georgia Libraries, Athens.

7. Mitchell to Commager, July 10, 1936; Mitchell to Herschel Brickell, July 7, 1936; Mitchell to Dixon, August 15, 1936; in Harwell, pp. 39, 19–21, 52.

8. Mitchell to Paul Jordan-Smith, May 27, 1936; Mitchell to Herschel Brickell, July 7, 1936, May 9, 1937; Mitchell to Ruth Tallman, July 30, 1937; in Harwell, pp. 7, 19–21, 144, 162. Margaret Mitchell, *Gone with the Wind* (New York: Macmillan, 1936), p. 675.

9. Farr, p. 157.

10. Selznick to Howard, January 6, 1937, *Memo from David O. Selznick,* ed. Rudy Behlmer (New York: Viking, 1972), p. 151; Mitchell to Brown, October 6, 1936, copy, Margaret Mitchell Marsh Papers; "treatment" by Sidney Howard, p. 37, Sidney Howard Papers, Bancroft Library, University of California, Berkeley.

11. Howard to Mitchell, November 18, 1936, Margaret Mitchell Marsh Papers; Selznick to Howard, January 6, 1937, Sidney Howard Papers; Wilbur Kurtz to Stacey, Wheeler, Menzies, Coles, Forbes, et al., memoranda, January 3, 14, 1939, November 15, December 21, 1938, copies, Margaret Mitchell Marsh Papers.

12. Brown to Mitchell, October 1, 13, November 16, 20, 1936; Mitchell to Brown, October 6, 1936, February 14, 1937, July 7, 1938, copies; Mitchell to Selznick, October 19, 1936; Mitchell to Russell Birdwell, November 1936, December 5, 1936; all in Margaret Mitchell Marsh Papers.

13. Kurtz memoranda, December 21, 1938, and n.d.; Kurtz to Dabney, December 22, 1938, copy; Kurtz to Susan Myrick, *Macon Telegraph*, December 27, 1938; Kurtz to Beverly M. DuBose, Trust Company of Georgia Building, December 28, 1938, copy; all in Margaret Mitchell Marsh Papers. Kurtz to Howard, February 8, 1938, Sidney Howard Papers.

14. George Brown Tindall, *The Emergence of the New South, 1913–1945,* vol. 10, *A History of the South*, ed. Wendell Holmes Stephenson and E. Merton Coulter (Baton Rouge: Louisiana State University Press, 1967), p. 552. Mitchell to Brown,

February 14, 1937, copy; Myrick to "Dear John," n.d.; both in Margaret Mitchell Marsh Papers.

15. Selznick to Howard, November 13, 1936, Sidney Howard Papers.

16. Myrick to Mitchell, January 11, 15, 1939, February 12, 14, 1939, March 12, April 17, 1939, Margaret Mitchell Marsh Papers.

17. Mitchell to Brown, April 17, 1939, Margaret Mitchell Marsh Papers.

18. Goodwin quoted in Harwell, p. 273; Selznick to Howard, memorandum, Sidney Howard Papers.

19. Myrick to Mitchell, report on Johnson, April 17, 1939; White to Selznick, June 18, 1939, copy; White to Howard, July 13, 1938; all in Sidney Howard Papers. On the UDC, see Mitchell to Selznick, January 30, 1939, copy; on the CSCCWI, see their undated memorandum; both in Margaret Mitchell Marsh Papers. For Roy Wilkins photograph, see *Crisis* 46 (December 1939): 381.

20. On Mrs. Roosevelt's maid, Lizzie McDuffie, see Mitchell to Katharine Brown, August 13, 1937; on McQueen's ambivalent behavior, see Myrick to Mitchell, February 12, 1939; both in Margaret Mitchell Marsh Papers. See also Victor Shapiro, "Diary of *Gone with the Wind*," Special Collections, UCLA; Cripps, pp. 359–62; Roland Flamini, *Scarlett, Rhett, and a Cast of Thousands: The Filming of Gone with the Wind* (New York: Macmillan, 1975), pp. 184, 216, 288.

21. Quoted in Cripps, p. 361.

22. Peter Noble, *The Negro in Films* (London: S. Robinson, 1948), pp. 75–79; Patterson quoted in John D. Stevens, "The Black Reaction to *Gone with the Wind*," *Journal of Popular Film* 2 (Fall 1973): 366–71. See Cripps, pp. 363–64 and notes 30 and 31, for a treatment of the Communist response, as well as that of other groups such as the National Negro Congress. For Moss's letter see *Daily Worker*, January 9, 1940. See also transcript of a panel on "cultural freedom" (to which I was referred by Hilmar Jensen, and in which Sterling Brown uses the film as a symbol of the status of the black artist), April 28, 1940, records of the National Negro Congress, box 21, Schomburg Collection, New York Public Library.

23. *Negro Actor*, quoted in Cripps, p. 364; *Crisis* 48 (January 1940): 17. Roy Wilkins of the NAACP concurred; he had expected "violently anti-Negro material" but found that "there is very little direct anti-Negro material" (Wilkins to Barbee W. Durham, January 31, 1940, copy, NAACP Records).

24. *Amsterdam News* (New York), March 2, 1940; *Afro-American* (Washington), February 10, 17, 1940.

25. For a sample of the black press, see *Pittsburgh Courier*, quoted in *Variety*, February 14, 1940, p. 27; *Amsterdam News* (New York), March 2, 1940; *Norfolk Journal and Guide*, February 24, 1940; *Gary American*, March 15, 1940; *Afro-American* (Richmond), April 20, 1940; *Afro-American* (Washington), March 9, January 20, 1940.

26. *Amsterdam News* (New York), March 16, 23, 1940; *Afro-American* (Phila-

delphia), March 30, 1940; *Norfolk Journal and Guide*, May 16, 1940; *Gary American*, March 15, 1940; *Afro-American* (Washington), March 9, 1940.

27. *Afro-American* (Philadelphia), March 23, 30, 1940; *Norfolk Journal and Guide*, March 23, 1940; *Afro-American* (Washington), March 23, 1940. Walter White to Walter Winchell, May 20, 1940, copy; George E. Haynes, Federal Council of Churches, to Walter White, March 28, 1940; Thurgood Marshall to Committee on Administration, memorandum, March 4, 1940, copy; "N.A.A.C.P. Hits Revival of 'Birth of a Nation'," press release, March 22, 1940; all in NAACP Records, Library of Congress.

28. *Opportunity* 18 (April 1940): 100; *Crisis* 47 (April 1940): 103; *Pittsburgh Courier*, March 9, 1940; *Afro-American* (Baltimore), March 9, 1940; *Afro-American* (Washington), May 18, 1940.

29. *Opportunity* 18 (April 1940): 100, and (February 1940): 56–57; Charles Rowan, "Has Slavery Gone with the Wind in Georgia?" *Crisis* 17 (February 1940): 44–45; *Cleveland Call & Post*, January 4, 1940; Andy Razaf, "Gone with the Wind," *Crisis* 17 (February 1940): 45.

30. Drafts of *Way Down South* and Lesser's editorial comments dated January–March 1939 are in the Langston Hughes Papers, James Weldon Johnson Collection, Beineke Library, Yale University. Here and there in Hughes's subsequent correspondence in the Beineke Collection and at Fisk University, Nashville, there are treatments, drafts, and outlines of projected films of his own: *The Negro Speaks of Rivers, The Chocolate Sailor, L'Amitié noire*, a story of the Kansas "exodusters," and an untitled "Paul Robeson Screenplay." Muse's letterhead resumé is in my possession.

31. Lenore Coffey to Walter Wanger, August 20, 1941, *Mississippi Belle*, file 2494, Warner Brothers Records, Doheny Library, University of Southern California, Los Angeles.

Race, Romance, and the Southern Literary Tradition Kenneth O'Brien

It was with great reluctance that Margaret Mitchell gave her un-wieldy tale of Pansy O'Hara's tribulations to Macmillan editor Harold Latham. In fact, she telegraphed him the next day requesting that he return the manuscript. He didn't, and Macmillan had its best-seller of 1936. Yet the extraordinary and unique record of pop-ular success and acclaim accorded the novel has not been paral-leled by critical esteem. Malcolm Cowley identified the elements that most bothered the critics. "*Gone with the Wind*," he wrote in the *New Republic*, "is an encyclopedia of the plantation legend." Unlike other authors, who had used only part of the legend, "Miss Mitchell repeats it as whole, with all its episodes and all its charac-ters and all its stage settings."[1] Recent surveys and analyses of twen-tieth-century Southern fiction have sustained Cowley's judgment by either ignoring the novel or dismissing it as mere "plantation ro-mance," a "highly romanticized portrait of the past that seems hardly aware of its own romanticism."[2]

In many ways, the film has met a similar fate. Practically ignored in Gerald Mast's *A Short History of Movies* and Robert Sklar's *Movie-Made America*, it has been attacked by both Andrew Sarris and Richard Schickel. According to Sarris, "We can certainly do without the oneliners about happy darkies, wicked carpetbaggers, white trash, and Southern slum clearance, nightrider style. The South of Margaret Mitchell is a still-born fantasy in which blacks lack even the villainous dignity of D. W. Griffith's *Birth of a Na-tion.*"[3] Schickel says, "Well, frankly, my dear I didn't (and don't) give a damn about the South's yokel notion that it once supported a new age of chivalry and grace." Since he thinks that the "historical evidence for that contention is slight," he could never join Mitchell in "mourning the age gone with her wind, which seemed to me far from an ill wind."[4]

The issue raised by such criticism has little to do with the artistic merits of either the novel or the film; rather, the works are criti-cized because of their thoughtless repetition of the convention-alities of the discredited and self-serving myths of the plantation South and the era of Reconstruction. But how well does Mitchell's work really fit into the literary world of the Southern romance of the late nineteenth and early twentieth centuries, the obvious frame of reference of the critics? How appropriate is it to dismiss

153

the novel, as did Cowley, as merely a particularly attractive rehash of the same old story?

Margaret Mitchell herself insisted that anyone who lumped *Gone with the Wind* with the romantic renderings of the region in earlier novels simply did not know the genre of "the gentle Confederate novel." There is truth in her contention. By examining the most archetypal product of that sort of romance by its most archetypal creator, we can identify Mitchell's break with that tradition and reformulation of a new set of literary and social values, recast within traditional forms.

Beginning in the 1880s and continuing for three decades, Southern writers and their tales of regional life enjoyed unprecedented popularity in national culture through novels and magazines. Through this literature, which focused on the antebellum and Reconstruction periods, the South seemed to be winning the war that it had lost on the battlefields. According to Albion Tourgee, an idealistic Northern emigré to the South during Reconstruction and a popular novelist in his own right, the South in the postwar era had become "the seat of intellectual empire in America," and the African had emerged as the "chief romantic element of our population."[5] Thomas Nelson Page was the leading exponent of the Southern school; indeed, his name has become synonymous with all its sentimental conventions. His novel *Red Rock: A Chronicle of Reconstruction*, published in 1895 and termed by one critic "the finest southern version of this era,"[6] is a summary of the literary conventions that characterized Southern attitudes toward the postwar past.

Even before the novel begins, Page establishes the framework of the literary and social conventions upon which he will build the novel. In the preface, he writes that during Reconstruction the people of the South "were subjected to the greatest humiliation of modern times: their slaves were over them—they reconquered their section and preserved the civilization of the Anglo-Saxon."[7] *Red Rock* is a tale of woe. Political power in the novel is held by Jonadab Leech, a Northern carpetbagger who has an honest Northern soldier transferred to the Western frontier after his interference with a black political rally. A coward who refused to serve in the military during the war, Leech rises to power through his ability to

use the black masses politically, inciting them to ever greater violence. Motivated by a dream of omnipotence, he is depicted as
seeking "wealth unlimited, position, unmeasured power" (p. 500).

If Leech fulfills the conventional role of the cynical, cowardly
Northern white man—the "outside agitator"—who plays on the
weaknesses of the South after the war, the freedman Moses plays an
even more significant stock role. He is the arrogant former slave
whose purpose is to overturn all the mores of Southern society. A
"Trick Doctor," he exercises his magic over the black masses. At a
political rally, he excites the black crowd by "tossing his arms in a
sort of frenzy" and calling them to "rise and prove they were the
chosen people" (p. 173). Listening to him, his black audiences begin "moaning and singing, hugging each other and singing"; worked
into a state of hysteria, they are "ready to follow him into any violence" (p. 328). He triply violates Southern social norms by his
race, class, and methods. "I'm as good as any white man and I'm
goin' to show 'em so," he says, aiming to demonstrate his triumph
by marrying a "white 'ooman and meck white folks wait on me"
(p. 291). His baseness, degeneracy, and perversion lead inevitably
to the classic convention of the genre—rape. The scene is charged
with animalistic fury as Moses, with "a snarl of rage," springs at his
victim "like a wild beast" (p. 173).

Within the conventions of the Southern romance, at least insofar
as Reconstruction is its theme, slavery and antebellum race relations are used as a dramatic and sociological counterpoint to indicate the horrors of a world turned upside down. Under slavery—
and with universally kind masters—blacks were invariably carefree
and childlike and were the loved and adoring intimates of their
white families. This tradition continues in the descriptions of the
loyal house servants who remain steadfastly attached to their old
masters after the war. Playing on one of the most persistent myths
not only of the romance but of Southern history and even of national popular culture, Page found it unnecessary to explain why
these "good" blacks would have been dominated by the "bad"
blacks, represented by the rudest field hands and savage witch doc-
tors. This division between "good" blacks and "bad" blacks relates
to the mass of black folks in the romance as well. Under the savage
leadership of a Moses, the freedmen threaten all order and decency;

155

under proper control, however, the former slaves are able to re-sume their valued position in society—and even in the economy. This proper control is exercised by white people. In one single pur-gative act of violence—their abduction of Leech—the Southern whites reassert order and in the process "restore" blacks to produc-tive subservience and regain the peace of prewar race relations: "One who has seen them [the freedmen] parading and yelling with defiance and delight the day that Leech led his handcuffed prisoners to the station to ship them off to prison, would not have recognized the awe-struck and civil people who now went back and forth so quietly to their work. It seemed a miracle" (p. 506).

Romantic subplots reinforce the general racial themes of all these stories. In *Red Rock,* Jacqueline Gray and Blair Cary, both represen-tatives of the Southern planter class, are united in marriage while Cary's friend marries the daughter of a well-intentioned Northern politician of the upper social class. Fittingly, both couples retire to the land, the restored plantation of Red Rock. The political meaning of these unions is clear: social redemption is associated with en-lightened upper-class rule and with the absolute rejection of black roles in politics. And it is critical to note here—for it is in the sharp-est contrast to *Gone with the Wind*—that the political purposes of *Red Rock* and of the Southern romances in general are paramount; the focus is on the horrors of black political initiative and the bless-ings of white authority, racial exclusion and subordination, and oligarchic control. Further, while the convention might only imply masculine authority, women's roles are clearly passive. Always de-fined as ladies, the young women, whether created by Page, Joel Chandler Harris, or Thomas Dixon, are unfailingly supportive of their dashing young suitors. They fit neatly into the conventions of the genre and typify the element of "free womanhood" as defined by Barbara Welter: sexual purity, religious piety, devoted domes-ticity, and submissiveness to both God and man. In Reconstruction literature, however, they play a further part, for they are the objects of black lust.

Thus all the conventions of the late-nineteenth-century Southern romance become apparent: the vileness of black authority; the trauma of its violent, irrational, emotional rule; its logical manifesta-tion in "witch doctor" leadership and in interracial rape; the bene-

156

fits of white order and conservative redemption; and the reasser-
tion of rational political processes. All the stock types emerge
clearly as well: the manipulative white carpetbagger, the hypnotic
black anti-Christ, the misguided black population, the long-suffer-
ing white folks, the upright young hero, and the innocent virgin.

On the surface, there is much in *Gone with the Wind* that is perfectly consistent with the scenes, stock types, and literary forms
used by Page. *Gone with the Wind*, like *Red Rock*, is essentially a
tale set in Reconstruction. Well over half the novel takes place after
April 1865, and an even larger piece occurs after Reconstruction
actually commences—after Sherman's destruction. And Mitchell
uses much the same technique as the Pagians in her counterpoint
between the quiet slaves and the licentious freedmen.

In her treatment of blacks as individuals and as a class, Mitchell is
faithful to the traditional view. Both Page and Mitchell portray
blacks as helpless innocents, children who are incapable of initiative and who require a strong guiding hand. This treatment by
Mitchell is true for the black masses as well as for individual blacks.
Mammy is a powerful figure but only within a well-defined structure. After the war, the degradation of Tara defeats her: "her shoulders dragged down . . . her kind black face was sad with the uncom-
prehending sadness of a monkey's face. . . ."[8] Although steadfast
and loyal, she is not capable of managing Tara in the absence of the
guidance of whites. The same is true for Pork. When asked, he cannot remember where yams are buried, and when Scarlett wants him
to catch a sow and her litter that have survived he is both "amazed
and indignant. 'Miss Scarlett, dat a field han's bizness,' he replied"
(p. 423). In time he adjusts to the new conditions, if not to field-
work, and he "forages" far and wide for food at night. Rather than
punishing him, Scarlett encourages him to steal. This situation provides Mitchell an opportunity to explain the proper relation of
black slaves to white masters; realizing that she is encouraging
theft, Scarlett recalls her mother's explanation of proper race relations. According to Ellen, Scarlett is "responsible for the moral as
well as the physical welfare of the darkies God has intrusted to your
care." Blacks, she continues, "are like children and must be guarded
from themselves like children . . ." (pp. 472–73). In a sense, that is
what happens at Tara during this period, inasmuch as Scarlett pro-

vides the leadership necessary for survival. In truth, Pork's contribution is reminiscent of the plantation tales of earlier literature, too, for blacks were always portrayed as thieves, however harmless the theft might be. Of the other slaves who remain, only Dilcey is able to help Scarlett, and this difference is explained by her Indian—in contrast to her African—heritage.

The incapacity for independent thought is another characteristic of Mitchell's blacks that draws on the earlier tradition. Thus in response to Pork's admonition that whiskey is not for ladies, Scarlett thinks, "How stupid negroes were! They never thought of anything unless they were told" (p. 409). Yet blacks are a necessary and valued part of Scarlett O'Hara's life. They are, in her judgment, "provoking sometimes and stupid and lazy, but there was a loyalty in them that money couldn't buy, a feeling of oneness with white folks . . ." (p. 472).

This quality of being "one with their white folks" captures another convention of the romantic genre: in a proper relationship, black-white relations were based on mutuality and even intimacy, particularly in slave times. Mammy, the major black character in the novel, is described as having been "raised in the bedroom of Solange Robillard, Ellen O'Hara's mother." Imperious, she "felt she owned the O'Haras body and soul." She and Ellen are co-equal moral arbiters of the world of Tara, and despite the fact that she is a "pure African" her sense of pride is equal to that of the O'Haras (pp. 22–23). With these sketches Mitchell emphasizes the intimate bond between slave and master as well as Mammy's importance to the household. Such intimacy is further evident at the picnic at Twelve Oaks, where "children, black and white, ran yelling about the newly green lawn, playing hopscotch and tag and boasting how much they were going to eat" (p. 94).

In actuality, Mitchell even exaggerates these black-white bonds beyond the tradition in the old romances. Uncle Peter, for example, rules the Hamiltons with an iron hand. According to Charles Hamilton, "He was the one who decided I should have a larger allowance when I was fifteen and he insisted that I should go to Harvard for my senior year, when Uncle Henry wanted me to take my degree at the University. And he decided when Melly was old enough to put up her hair and go to parties. He tells Aunt Pitty

158

when it's too cold or too wet for her to go calling and when she should wear a shawl. . . . The only trouble with him is that he owns the three of us, body and soul, and he knows it" (p. 144).

Likewise, Mammy is an uncompromising power within the O'Hara household. She is, more significantly still, virtually a co-conspirator in Scarlett's scheme to save Tara by stealing Frank Kennedy from her sister Suellen: Mammy "understood and was silent," and Scarlett found in her "a realist more uncompromising than herself" (p. 599). Given her role as the family's "moral arbiter," her support for this deceit is especially important. The identity of the "real master" is also apparent in Mitchell's treatment of Gerald O'Hara's relations with his slaves. Although he constantly threatens dire whippings and selling slaves south, "there had never been a slave sold from Tara and only one whipping. . . ." Because the slaves understood Gerald, "they took shameless advantage of him" (p. 51).

In contrast to the innocence, ignorance, and benign "overlordship" of blacks in slavery, Mitchell describes a bestial or savage side of black character that is also consistent with the tradition. Even in her depiction of slavery, Mitchell uses animal imagery to describe blacks—elephants, panthers, and faithful dogs. For Reconstruction, her terms become more threatening: blacks are like gorillas or monkeys on a rampage through a treasure house; society is being besieged by savages squatting in breechclouts. Indeed, as much as Page and the others, Mitchell treats Reconstruction as having excited the basest animal instincts in the black population. Moreover, she writes that Reconstruction unleashes the basest class within the black community, that a sort of social revolution takes place even among the freedmen. Those who rampage are the former field hands, whom Mitchell describes as the dregs of black society, the culls in a kind of Darwinian selection process. Repeating another convention of the genre—and another of the most persistent myths about black society—Mitchell has her field-hand freedmen repudiated even by other blacks, at least by the "house servants." In the process, of course, she reaffirms the attachment of these black "aristocrats" to the white master class.

In the Page tradition, the upheaval of the servile population is epitomized by outbreaks of black violence against whites, usually involving rape. In *Gone with the Wind*, one character is forced to leave the South after he kills his old "black buck" foreman for an insult directed at his sister-in-law. In another scene, a rape suspect is reported to have been lynched "to save the as yet unnamed victim from having to testify in open court" (p. 745). Mitchell even goes so far as to ally Rhett Butler with these sentiments when he admits that he "did kill the nigger" who "had been uppity to a lady" (p. 623). All this is rather old stuff, material similar to that produced by innumerable Southern white authors in the 1890s. Mitchell uses sexual peril in a stock manner to explain the rise of the Klan, an organization in *Gone with the Wind* that is led by the best elements of the Old South. It is, Mitchell writes, the "large number of outrages on women and the ever-present fear for the safety of their wives and daughters that drove Southern men to cold and trembling fury and caused the Ku Klux Klan to spring up overnight" (p. 656).

Even Scarlett falls victim to a sexual attack. Despite warnings that it is not safe for her to travel alone, she continues to drive by Shantytown on her way to her mill, and on one occasion she arranges with an old Tara field hand, Big Sam, to stop and pick him up on her return. When she stops, however, she is met not by Big Sam but rather by a "big ragged white man and a squat black negro with shoulders and chest like a gorilla." They want her money; when she refuses, the black attacks. With "his black face twisted in a leering grin," he seizes her: "The negro was beside her, so close that she could smell the rank odor of him as he tried to drag her over the buggy side. With one free hand she fought madly, clawing at his face, and then she felt his big hand at her throat and, with a ripping noise, her basque was torn open from the neck to the waist. The black hand fumbled between her breasts, and terror and revulsion such as she had never known came over her and she screamed like an insane woman" (p. 788). Ultimately, she is saved by Big Sam, but later that night she remembers her assailant's "malignant black face" and "thought of the black hand at her bosom and what would have happened if Big Sam had not appeared" (p. 792).

On the surface, this scene meets all the requirements of conventional rape as depicted in the traditional romance. But on closer examination it reveals the ways in which Mitchell transforms the

160

meaning of the action. In her hands, the rape attempt is something altogether different from Page's treatment. In this regard, this episode serves as a useful and important introduction to the ways in which Mitchell, even while working within the old formulas, alters their meaning and significance.

First, the attack is biracial. Two men, one black, one white, participate. The latter holds the reins of the horse while the black (who is presented in this scene for the first time in the novel) physically assaults Scarlett. Second, the scene is more clearly drawn in terms of a criminal or social violation rather than merely a racial act. Shantytown, the area in which the attack occurs, is described as the home of "outcast negroes, black prostitutes and a scattering of poor whites of the lowest order" (pp. 777–78). With the identification of the area as "the refuge of negro and white criminals," race is subordinated to economic and social factors. Third, the fact that the assailants are strangers also breaks significantly with the tradition; in the Page-Dixon school, the rapists are invariably familiar and even well known to the victims. By this means, Mitchell isolates the affair from the main flow of the narrative or plot line. It is simply one more dramatic event rather than an integral part of the plot. The scene ends with Scarlett's rescue by another black, which undercuts the theme of racial villainy still further.

By presenting the scene this way, Mitchell shifts the motivation from racial differences to criminal behavior in general. But the matter of criminal behavior is not limited to the two ruffians, nor does it result only from the upheaval of Reconstruction. In an even more extraordinary departure from tradition, the "victim" herself becomes responsible for the attack, which is even described as punishment. India Wilkes screams at Scarlett, "What happened to you this afternoon was just what you deserved and if there was any justice, you'd have gotten worse" (p. 794). Archie, the misogynist mountain white who serves as Scarlett's protector at Melanie's insistence, raises the same issue: "It's all yore fault, and thar's blood on yore hands." Why was Scarlett to blame? Because she had been "gallivantin'" this afternoon" in a dangerous part of town (p. 798).

This is not the only time that Scarlett is assaulted, and the second occasion modifies still further the conventions associating rape with race. The scene is Rhett's drunken, enraged attack. Without presenting anatomical detail, Mitchell leaves no doubt as to what occurs:

> He swung her off her feet into his arms and started up the stairs. Her head was crushed against his chest and she heard the hard hammering of his heart beneath her ears. He hurt her and she cried out, muffled, frightened. Up the stairs, he went in the utter darkness, up, up, and she was wild with fear. He was a mad stranger and this was a black darkness she did not know, darker than death. He was like death, carrying her away in arms that hurt. She screamed, stifled against him and he stopped suddenly on the landing and, turning her swiftly in his arms, bent over her and kissed her with a savagery and a completeness that wiped out everything from her mind but the dark into which she was sinking and the lips on hers. . . . She was darkness and he was darkness and there had never been anything before this time, only darkness and his lips upon her. . . . Suddenly she had a wild thrill such as she had never known, joy, fear, madness, excitement, surrender to arms that were too strong, lips too bruising; fate that moved too fast. For the first time in her life, she had met someone, something stronger than she, someone she could neither bully nor break, someone who was bullying and breaking her.
>
> [pp. 939–40]

The repeated use of the word *darkness* in this scene suggests racial associations, but in this specific context, the sexual assault is being committed by Rhett Butler, the white husband and hero. In this sequence, Mitchell portrays rape as an integral facet of human sexual relations, having nothing to do with race.

This shift in both rape scenes away from racial associations represents a still more profound alteration in Mitchell's treatment of blacks and the period of Reconstruction from that drawn by the Southernists. *Red Rock*, Joel Chandler Harris's *Gabriel Tolliver*, and even Thomas Dixon's *The Leopard's Spots* all focus on Reconstruction as a racial tale, and the purpose of each novel is to examine the racial dynamics of the era. Whatever their conclusions (and they are quite different), these novelists agree that the period was a laboratory of racial experimentation. Such is simply not the case with *Gone with the Wind*.

As extraordinary as it may sound, Mitchell's novel would still hold together and still make sense if all the comments on black character were eliminated or even if black characters disappeared. Race relations—inseparable from the earlier novels—are largely background material for Mitchell. Even the structure of *Gone with the Wind* emphasizes this characteristic. Thus, in the sections on Reconstruction, politics and racial affairs are not at all integrated into the narrative but exist as long descriptive passages quite at variance with the other writing in the novel. The "tragedies loosed upon Georgia" are only backdrop against which Mitchell projects Scarlett O'Hara's story. Race, and politics too, are essentially negligible elements in *Gone with the Wind*, and nothing could make a sharper contrast with the main themes of the earlier works.

But if politics and race are really unimportant, what does hold the story together? In what positive ways does Mitchell alter the regional romance? For Mitchell, the traditional Southern tale of Reconstruction became the vehicle for telling Scarlett O'Hara's story, specifically the struggle of one individual against the confines of Southern womanhood.

Scarlett's battles against society begin long before she ever meets Rhett Butler and, of course, long before Sherman comes along to provide the rationale for her struggle, as others have noted. In her, the two cultures of upcountry Georgia are combined—the aggressive, male-dominated society of Clayton County and the passive, female-oriented coast culture of Savannah. It's "a man's world," she says, and therefore she rejects the feminine model. The man "owned the property," but the woman "managed it." And, as the man "took credit for the management," the woman was forced to praise his "cleverness." To succeed within this structure, Scarlett had to mask her "sharp intelligence" and appear "demure, pliable, and scatterbrained" (p. 42). At "no time before or since," writes Mitchell, "had so low a premium been placed on feminine naturalness" (p. 80).

Although she seems successful as a belle, she hates the role. "I'm tired of saying 'How wonderful you are!' to men who haven't got one-half the sense I've got, and I'm tired of pretending I don't know anything so men can tell me things and feel important while they're doing it . . ." (p. 79). She has a go at every possible role that Southern society demanded of its women and fails at each. Widowhood is

163

as distasteful to her as bellehood: "A widow," she thinks bitterly, "had to wear hideous black dresses without even a touch of braid to enliven them, or a flower or a ribbon or lace or even jewelry. . . . Widows could never chatter vivaciously or laugh aloud." They were permitted only a "sad, tragic smile" (pp. 133–34). Motherhood is only a bother and a burden, and she cannot find camaraderie with other women. At the bazaar, she has a "sudden flash of self-knowledge that made her mouth pop open with astonishment" when she "realized that she did not share with these women their fierce pride, their desire to sacrifice themselves and everything they had for the Cause." To her, the war is not "a holy affair, but a nuisance that killed men senselessly and cost money and made luxuries hard to get" (p. 173). There remains ladyhood, and this she rejects from the outset.

While failing at every role that Southern womanhood demands of her, Scarlett is not unsuccessful. When Tara is threatened, she and she alone evidences the courage and ability to save it. Her solution is to steal her sister's beau, Frank Kennedy, and go on to bigger things. When she begins to manage her husband's business, he is resentful and exhibits the "usual masculine disillusionment in discovering that a woman had a brain." "With the idea that she was as capable as a man," writes Mitchell, "came a sudden rush of pride and a violent longing to prove it" (p. 620). As merchant, as businesswoman, as manager of her prized sawmills, Scarlett O'Hara Hamilton Kennedy Butler has few peers, male or female. Her successes are all associated with Atlanta, and its rebirth during Reconstruction as the business capital of the Lower South; the parallel between the city and the heroine is intentional on Mitchell's part. "Like herself, the town was a mixture of the old and the new in Georgia, in which the old often came off second best in its conflicts with the self-willed and vigorous new" (p. 143).

Many of the conflicts within Scarlett are bound together in her relationship to Rhett Butler, the outcast son of the coast culture. She is no Lady; he is certainly no Gentleman, and as outsiders these two characters provide the perspective from which Southern social attitudes are to be understood. They mock society's sensibilities and pretensions, and, for this reason, Mitchell was always fearful of the Southern reaction to her work. When Rhett tells the hot-blooded young Rebels that "all we have is cotton and slaves and arrogance," he is saying little more than the unpleasant truth they could never bear to hear (p. 111). His "contempt for the braggings of children" (p. 110) is both understood and shared by Scarlett. Throughout the novel, their clear vision, their unique ability to penetrate the trappings of reality is what separates Rhett and Scarlett from all others. Together, they "outraged every tenet" of the unwritten code that governed Southern society. Paying him the highest possible compliment, Scarlett recognizes that Rhett is "the only man I ever saw who could stand the truth from a woman" (p. 837).

In the end, Margaret Mitchell could not unite her instinctual and insightful perceptions to create a pointed and consistent reworking of the Southern tradition. In too many ways, she relied on that tradition and escaped confronting its implications. Thus we have the strangely ambiguous and unsatisfying conclusion to the novel, with Rhett looking to find "the utter boredom of respectability . . . the calm dignity life can have when it's lived by gentle folks, and the genial grace of days that are gone . . ." (p. 1034) and with Scarlett seeking solace in Tara and "tomorrow." In their own different ways they are returning to the Old South.

More important, there is the strange evidence of Margaret Mitchell's various reactions to comments on her creation. While she denied categorically that she ever demeaned blacks, she wrote an effusive letter to Thomas Dixon, the worst of the fiction-writing race-baiters, thanking him for his praise of her work. She found it "very exciting" and recalled the influence of his work on her at a very young age.[9] Even more curious is her disavowal of Scarlett, whom she characterized in a letter as a "far-from-admirable" woman.[10] In response to criticism of Scarlett's moral nature, she explained to another correspondent that Melanie Wilkes and the matrons of Atlanta were the true heroines in the novel.[11] Yet at the Atlanta premiere of the film, she acknowledged her heroine to wildly cheering friends as "my Scarlett, my poor Scarlett."[12]

In this sense, the tragedy of *Gone with the Wind* is not simply the "tragic era" of Reconstruction, nor the vanished era of magnolias and mint juleps. Mitchell's depiction of the vigorous, crude Georgia planter elite, her relegation of race relations to the periphery of the novel's action, her concentration on the development of a postwar urban business culture, and, most important, her exploration of the myth of Southern womanhood—all make *Gone with the Wind* profoundly different from anything in the older tradition. The tragedy for us is that, while Mitchell could identify and probe significant themes in Southern life, she could not do so with the will or talent necessary for an important literary creation.

Notes

1. Malcolm Cowley, "Going with the Wind," *New Republic,* September 16, 1936, pp. 161–62, reprinted in this volume.

2. Richard Gray, *The Literature of Memory* (Baltimore: Johns Hopkins University Press, 1977), p. 107. For other such references, see Jay B. Hubble, *Southern Life in Fiction* (Athens: University of Georgia Press, 1960), p. 29; Phillip Butcher, *George Washington Cable* (New York: Twayne Publishers, 1962), p. 166; Jerome Stern, "Gone with the Wind: The South as America," *Southern Humanities Review* 6 (Winter 1972): 5–12.

3. Andrew Sarris, "Films," *Village Voice,* October 26, 1977, pp. 38–39. Other references include Roger Rosenblatt, "Reconsideration: *Gone with the Wind*, The Movie," *New Republic*, January 25, 1975, pp. 19–22; Peter Noble, *The Negro in Films* (Port Washington: Kennikat Press, 1969), pp. 75–79.

4. Richard Schickel, in Gavin Lambert, "The Making of *Gone with the Wind,*" *Atlantic Monthly*, March 1973, p. 71.

5. Albion Tourgee, "The South as a Field for Fiction," *Forum* 6 (December 1888): 406.

6. Theodore L. Gross, *Thomas Nelson Page* (New York: Twayne Publishers, 1967), p. 79.

7. Thomas Nelson Page, *Red Rock: A Chronicle of Reconstruction* (New York: Scribner's, 1899), p. viii (hereafter cited in text).

8. Margaret Mitchell, *Gone with the Wind* (New York: Macmillan, 1936), p. 415 (hereafter cited in text).

9. Richard Harwell, ed., *Margaret Mitchell's "Gone with the Wind" Letters, 1936–1949* (New York: Macmillan, 1976), pp. 52–53.

10. Finis Farr, *Margaret Mitchell of Atlanta* (New York: Morrow, 1965), p. 163.

11. Harwell, pp. 123–24.

12. Farr, p. 12.

The "Simple Story's" Ideology: *Gone with the Wind* and the New South Creed

Richard King

"'The Wind'," wrote James Agee in 1944, "was perhaps the greatest entertainment natural in screen history." Much the same might be said of the novel's place in American literature. Its strength is that of all enduring popular art: the presentation of striking and memorable images, characters, and situations in a style neither difficult to follow nor hard to understand. *Gone with the Wind* is a cracking good story, offering vivid examples of grace (or at least courage) under pressure, cowardice, loyalty and perfidy, scrappy underdogs and rapacious occupiers, high sentiments and low cynicism. Nor was it surprising that a novel set during the harrowing years of the Civil War and Reconstruction should find a response in the 1930s, a decade of unprecedented economic and social distress.

Neither Margaret Mitchell nor her novel made any pretenses toward high art of the modernist variety. She complained that contemporary literature was needlessly obscure and trafficked in sordid themes. And, when questioned, she admitted that she had read neither *Vanity Fair* nor *War and Peace,* two classics which overheated supporters were known to compare with her gigantic novel. All she claimed was to have told a "simple story" based on conversations with survivors of the war and Reconstruction, extensive research, and several years of hard work.[1] If, as the story goes, every Southerner has an unfinished novel in a desk drawer, Mitchell's was the legendary fulfillment of such literary dreams.

Yet the naïve popular artist who tells the "simple story" is as illusory a creature as the value-free social scientist or the objective historian. Artlessness is itself a technique and a style; and what appears to be "realistic" fiction is highly stylized and composed. Novels working with the realistic conventions, such as *Gone with the Wind*, are shaped by both personal and collective visions and assumptions. Indeed, the invocation of simplicity by a novelist signals that what follows partakes of the mythic and ideological.[2]

I will expand this theme by placing *Gone with the Wind* in the intellectual context of the Southern Renaissance, specifically the varieties of historical consciousness articulated in that literary and intellectual movement. The novel fits within a second context as well, what I call the Southern "family romance." I will treat the novel as it both expresses and departs from the family romance, with particular attention to the role of women in the patriarchal tradition. Far from being a simple story, *Gone with the Wind* is a complex, often confused expression of the Southern cultural tradition in crisis.

The Varieties of Historical Consciousness

In the 1930s and 1940s, Southern intellectuals and writers engaged in a root-and-branch reassessment of the South's cultural tradition. How they came to terms with that tradition reflected the underlying mode of historical consciousness by which they grasped the past.

A common, though by no means dominant, form of Southern his-torical consciousness can be characterized by Nietzsche's "monumental" rubric. Monumentalism (or what Barrington Moore has called "Catonism") measures the unsatisfactory present against a heroic past. Its Southern incarnation was accompanied by an elegiac sensibility that sought to revivify the heroic ethos of the planter aristocracy and its valiant struggle against the forces of modernity, represented historically by the rapacious economics and misguided racial notions of the North. Some of the Vanderbilt Agrarians clearly articulated a kind of monumentalist view of the past. The early Faulkner vents Catonist views in the despairing figure of Quentin Compson, Sr., and the hallucinatory maunderings of Gail Hightower. The work that perhaps best expresses this despairing monumentalism is Will Percy's *Lanterns on the Levee.* In his autobiography, Percy bemoans the loss of tradition and civility in the modern, mob-ruled world. "A tarnish," he writes, "has fallen over the bright world: dishonor and corruption triumph; my own strong people are turned into lotus-eaters; defeat is here again, the last, the most abhorrent."

At the other extreme stood the ideology of liberal modernization developed by the Chapel Hill Regionalists. For Regionalists such as Howard Odum and Rupert Vance, the Southern past was more a burden than a repository of exemplary figures of action. Only through economic diversification and regional planning could the South's natural and human resources be used to their fullest. To invoke Nietzsche again, their form of historical consciousness was a "critical" one. It subordinated the monuments of the past to the needs of the present and future.

168

This spirit of critical realism was deepened and nuanced by Lillian Smith, W. J. Cash, H. C. Nixon (the only Agrarian to make the symbolic journey from Nashville to Chapel Hill), and C. Vann Woodward, among others. Though by no means of one voice, they severely criticized the regional leadership of the past and called for a new spirit of critical inquiry to guide the twentieth-century South and a revival of the democratic-populist tradition in Southern politics. Unlike the monumentalists, the modernizers felt uncomfortable with traditional Southern racial attitudes and practices; some even went so far as to suggest alternatives to the hallowed tradition of racism.

The modernizers were generally hostile to *Gone with the Wind*. Just beginning her own probings of the Southern tradition, Lillian Smith panned the novel: it "wobbles badly like an enormous house on very shaky underpinnings. . . . [it is] slick, successful, but essentially mediocre fiction." Still an obscure journalist, W. J. Cash felt that Miss Smith had taken the "correct measure" of *Gone with the Wind*. Later, however, Cash so enjoyed a day's visit with Mitchell, a woman of considerable charm, that he qualified his assertion that the novel was "sentimental."

Between the visions of the monumentalists and the modernizers in the 1930s stood a tragic mode of historical consciousness that was split between past and present. The representative texts are Allen Tate's *The Fathers* and Faulkner's *Absalom, Absalom!* In his biographies of Stonewall Jackson and Jefferson Davis, his essays, and his novel, Tate subjected the Southern tradition to an extended critique. Though preferring the antebellum order to traditionless modernity, Tate contended that the Old South's basic flaws had been intellectual and political. In *The Fathers,* Major Lewis Buchan lacks the proper sensibility to cope with the disappearance of his world of formal order and fixed values. And his son, Lacy, can never quite decide where he should locate himself vis-à-vis his family tradition. Faulkner's Quentin Compson is caught between a deep longing for the certainties of the Southern past and a repugnance (mixed with attraction) before one of its representative types, Thomas Sutpen. Quentin can neither share his father's despairing monumentalism nor accept wholeheartedly the demonic picture of Sutpen proposed by Rosa Coldfield. His recollections lead only to repetitions. Thus Tate and Faulkner were too intelligent, their visions too complex, to join in easy celebration of the Southern past, yet they could not quite cut loose from it either. Of Ellen Glasgow, similar things could be said.

What then of Mitchell's *Gone with the Wind*? Though the novel displays aspects of the monumentalist and modernizing consciousness, it did not in truth fit comfortably in either camp. Nor did *Gone with the Wind* express the tragic ambivalence found in Tate and Faulkner. Rather, it exemplifies the historical consciousness underlying the "New South creed." Though bearing its own share of nostalgia, the obscure object of the novel's desire is as much New South promise as it is Old South tradition. As Paul Gaston has noted, the New South advocates celebrated the antebellum South but also sanctioned industrial development under the dispensation of laissez-faire capitalism. They shed no tears for the demise of the peculiar institution of slavery yet projected a South of white supremacy and black subordination, a sort of middle-class paternalism. They urged the South to rejoin the Union yet were ardent Southern patriots. In short, where the tragic stance of Tate and Faulkner could settle for neither past nor present, the New South vision wanted it both ways. In this sense, *Gone with the Wind* provides the literary account of the origins of the urban, commercial, and financial middle class that arose from the destruction of the prewar planter class; it illustrates the peculiar uses to which the plantation tradition and the legacy of the Civil War were put in the consciousness of that new middle class.

The *locus classicus* of the New South spirit was, of course, Atlanta, with Birmingham and Chattanooga as industrial outposts. The title of Mitchell's novel would suggest that it was a sentimental evocation of the planter aristocracy. Yet in the figures of Scarlett and Rhett, the novel apostrophizes the bustling commercialism and capitalist ambience of postwar Atlanta. Scarlett O'Hara illustrates vividly the divided allegiances of the novel and of the ideological system that emerged after the war. Although she glories in the social whirl of the antebellum days—an aspect of the novel and the film that lingers in the popular mind—she resolutely sets her face toward the future when that world collapses. There was "no going back and she was going forward."[3] She willingly departs from what

170

one character in Stark Young's *So Red the Rose* called the "perfect academy of memories" and, at first reluctantly, then eagerly, enrolls in the school of hard knocks. The historical context in which Scarlett flourishes was what Cash called "the frontier the Yankee made," a situation of social chaos and well-nigh mortal damage to the South's traditional institutions.

Indeed, the latent energies which the New South would tap are foreshadowed early in the novel. Of Scarlett, Mitchell writes in the second paragraph of the book: ". . . her true self was poorly concealed. The green eyes in the carefully sweet face were turbulent, willful, lusty with life, distinctly at variance with her decorous demeanor" (p. 3). Later Mitchell reinforces this contrast between appearance and reality when she describes the Georgia spring: "Along the roadside the blackberry brambles were concealing with softest green the savage red gulches cut by the winter's rains, and the bare granite boulders pushing up through the red earth were being draped with spangles of Cherokee roses and compassed about by wild violets of the palest purple hue" (p. 82). And, finally, not only nature but the man-made world, the city of Atlanta with which Scarlett is always closely identified, exemplifies this contrast between appearance and reality, present and future: "There was something exciting about this town with its narrow muddy streets, lying among rolling red hills, something raw and crude that appealed to the rawness and crudeness underlying the fine veneer that Ellen and Mammy had given her" (p. 152).

Thus Mitchell's Scarlett was destined for a life at odds with the manners and morals of the antebellum South, at least with those of the planter aristocracy. Like Tate's George Posey in *The Fathers* or Faulkner's Thomas Sutpen in *Absalom, Absalom!* or Thomas Wolfe's Eliza Gant, Scarlett is heedless of the forms that the Old South used to hedge in natural man's asocial and individualistic impulses. As conservatives, Tate, Young, and Will Percy saw traditional Southern culture resting upon manners, not morals, its social traditions emanating from the family rather than from individual judgment. Scarlett has no use for such a vision. "She cared," writes Mitchell, "no more about family than her father" (p. 136). The goal of life was survival, not style; its quality was measured by success, not honor. The trappings could be added later.

As stated earlier, the commercial and financial bourgeoisie of Atlanta gave formal obeisance to the Old South ethos, but they damned it with fulsome praise. Gentility of spirit replaced the spirit of aristocracy. For all her pride in the novel's historical accuracy, Mitchell tipped her hand when she wrote that *Gone with the Wind* "was probably as Victorian a novel as was ever written. . . ."[4] That is why, for all their monumentalizing tendencies, Young in *So Red the Rose* or even Tate in *The Fathers* probably struck nearer the truth about the aristocratic way of life than did Mitchell. Young pictures an aristocracy of men and women who enjoy drink and, one suspects, even sex. Aristocrats, whatever else they are, are not prudes, prudery being the besetting vice of the Victorian middle class. In *The Fathers* it is the rootless George Posey, not the aristocratic Lewis Buchan, who is embarrassed by the copulation of animals and who cannot face death because he lacks any way of handling it. Mitchell's upper classes, whatever their lineage, resolutely deny body or animal spirits. They are middle-class Victorians in aristocratic garb.

Another indication that Mitchell missed something essential about the aristocracy is her depiction of its true-blue representative, Ashley Wilkes. Ashley appears an overly refined and etiolated devotee of poetry and opera, a sufferer from *Weltschmerz* who has lost out in the struggle for survival in a world he never made. Though Ashley is not implausible as an individual, he is hardly typical; in truth, he comes nearer the Catonist sensibility of the 1930s than he does to the more combative style of the Southern planters. We see the aristocratic order at its height as the novel opens, and we see its lingering hold during Reconstruction. (Scarlett thinks in exasperation, "Why can't they forget?" [p. 740].) The women—not the men—who survive are heroines of sorts. But for Scarlett—and for Mitchell—it all seems a waste of time. Though the title of the novel urges the reader to look back in nostalgia, its final message is much nearer to "tomorrow is another day," an earlier working title of the book.

Finally, like most Southerners of her time, liberal or not (with the honorable exception of Lillian Smith), Mitchell appealed to Southern chauvinism, which still nurtured the bleak memories of Reconstruction. In a decade suspicious of capitalism, modernizers could inveigh against Yankee-imposed capitalism because it was unfettered and rapacious, while monumentalists could object to it because it was financial and industrial. But all could agree to dislike Reconstruction because it was imposed from the outside. *Gone with the Wind* pokes malicious fun at the carpetbaggers yet offers Scarlett as a figure of financial cunning and energy, thus suggesting that Rebels can beat Yankees at their own game. At least she is a home-grown entrepreneur.

Only a handful of critical voices in the 1930s—Nixon, Woodward, Arthur Raper, Ira Reid, and Cash—suggested that, though the South remained an economic colony of the North, its skewed economic and social development—what André Gunder Frank has called "underdevelopment"—was the handiwork of an indigenous Southern elite of black belt latifundists—iron, coal, and textile industrialists and a host of smaller fry (like Scarlett O'Hara) who seldom shrank from using even convict labor in their pursuit of the main chance. Indeed, Mitchell feared that her novel would meet local criticism because it suggested that several Atlanta fortunes had been made during Reconstruction. She needn't have worried. Though the intellectuals of the 1930s were almost unanimous in rejecting the New South vision in unalloyed form, the novel's great popularity in the South testified to the still-powerful hold of that ambivalent vision on the literate South as a whole.

The Southern Family Romance

An examination of the modes of historical consciousness during the Southern Renaissance has affirmed Mitchell's primary debts to the New South's ambivalence toward Southern tradition. But of equal importance is the content of that tradition, which entailed the cultural vision of a collective "family romance." This was the fantasy that lay at the heart of Southern culture, making up what Raymond Williams has called the "structure of feeling and experience" of a culture. It expressed the assumptions underlying the white South's conception of itself and of the relationships between male and female, black and white, parent and child, past and present.

How did this family romance originate? First, in an agrarian, institutionally underdeveloped, and patriarchal culture such as the South's, the family has historically been the central institution: one's family was one's destiny. The centrality of the family was established in the plantation South, and the paternalistic ideal was one of the principal components of the planter ideology. As Eugene Genovese and others have emphasized, the ideology of the family was expressed most clearly in the work of George Fitzhugh. But whether articulated in Fitzhugh's theory or held at a scarcely conscious level, the notion that Southern society was less a compact among equals than a metaphorical family of organically linked unequals survived the Civil War and Reconstruction. The concept was popularized and then became a staple of sentimental, popular literature in the South and the North. Thus the family romance, the South-as-family, paradoxically found a reception in a historical setting that bore increasingly less resemblance to its conditions of origin.

Finally, the term *family romance* refers to the white Southern tendency to idealize the family and its past. Freud used the term to describe the tendency of young children to reject their actual parents and fantasize royal or elevated origins for themselves.[5] This idealizing tendency was at work in the South at a collective level. The sociologist Hortense Powdermaker reported as late as the 1930s—and native Southerners will be able to extend her observation to a later period—that Southerners, particularly middle-class ones, were obsessed with establishing their genealogical connections with aristocratic ancestors.

The Southern family romance was dominated by heroes of a generation that had fought the Yankees and defended white purity in the dark days of Reconstruction. One thinks here of Faulkner's Sartoris saga or Will Percy's evocation of his grandfather in *Lanterns*. These were the men whose portraits presided over the present generation in so many Southern novels. The white woman, the mother, was a shadowy figure who took a back seat, albeit an honored one, in the cultural mythos. Indeed, with few exceptions, it is difficult to think of a memorable female character, at least a white mother, in the literature of the 1930s. For instance, Tate's *The Fathers* opens with the death of Mrs. Buchan, and we never see Ike McCaslin's mother.

The other side of the notion of past glory and a heroic generation of founders was the sense of loss or decline, the Catonism of a

174

Percy. And indeed, "an anxiety of influence" haunted the Southern family romance.[6] There was a pervasive sense that the sons and grandsons had failed to match the heroic example of the founding fathers of the tradition. As the third and fourth generations came on the scene after World War I, this sense of estrangement from the tradition and anxiety over its still potent influence had grown overwhelming. As Walker Percy says in *The Last Gentleman,* the grandsons had grown "ironic." John Irwin's cogent formulation of the central problematic in Faulkner's work—"whether a man's father is his fate"—could apply equally to many of the Southern Renaissance's seminal texts.

There is yet another element of the family romance that bears examining—race. In the family romance the white caste became the "parent" caste, and blacks were considered to make up the "child" caste. Blacks were seen as amiable and impulsive, loyal but undependable, and in need of a firm parental, i.e., white, hand. As John Dollard first observed, miscegenation was unconsciously identified with violation of the incest taboo. Miscegenation and incest came together in the sexual relationship between white women and black men, symbolic mothers and symbolic sons. But if this was what Pierre van den Berghe has called the "paternal" racism, which operated with Oedipal imagery, nonetheless a "competitive" type of racism tended to dominate in times of confusion and dislocation. According to this second interpretation, blacks were characterized in pre-Oedipal and phobic terms: they were animals, dirty or diseased.[7] Underlying both types of racism was the opposition between nature and culture: black signified the pre- or anticultural; white stood for order and culture.

Thus the great fear of rape in *Birth of a Nation,* which also makes an obligatory if less crucial appearance in *Gone with the Wind,* becomes comprehensible: it was the greatest symbolic threat to the cultural order. As a covert form of incest, rape threatened to collapse culture back into nature. Moreover, it was, as Cash points out, more than a mere psychological projection of white desires and guilts onto blacks, for it also threatened the racial purity of the dominant caste and was seen to pollute the line of paternal succession running from white father to white son. This is the source of Sutpen's great fear. Faulkner's obsession with incest and miscegenation is not gothic titillation but represents his exploration of the nature/culture demarcation and the disorder attendant upon its violation.

Finally, the family romance could appear in inverted form. As Otto Rank points out, in myths and legends the foster parents or "kind animals" rear the abandoned hero as their own.[8] In the inverted version of the Southern family romance, the older black man became a kind mentor, a figure of untutored wisdom, and the black woman became "mammy," the nurturing mother to the white upper and middle classes. Many of the important works of the Renaissance articulated this inverted family romance in which the white mother, as I have observed, all but disappeared and the black "mother" assumed a dominating role. This can be seen most clearly in the work of Lillian Smith, who ended by placing the black woman, not the white father, at the center of the Southern family romance.

If confrontation with the family romance was a central theme in the intellectual history of the Southern Renaissance, how then did *Gone with the Wind* deal with this cultural problem? Here again, in her affirmation of some parts, rejection of others, Mitchell reflects the ambivalence of the New South.

She challenged few of the racial conventions of the family romance. Thus Mammy is the nurturing spirit who cooperates with her mistress in trying to curb Scarlett's animal spirits. Later, on returning to Tara and discovering that her mother is dead and her father unhinged, Scarlett is consoled by the thought that "Soon Mammy would be with her—Ellen's Mammy, her Mammy. . . . Scarlett ran to her, laying her head on the broad, sagging breasts which had held so many heads, black and white. Here was something of stability, thought Scarlett, something of the old life that was unchanging" (p. 415). Yet Mammy is actually incapable of nurturing in a useful way in this crisis: she is as bewildered by the turn of events as everyone else. The last emblem of the old order has faded. From then on Mammy lumbers in and out of the action, but she is hardly a figure of power or comfort, except perhaps in Scarlett's imagination. Uncle Peter too assumes a quasi-parental role in his nurture of Aunt Pitty, and he takes pride in recalling his old master's deathbed wish: "You, Peter! You look affer mah chillun" (p. 673).

Other than this demotion of Mammy at a critical juncture, Mitchell's blacks fulfill the other roles dictated by the family romance. There is no confusion or ambiguity here. Besides Mammy, there are the faithful Uncle Peter, the loyal Sam, and egregious Prissy. A ludicrous bunch altogether, they shuffle about, mumbling phrases such as "Fo' God, Miss Scarlett." They are depicted as simpletons, grown-up children. Significantly, Scarlett invokes family relationships to rebuke some Yankee women for insulting Uncle Peter: he is "one of our family . . ." (p. 672). She observes how affected Peter is by their insults and thinks, "It was as though someone had been senselessly brutal to a child" (p. 673). But in the chaotic world of postwar Georgia, there were freedmen who appeared in different guise. Mitchell describes them as "scarcely one generation out of the African jungles" (p. 656); the black man who attacks Scarlett has a "chest like a gorilla" (p. 787), and destruction attributed to ignorant freedmen is likened to that of monkeys loosed among treasures. These racial attitudes are thoroughly consistent with the New South vision of free but subordinate blacks.

In other areas Mitchell modifies the conventions of the family romance. Though the family romance glorified kinship, blood, patriarchs, and dynasties, there is little or nothing of this in the novel. On the contrary, Mitchell actually reverses many of the images and roles of the tradition. Scarlett has little family feeling—she cares nothing for her own children and steals her sister's beau without a thought. Although her sidekick Rhett makes motions toward returning to the family fold at the novel's end, throughout the narrative he has been a black sheep, repudiating the stifling conventionalities of his Charleston family. Much the same holds true for the dominant figures in Mitchell's antebellum society. None of the planters, besides the Wilkeses, is to the manner born. They are arrivistes, denizens of the backwoods, rough-and-tumble part of Georgia, who gaze ambitiously upward at their social superiors and dismiss those beneath them. They are rootless and have in common their lack of blood or kinship ties. Thus Mitchell's picture of the antebellum planter class has much in common with the one Cash later sketched. There is no reference at all to dynastic ambitions and continuity of a family line. There are no patriarchs. Rather than a graceful and powerful father figure, a sort of happy union of Sutpen and Sartoris, Gerald O'Hara is a likable Irish immigrant, to whose bluster and bragging no one, not even the slaves, pays much attention.

Nor, indeed, is there a lost age of heroism in the novel. Mitchell was sharp-eyed enough to recognize how the collective Southern memory contained large elements of fantasy, how the children learned to glorify the war, and how the myth of the Lost Cause was stronger after defeat than Confederate nationalism had been during brighter days. The surprisingly realistic Ashley and the cynical Rhett both know that war will mean the doom of the old order, but both consider its destruction inevitable. Moreover, the renegade Charlestonian constantly inveighs against the "betraying sentimentality" of the Southern mind. But Mitchell compromises their positions by having both men fight for a cause they know is doomed.

These compromises and inconsistencies in the characters of Butler and Wilkes deny them the role of heroes in the sense of the family romance; *Gone with the Wind* is actually devoid of heroes altogether. Still, though male society in Clayton County and Atlanta is filled with blusterers, callow youths, cynics, incompetents, and fumblers, a strong figure of authority does preside over *Gone with the Wind*'s early pages at least—Ellen O'Hara. Not only does she play Lady Bountiful to her plantation family, she also manages the business end of things as well. To the adolescent Scarlett, Ellen is the cynosure of virtue; at evening prayers, Scarlett often confuses her in her mind's eye with the Virgin Mary. As heroic matriarch, Ellen elicits awe and is both ego-ideal and superego. But she never comes to life in the novel and dies early. Apparently Mitchell cared little for her and wrote to one correspondent that "Ellen . . . was very dark, completely without humor and with no vivacity."[9] Another older woman, Grandma Fontaine, displays a certain tough conventional wisdom when she warns Scarlett of the costs of her single-minded pursuit of survival. But the rest of the women, except for Melanie, are an assortment of biddies and busybodies, the worst of the lot being Aunt Pittypat Hamilton. Still, near the close of the novel, Mitchell offers a panegyric to Melanie, whom she considered the true heroine of her work: "She [Scarlett] was seeing through Rhett's eyes the passing, not of a woman but a legend—the gentle, self-effacing but steel-spined woman on whom the South had built its house in war and to whose proud and loving arms it had returned in defeat." [10]

Though figures of admiration, Ellen and Melanie are proper Victorian women, rendered without sexual desire or awareness. To this extent they exemplify rather than work against the grain of the Southern family romance in which the white woman was denied sexuality. Scarlett scorns Melanie's childlike figure with scarcely any breasts: she is an androgynous angel, maternal and warm yet asexual. Scarlett herself is quite the social rebel, but her sexual experience and sophistication are minimal. Her energy and vivacity come from her father, about whom there "was something vital and earthy and coarse," qualities she "possessed in some degree . . . despite sixteen years of effort on the part of Ellen and Mammy to obliterate them" (p. 31). But these qualities are redirected from the affective realm into the world of business and commerce.

What about Scarlett, who clearly stands at the emotional center of the book, Mitchell's attempt to make Ellen and Melanie the heroines notwithstanding? Scarlett chafes against the submissive role that the South has laid on its women and realizes quite soon that she is better than most of the men in her world. But though often shrewd, she is intelligent neither about herself nor about others. As Mitchell repeatedly stresses, Scarlett is "unanalytical," surely one of the understatements of Southern literature. Just as her father is always "on stage" for his admiring wife, Scarlett always plays to her male audience, while secretly holding them, and her female contemporaries, in contempt. Not only does she play to men, she comes to play the male role herself. She assumes the same role her mother had, yet the difference between her and her mother marks an implicit critique of the mother's role in antebellum Southern ideology and life.

But though Scarlett appears quite "liberated," her freedom is more social than psychological. Ostensibly the most realistic and hardheaded of women, she is enslaved by the romantic desire to be swept off her feet by Ashley, the narcissistic creation of her essentially commonplace sensibility and the symbol in the novel of everything that Scarlett lacks and can never quite understand. Since

Ashley fails her repeatedly (and by implication the Old South ethos can offer nothing essential to New South ambitions), Scarlett must become a male version of herself, a tougher New South repetition of her mother.

Scarlett's success and the way she flouts it seem designed to smoke out the man who can master her. When Rhett seduces/rapes Scarlett, Mitchell seems to imply that this is what all strong women want and need: "For the first time in her life she had met someone, something stronger than she, someone she could neither bully nor break, someone who was bullying and breaking her" (p. 940). This passage indicates the extent to which Scarlett's is merely a rebellious conformity, an advance better only than retreat. The unequal relationship of male and female in Mitchell's version of the family romance allows individual deviation from sexual roles if, as in this case, the rebellious woman is brought back in line psychologically. The prodigal son of the aristocracy, Rhett, has the last word. It is not a strong one, but it is the last one.

Thus Mitchell's intentions concerning Scarlett exemplify the wider confusions in the New South version of the family romance. But if there was confusion in literary characterization, Mitchell was no clearer in her private correspondence or her public comments about Scarlett. In a letter of July 1936 she claimed that Scarlett was a "normal person,"[11] but she countered later by writing to a friend that "Scarlett was not a very nice person."[12] Then, early in 1937, Mitchell came down squarely on both sides by allowing that Scarlett "had good traits . . . balanced by her bad qualities."[13] Then at the film's premiere Mitchell repeatedly thanked her audience and the filmmakers for what they had done for her and "my Scarlett."

Behind this waffling stood Mitchell's reaction to a psychiatrist's analysis of Scarlett's "inward hollowness and serious lack of insight." Rather than taking umbrage, Mitchell heartily concurred that Scarlett was a "partial psychopath," a denunciation that Scarlett's most serious detractors would scarcely have hazarded.[14] The author of *Gone with the Wind* went on to express bewilderment, even concern, that her creation had been taken to the public's heart and was particularly surprised that Scarlett had been described as "passionate and wanton" since Mitchell thought it obvious that

180

"Scarlett was a frigid woman." Scarlett's letter "S" was for survival, not sexuality.

One need claim no diagnostic exactitude to assert that Scarlett resembles the hysterical character type so prevalent in Victorian society. (The emphasis should be upon "character type," a term that denotes a social role, not a clinical neurosis.) Carroll Smith-Rosenberg has claimed that hysteria offered Victorian women a way of escaping the contradictory tasks imposed upon them.[15] As a mother, the Victorian woman was required to be strong, self-reliant, protective, and efficient in managing the home and hearth; yet as a wife she was to be emotional, dependent, and gentle. In the world of Reconstruction, it was plausible for a woman such as Scarlett to attempt to escape this cultural double bind by assuming the strong, self-reliant role and shifting its field of action to the public world of business. Though Scarlett suffers none of the fainting spells or migraines that often accompanied hysteria, she is the archetypal "tease," unable to establish lasting relationships, emotionally dissociated, egocentric, narcissistic, and frigid. It is difficult to say whether she uses her society or her society uses her.

Thus *Gone with the Wind* ultimately falls somewhere between a critique of and a reaffirmation of the Southern family romance. It thus mirrors the ambiguous message of the New South creed. This is not to say that *Gone with the Wind* is not a great novel because of its ideological underpinnings. It is rather that Mitchell's book offers nothing that challenges deeply held beliefs nor does it force the reader to see the world in a new light. Memorable though not deeply explored characters are set against a historical background that elicits almost automatic responses. The novel does the feeling and the thinking for the reader. Said another way, *Gone with the Wind* offers something for everyone. Ambiguous without being complex, it allows those nostalgic for a lost way of life their innings yet apotheosizes its very negation, the woman on the make. But then it turns around and gives the raven-haired hussy her comeuppance—and ends with her indomitably setting forth again. Every reader finds something to like and to hate—devotees of the Old South and celebrators of the New, the conventional and the rebellious, men and women, North and South. (Only black readers are left without their champions.) But then fantasy and myth are ever doing this, even if they appear in realistic fictional guise or as a "simple story."

Notes

I would like to thank Louis Strawbridge and Darden Pyron for reading and criticizing earlier versions of this essay.

1. Biographical information on Mitchell is taken from Finis Farr, *Margaret Mitchell of Atlanta* (New York: William Morrow, 1965), and Richard Harwell, ed., *Margaret Mitchell's "Gone with the Wind" Letters, 1936–1949* (New York: Macmillan, 1976).

2. The French critic Roland Barthes has been most insistent in his critique of realism as thoroughly ideological, i.e., bourgeois. Its central impulse, he claims, is to disguise its own artifice and to transform the contingently cultural and the historical into the natural and the universal. See Barthes, *Writing Degree Zero* (New York: Hill and Wang, 1968) and *Mythologies* (Frogmore, U.K.: Paladin, 1976). For a less polemical distinction between the traditions of realism and modernism, see David Lodge, *The Modes of Modern Writing* (Ithaca: Cornell University Press, 1977).

3. Margaret Mitchell, *Gone with the Wind* (New York: Macmillan, 1936), p. 428 (hereafter cited in text).

4. Harwell, p. 192.

5. Sigmund Freud, "Family Romances," in *The Sexual Enlightenment of Children,* ed. Philip Rieff (New York: Collier, 1964), pp. 41–45.

6. See Harold Bloom's *The Anxiety of Influence* (New York: Oxford University Press, 1972) for his theory of poetic influence, which I have extended to the more general realm of cultural influence.

7. See John Dollard, *Caste and Class in a Southern Town,* 3d ed. (Garden City, N.Y.: Doubleday Anchor, 1957), pp. 434–46; Pierre van den Berghe, *Race and Ethnicity* (New York: Basic Books, 1970).

8. Otto Rank, *The Myth of the Birth of the Hero and Other Writings,* ed. Philip Freund (New York: Vintage, 1959). In *The Ego and the Mechanisms of Defence* (London: Hogarth, 1976), Anna Freud discusses the ways in which "kind animals" are produced in dreams and fairy tales.

9. Harwell, p.105.

10. One cannot help noting that this passage is a prime example of the way Mitchell's prose fails her at crucial points. It is pure cliché, especially the pseudo-Biblical "builded."

11. Harwell, p. 29.

12. Harwell, p. 68.

13. Harwell, p. 112.

14. Farr, pp. 192–93.

15. Carroll Smith-Rosenberg, "The Hysterical Woman: Sex Roles and Role Conflict in 19th Century America," *Social Research* 39 (Winter 1972): 652–78. In "The Hysterical Personality and the Feminine Character: A Study of Scarlett O'Hara," *Comprehensive Psychiatry* 17, no. 2 (March–April 1976): 353–59, Charles Wells claims that, though Scarlett's appearance and behavior fit the category of hysteria, other crucial factors are lacking. He suggests that her "hysteria" is an example of conformity to the social role expected of women rather than a deeply rooted neurosis.

The Inner War of Southern History

Darden Asbury Pyron

The Southern plantation legend is a part of the national parlance: the South as a land of courtly lords and gracious ladies, dazzling fêtes at pillared mansions, faithful retainers in the kitchens and happy servants in the fields; a world of style and quality, unconstrained by the routine of daily work and petty calculations of common folk hustling to survive or thrive. This vision of the South—rather apart from its material reality—has had a life of its own in American intellectual history.

For more than one hundred and fifty years in both high and low culture—from Henry Adams to the dime novel—this ideal of an aristocratic South has served as a counterpoint or alternative to urban, industrial, middle-class values of mainstream culture in the United States.[1] And since 1936 this imagery has been linked almost inseparably to *Gone with the Wind*. Indeed, it reached its apotheosis in the prologue (written not by Margaret Mitchell but by the urban Ben Hecht of *Front Page* fame) to David Selznick's film version of Margaret Mitchell's work:

> There was a land of Cavaliers and
> Cotton fields called the Old South . . .
> Here in this patrician world the
> Age of Chivalry took its last bow . . .
> Here was the last ever to be seen
> of Knights and their Ladies Fair,
> of Master and Slave . . .
> Look for it only in books, for it
> is no more than a dream remembered,
> a Civilization gone with the wind. . . .[2]

If the film sealed the identification between *Gone with the Wind* and the willowy Old South ideal, this interpretation existed long before Selznick's first cameras were loaded. For example, in September 1936 Malcolm Cowley railed against the novel as an "encyclopedia of the plantation legend," which lent new credence to the false, vicious, and "generally pernicious" myth of the aristocratic Old South.[3]

This essay originally appeared in *Southern Studies: An Interdisciplinary Journal of the South* 20 (Spring 1981): 5–19.

185

This is not at all what Margaret Mitchell intended. On the contrary. She scoffed at what she called the "lavender-and-old-lace-moonlight-on-the-magnolia" tradition, ridiculed the sweet sentimentality of the "gentle Confederate novel" of the "Thomas Nelson Page—type," and scorned "professional Southerners." Long before the film's production, she complained about readers wanting a movie-set version of the South: ". . . it's hard to make people believe that North Georgia wasn't all white columns and singing darkies and magnolias, that it was all so raw and new." And as for the film version itself, she "yelped with laughter" at the contrast between Selznick's gaudy elegance and the "healthy, hard, country and somewhat crude civilization" that she had wanted to describe.[4]

Although this interpretation puzzled and, in the case of Cowley's condescension, rankled her, Mitchell made no public defense of her social intentions in the novel; yet sympathetic readings won her special enthusiasm. One that drew her attention was written by Virginius Dabney in his 1942 examination of Southern society, *Below the Potomac.* Himself a significant and largely unexplored character in Southern intellectual history, Dabney was the liberal editor of the Richmond *Times-Dispatch.* His career bears striking parallels to Mitchell's. A product of an urban environment with roots in the country, a journalist who was skeptical of traditional pieties, a progressive who eventually soured on reform, and almost exactly Mitchell's age, Dabney had attacked the national tendency to mythologize the antebellum South in his chapter entitled "The South that Never Was." He had used the prologue to Selznick's film as a case in point. It was a classic national misrepresentation of the Southern past, he wrote, and a grotesque distortion of the social milieu that Mitchell had described in her novel.[5] The analysis delighted Mitchell, and she resketched for the sympathetic Virginian what she had tried to do. She had been embarrassed, she wrote, at "finding myself included among those writers who picture the South as a land of white columned mansions whose wealthy owners had thousands of slaves and drank thousands of juleps—if indeed it existed anywhere." She protested that she had taken great pains "to describe North Georgia as it was" with its farmer population of "sturdy yeoman stock" living in rambling comfortable houses only a step removed in time and spirit from Indians and log cabins. But

186

everyone went on believing in the Hollywood version: "people believe what they like to believe and the mythical Old South has too strong a hold on their imaginations to be altered by the mere reading of a 1,037 page book."[6]

Mitchell and Dabney were correct—national biases have distorted *Gone with the Wind*; yet Mitchell's antebellum world is more complex than she implies in her letter. If it is far from the aristocratic world that Hecht and Cowley saw, elements of that order and that tradition intrude upon the simple society that Mitchell thought to draw. These two orders war with one another in the novel. Mitchell describes a society split by bitter and subtle intra-regional, class, and sexual conflicts, and individual Southerners who are equally torn within themselves or pitted against the social order. These polarities describe a reality of the 300-year-old Southern historical experience; and, still more profoundly, they betray an intellectual dualism that haunts and dominates Southern thought and action, accounts for contradictions within the Southern character, and describes an intellectual conflict between regional thought and the dominant Lockean values of national culture. This study examines *Gone with the Wind* as a collective intellectual biography of a people as much at war with themselves as with Yankees and of the way in which they reconcile this conflict collectively and individually.

Historically, intra-regional divisiveness has been one of the most pronounced characteristics of the regional experience. While from a national perspective, one slaveholder might not have appeared significantly different from another, a Virginian from an Alabamian or one white Southerner from another, nuances and distinctions within regional society are inseparable from Southern history. The classical polarities are the Upper South versus the Lower, the Atlantic seaboard versus the transmontane region, the coastal and delta areas versus the interior, and Charleston and Virginia against everybody. These geographical distinctions have also carried connotations for class and social standing. This is indicated in the Southern adage about South Carolina and Virginia being mountains of conceit beside North Carolina's valley of humility. Indeed, these two "mountains of conceit" have traditionally represented the essence of the aristocratic ideal in the South. They produced the original great slave plantations based on agricultural monoculture, the mansions that were models of careless wealth and lavish living and are still the arrogant pride of the James, Ashley, and Cooper rivers; and they produced an elite within the white minority to whom society naturally deferred. Moreover, as the initial English settlements in the South, they have been closely associated with tradition and even history itself. One might note that even in recent Southern history, to own a house on the Battery or to make one's debut at the St. Cecilia Ball in Charleston, to carry Virginia names like Randolph, Fitzhugh, Lee, or Blanding, to have family or professional connections in either area, or to speak with the "r"-less accents associated with these areas still carries weight among Southerners.[7]

If Charleston or low country South Carolina and Virginia are the epitome of the high-cultural, aristocratic ideal in the South, the back or upcountry—the interior—represents the antithesis of those values. This area has been characterized historically by the small farm and the yeoman, fewer blacks and slaves (or none at all), more recent settlement, and religious and political dissent. At its extreme, it is hillbilly, yokel country, representing a kind of yahoo egalitarianism and perpetual frontier spirit. It is Indian fighting, eye gouging, and home brewing, a hectic form of "laissez-faire" nurtured in mountain coves, and a visceral, inconstant radicalism that blows hot and cold as well as right and left.

These intra-regional and cultural distinctions form the basis of the social structure of Mitchell's South in *Gone with the Wind*.[8] Within the context of these intra-regional hierarchies of values, it is critical that Mitchell sets the novel in the interior and constantly plays backcountry values against the aristocratic ones of Charleston and Virginia. Two hundred and fifty miles inland from the drawling aristocrats of Charleston and Savannah, Mitchell's North Georgia setting represents the spirit of Augustus Longstreet and Davy Crockett rather than William Grayson or Thomas Nelson Page. Repeatedly Mitchell describes her South as a frontier. Brawling, restless, democratic, and egalitarian, it places a premium upon activity, energy, and drive. Wide open and fluid, it attracts people from all backgrounds and circumstances, Frenchmen and Irishmen, Roman Catholics and Presbyterians, Yankees and Southerners, members of old families and newcomers with no families at all—hunters, frontiersmen, and poor immigrant boys. This cultural melting pot allows anyone to achieve wealth and power, even ignorant bogtrotters, according to the advice and example of Gerald O'Hara. Indeed, the bogtrotter on the make is thoroughly descriptive of Mitchell's typical planter. Ambition, ruthlessness, amorality, selfishness, and disregard of the commonweal are hallmarks of her backcountrymen. While open at the top, her social order is equally open at the bottom, and no claims to birth or manners can prevent the lazy or altruistic from collapsing back into white trashdom.

While mostly interested in stressing the roughneck origins of her backcountry planters, Mitchell also includes yeomen in their original state in *Gone with the Wind*. "The Troop," the county cavalry unit, is full of them. Containing almost no rich planters, it consists mostly of hunters from the backwoods, swamp trappers, crackers, and, horror of horrors, even some poor white trash, although Mitchell adds they would have been few, and, wittily, they would have been above the average of their class. The same yeoman worthies appear again later in a literary tableau-vivant reminiscent of the American regionalist painters or the folk muralists of her generation:

> Many small farmers from far across the river were present and Crackers from the backwoods and a scattering of swamp folk. The swamp men were lean bearded giants in homespun, coon-skin caps on their heads, their rifles easy in the crooks of their arms, their wads of tobacco stilled in their cheeks. Their women were with them, their bare feet sunk in the soft red earth, their lower lips full of snuff. Their faces beneath their sunbonnets were sallow and malarial-looking but shining clean and their freshly ironed calicoes glistened with starch. [p. 707]

These utterly non-aristocratic Southerners appear as individual actors in Mitchell's drama as well. The wife-killing, black-baiting, Yankee-hating Archie is a vividly sketched "mountain man" in Reconstruction Atlanta, and the illiterate small farmer Abel Wynder is second in command, under Ashley Wilkes, of the county cavalry unit; indeed, his selection serves as the occasion for a little election sermon on the South as a meritocracy. Far more significant in the narrative is the yeoman Will Benteen, a South Georgia Cracker.

189

Tireless, faithful, grave, intelligent, and wise, he embodies a Southern version of Roman virtue. It is he who restores the plantation after the war: "Tara's bloom was not the work of a planter aristocrat, but of the plodding, tireless 'small farmer' who loved his land" (p. 703).

While the yeoman citizenry and frontier values of the upcountry constitute the substance of Mitchell's South, she also describes a contrasting aristocratic social order. She identifies it geographically with the two traditional fonts of aristocratic ideals in the South—Virginia and Charleston, with which she includes Savannah. Placing the aristocratic tradition outside the physical setting of the novel underlines its isolated, anomalous qualities. Mitchell's actual descriptions reinforce these characteristics: aristocrats and aristocratic values are the exotic products of peculiar local circumstances. Unrealistic dreamers, her aristocrats lack life and vitality. She characterizes them alternately as ethereal, wraith-like, ghostly, and almost physically transparent.

The Wilkeses personify the Virginia cavalier tradition. From their first appearance in the novel, they are identified as exceptional and queer, these qualities being associated with their Virginia ancestry: "Well—you know how the Wilkes are," the rough-and-tumble Tarleton twins remark, ". . . Mother says it is because their grandfather came from Virginia" (p. 16). Culturally and physically the family is overbred, inbred, overrefined, attenuated, and bloodless. They are compared to such passive creatures as does, rabbits, and lap dogs. Unable to adapt to changing circumstances, they are also doomed, individually and as a family. Fulfilling prophecies about their extinction, they have trouble reproducing: Melanie Wilkes barely survives one childbirth and a second pregnancy actually kills her. Less than a man, even less than a woman, Ashley Wilkes, in Old Miss Fontaine's description, is socially if not sexually impotent. He can ride a horse better than any man in the county, but he pursues such manly activities without feeling or commitment. He is unable to balance account books, run a business, or even perform odd jobs around the farm like splitting wood. Indeed, the ultimate measure of Mitchell's backcountry soil's bounty might not be that bogtrotters can become wealthy but that the high-born Wilkeses can turn a profit so as to support their predilections for Bulwar-Lytton and other alien exotica.

Ellen Robillard O'Hara represents the other peak of Southern aristocracy—the rice country nabobs of Charleston and Savannah. For all her good works and rustling crinolines, she is distant and aloof. Lacking passion and color, she is described as lacking life itself. In keeping with this characterization, she seems actually to gain power over her family when she expires physically at age thirty-five. She remains an anomaly in the backcountry. These characteristics are the ones that Mitchell applies repeatedly to the low country aristocracy. Described as shadows that meld with the Spanish moss of live oak trees, her nabobs as a class are a brooding presence lurking just outside the narrative. They share many qualities with their cavalier cousins. Like the Wilkeses, who are spavined, pallid, and anemic, the residents of the low country's malarial marshes are also associated with illness and disease. They are represented as pompous, stilted reactionaries: they are obsessed with tradition and puffed up with pretentious family pride. Life in their society is stifling; it is compared to living in a prison. It is as artificial and doomed as that represented by the Wilkeses. If, however, the passing of the doe-eyed Wilkeses might generate nostalgia and regret, the extinction of the "lumbering dinosaurs" of the tidal marshes is cause for celebration: thus Rhett Butler expresses Oedipal delight at the death of his "old school gentleman" father who typified the rigidity, brittleness, and hidebound qualities of coastal society.

Mitchell's attitude toward aristocracy also coincides with her treatment of slavery. In no area has *Gone with the Wind* been more criticized than in the neglect and misapprehension of black bondage in the South. The racial attitudes in the novel relate to the post-Reconstruction ideology of the New South creed as Richard King has treated it, to the "savage ideal" described by W.J. Cash, and to the white "Volksgeist" that manifested itself nationally in the 1920s and 1930s.[9] All of these were a part of Margaret Mitchell's world view which she wrote into the novel. But her attitude is likewise both a cause and an effect of the intra-regional biases that underlie her work. If Mitchell failed to appreciate the importance of slavery

in antebellum society as a whole, the institution was less immediately relevant and even less visible in the interior where she set
her novel. As stated earlier, slavery and blacks had their clearest
political, social, economic, and numerical impact in the Tidewater
and the deltas, along the navigable rivers, in Virginia and around
Charleston—the centers associated with traditional aristocratic
power. By the 1850 census, for example, as recorded by David Donald, slave population was virtually nonexistent in some areas of the
backcountry, and around the Atlanta area it constituted between 9
and 36 percent of the population. In contrast, the slave-white ratios
were almost exactly reversed in the plantation country of the
Georgia-Carolina coast, where slaves ranged from a "low" of 66 percent to a high of 88 percent of the total population.[10]

Reflecting these backcountry characteristics, slavery as an economic system simply does not exist in *Gone with the Wind*. There
is no suggestion of slave labor in the creation of the novel's estates;
thus "Tara's broad acres" are created by Gerald O'Hara's entrepreneurial skill—his "shrewd Irish brain"—with no reference to
slavery. Slaves are merely social ornaments for upwardly mobile
white farmers. Symbolically, Gerald's first slave—after he is already
on his way to his fortune—is a valet. Although Pork helps the family
survive by foraging after Sherman passes through, he is incapable of
sustained labor of any sort, unable even to mend a shirt. This is true
of all Mitchell's black characters with one exception—Dilcey, who
is doubly exceptional in that she is twice described as bronze
rather than black, more Indian than African. If individual slaves are
physically or economically ineffectual, however, this merely echoes
the explicit attributes of Mitchell's white aristocrats, most notori-
ously Ashley Wilkes, who is cut from the same social cloth as Pork.
Further underlining the relationship between the white aristocrats
and the slaves, the black characters are all associated with tradition,
the old ways, and the codification of behavior, and they are as lost as
the gentry in a new world order.

Mitchell goes beyond the matter of the mere economic irrelevance of slavery, for even as a social or political system the institution is virtually ignored. This is perhaps her greatest flaw: she ne-
glects a brooding off-stage presence for blacks that she allows for
even her shadowy aristocrats—the invisible presence that lurks be-

tween the lines of most exemplars of the Southern mind from the eighteenth century down to the present. Slaves are important only as individuals, and the primary black actors—Mammy, Pork, Uncle Peter, Dilcey, even Prissy—are "house servants," and by Mitchell's conventional definition, "members of the family," pets, and thereby hardly slaves at all. Of "real" slaves—field hands and black workers—Mitchell has almost nothing to say. None except Big Sam has an identity, and only a few others have names. Not until the section on Reconstruction does the narrative treat this class of blacks in any detail, and even here the flashback is quick and cursory: field-hand blacks, the insolent freedmen of Reconstruction, all come from the class of field hands who were "the least honest and trustworthy, the most vicious and brutish" (p. 654).

If Mitchell misses blacks and slavery as one of the most profound components of inner Southern divisiveness, she describes another that is virtually as important: gender distinctions which from early in the regional experience supercharged the conflict within Southern values.

From such evidence as John Smith's history of Virginia, published in the early seventeenth century, it is clear that chivalric notions of love, romance, and adventure were an integral part of the Southern world view from its earliest intellectual foundations. In this set of ideas, dating from the courtly romances of the twelfth century, women were identified as both the objects and the means of a man's success in the world.[11] As Edmund S. Morgan has indicated in his history of colonial Virginia, the particular position of women in that society tended to exaggerate or even add a new dimension to the sexual differentiation of the chivalric tradition: given different death rates between men and women, females—and marriage—became a primary means by which a man might acquire wealth and property.[12]

Before the close of the seventeenth century, the acquisition of wealth through marriage had developed into a consuming interest in passing on an estate or augmenting a child's estate through a good match. Almost simultaneously, the notion of acquiring or passing on a name—the idea of achieving social as well as economic legitimation—became a folk institution within the South.[13] But the ideal of gentility, prestige—a name—rose, literally, at the expense of estates and property: reaffirming still another motif of the chivalric ideal, property represented avarice and was thereby a sure sign of one's ignobility. Personal dissolution, careless generosity, and ostentatious display, then, became fixed as classic characteristics within a regional mind-set.[14]

The social implications of this system are far-reaching. It helps to account for the imperative for new blood, or new families, to avoid absolute stagnation or social implosion. It gives meaning to the constant rise and fall of fortunes, the proliferation of "names" yet the stability of the social order. It also contributes still further to gender differentiation and the association of gender roles with the other polarities of Southern thought. If physical property was highly suspect, women came to fill the needs of ownership: they brought property with them (thereby allowing a man to avoid direct contamination by acquiring his own wealth), represented prestige as a substitute for property, became estate managers (in much the way Greek slaves assumed managerial functions in Imperial Rome), and actually functioned themselves as a kind of property.[15]

Within this framework, marriage continued to serve as a primary means of a man's ascension in the social order, but even more it served an intellectual or social imperative: reuniting the disparate elements within the Southern personality, or halting the centrifugal forces within the regional experience. This institutional purpose of marriage is indeed one of the constant themes of Southern social history that repeats itself over and over again from the earliest days to the present. Random examples include: the marriage of the familyless Tuckahoe Peter Jefferson to the F.F.V. Martha Randolph; of the backwoodsman John C. Calhoun to his haughty, low-country cousin Floride; of the crude, illiterate tailor Andrew Johnson to his Victorian schoolmarm; and, in the modern era, another spate of Johnson couplings—the hill-country Sam Houston Johnson to the genteel Rebekah Baines, and their raw-boned offspring, Lyndon, to the cultured Lady Bird.

Paradoxically, even while binding up the passions of the Southern experience, marriage tended to formalize the very compartmentalized or fragmented roles that were recombined. It was a formal union of stylized parts in which ideas of love, fancy, or affection were secondary. Margaret Mitchell was keen to all the nuances of

194

meaning in the association of gender roles with class, social, and even intra-regional distinctions, and in the implications—cultural, psychological, and even political—of marriage for the Southern mind.

The "successful" marriage of Gerald O'Hara and Ellen Robillard is the key to understanding Scarlett's character, and it thereby becomes the central metaphorical device for understanding Southern history and the internalized contradictions in the Southern mind. The two parts of the union embody the stereotypical polarities of the Southern tradition: Gerald is all maleness, the new man, self-made, the backcountry; Ellen represents femaleness, tradition, family, the coast. The match is a *mésalliance,* and Mitchell exaggerates its incongruity by stressing the physical and personal differences in the two: ruddy-dark, short-tall, old-young, loquacious-taciturn, loud-soft, physical-spiritual, spontaneous-disciplined, coarse-refined. They even smell different—Gerald of horses, Ellen of lemon verbena. It is, moreover, a formal union sealed by fate rather than by romantic choice. When Gerald goes out looking for an aristocratic wife (as he had gone out to buy slaves) as a means of climbing the social ladder, he is successful mostly because of Ellen's fatalistic desire to escape Savannah after the death of her cousin-lover, whom she had been forbidden to marry. Romantic love and passion play no part in the union; it is a formal arrangement based on mutual obligation, duty, and loyalty: even after seventeen years of marriage, the pair still refer to one another as Mr. O'Hara and Mrs. O'Hara.[16] The marriage between Suellen O'Hara and the "South Georgia Cracker" Will Benteen continues the theme of wedding two conflicting cultural traditions. Although Mitchell treats this second-generation coupling in a significantly different way, both Suellen and Will represent polar social values, and their match, even more than the first, is a passionless "social necessity."

While true to an actual social custom in the South, such marriages also symbolize a central problem in Southern intellectual history: as in the marriage of Gerald O'Hara and Ellen Robillard, the region itself becomes a mésalliance. The result is a philosophical or social dualism to which we might most appropriately apply the concept of "syzygy," as Michael Kammen has used it, to indicate the coexistence of opposites or the binding together of polar forces without the loss of identity.[17] Internalized in the psyches of the children of such a union, this dualism accounts for the most peculiar characteristics of Mitchell's characters. Torn between the values represented by her mother and her father, Scarlett simply refuses to think about it and obscures the paradox in the mindless busyness of her life. Conversely, Ashley Wilkes contemplates the world and the contradictions freeze his will. Their polar reactions represent historical responses in the Southern tradition—the wild charge on the one hand, the retreat to fantasy and abstraction on the other. Between the two extremes, Rhett Butler is as keen as Ashley to reality, yet as predisposed as Scarlett to the fight. The result in his character is near-schizophrenia, as he shifts from role to role in search of equilibrium. Ultimately, irony is the expression of the dualistic tension in his character. His words are two-edged swords, and he confuses and confounds with his ability to alter the meaning of what he says with a gesture, smile, or shrug. The ultimate irony in Rhett's life, however, is his belief that escape is possible, and he finally bows to the inevitable and returns to the very society that he has scorned throughout the narrative.

These avoidances, submissions, surrenders, and compromises raise central problems with the novel—and, indeed, with Southern history. Within a liberal Lockean framework they symbolize a failure of the will—the character's and the author's. Writing from this perspective, critics have censured the novel on moral as well as artistic grounds. In the preeminently liberal *New Republic,* John Peale Bishop in 1936 criticized Mitchell's "moral uncertainty" in seeming to approve of Scarlett's persistence while at the same time she implies "that civilization consists precisely in an unwillingness to survive on any terms save those of one's own determining.[18] James Boatwright, writing for the same journal almost thirty years later, was even more critical. He dismissed the novel as a "camp classic" that "flirts with the terrible ambiguities of freedom without believing that it is really possible."[19]

These criticisms are both perceptive and misleading. It is true that in her point-counterpoint between the past and the future, yeomen and aristocrats, businessmen and planters, men and women, individuals and society, freedom and order, Mitchell does not impose literary harmony. Her perspective shifts; her descriptions contradict her characterizations, and her values change from episode to episode. At the same time, even these literary shortcomings echo the dissonances of Southern society itself. Moreover, while *Gone with the Wind* affirms the rules of home and history, their content is very different from the cozy hearth and picturesque tradition implied by liberal critics: home is cold ashes and a withered tit; history is defeat, loss, and the inevitability of death. Finally, the process that Boatwright describes in demeaning sexual terms as a "flirtation" is no trivial affair at all. Within a specific regional context of distinctive social ideas and intellectual assumptions, the struggle for liberation seems both inevitable and hopeless. If not tragic, it is, at least in Southern terms, epic.[20]

The social setting from which Mitchell wrote was significantly different from the national perspective. In the place of a national Lockean ideal of society as merely the aggregate of autonomous individuals where to think free is to be free, in the South society itself is the primary autonomous unit. Organic in time and space, it is superior to its constituent parts and dictates roles that individuals are to play. Roles and relationships are preestablished. Playing parts is then the *sine qua non* of the Southerner's life. In this world the premium is upon acting rather than producing, being rather than making, style rather than substance. Life itself takes on a quality of art, one result being the softening of the distinctions between reality and fantasy, yielding the hazy ambiguity of Southern thought and action. Creativity derives from playing parts intensely or by exercising the discipline that melds the actor with the role. Subtlety and nuance also count—the gesture and tone of one's performance. One might also vary the drama by playing another part or by stepping periodically out of character. Nevertheless, the individual's range of legitimate action is ultimately prescribed, and these limits can produce sharp tension between the actor and his role or the actor and the whole drama. The tension can debilitate and reinforce tendencies towards fatalism and lethargy; it is, conversely, another source of the violence, both social and individual, within the Southern character.

Within this social system, Ashley's transparent despair, Rhett's schizophrenic tendencies, and Scarlett's recurring nightmares of foggy voids are most appropriate, while Ellen's and Melanie's steel-stayed discipline is a means of surviving the same social forces. The alternative to all this is exile, and the paradoxical theme of "going north toward home" for one's survival as a Southerner, a standard theme in Southern intellectual history, also figures in *Gone with the Wind*: Ashley's projected move to New York is equated with his survival; to remain at home he subjects himself to the inexorable working of the social order. Failing to break away, he concedes his helplessness, impotence, and defeat.

Gone with the Wind describes the paradoxes of Southern life and thought, but even in its form or formlessness it unself-consciously underlines the conflicting allegiances of the dualistic Southern mind. Margaret Mitchell's genius, and perhaps her curse as well, was her ability to describe in national terms and commonplace language the essence of the Southern character. If her national dress for the Southern manikin has obscured that character, this, too, is not unfitting, for the conflict between the nation and the region is not the least of the paradoxes that informs the Southern temper.

Notes

1. C. Vann Woodward, *The Burden of Southern History*, rev. ed. (Baton Rouge: Louisiana State University Press, 1968); W.R. Taylor, *Cavalier and Yankee: The Old South and American National Character* (New York: George Braziller, 1956).

2. Quoted in Sidney Howard, *GWTW: The Screenplay, Based on the Novel by Margaret Mitchell*, ed. Richard Harwell (New York: Macmillan, 1980), p. 51. See also Gavin Lambert, *The Making of "Gone with the Wind"* (Boston: Little, Brown, 1973), p. 88; Rudy Behlmer, ed., *Memo from David O. Selznick* (New York: Viking Press, 1972), p. 214.

3. Malcolm Cowley, "Going with the Wind," *New Republic,* September 16, 1936, p. 161 [reprinted in this volume].

4. Richard Harwell, ed., *Margaret Mitchell's "Gone with the Wind" Letters, 1936–1949* (New York and London: Macmillan, 1976), pp. 5, 172, 8, 249–50, 36; see also pp. 137, 254–55, 370.

5. Virginius Dabney, *Below the Potomac* (New York and Toronto: Appleton-Century, 1942), p. 2.

6. Harwell, pp. 357–59.

7. See Raven I. McDavid, "Postvocalic -r in South Carolina: A Social Analysis,"

American Speech 23 (1948): 194–203, reprinted in Dell Hynes, *Language in Culture and Society: A Reader in Linguistics and Anthropology* (New York: Harper & Row, 1964), pp. 473–80. This perceptive analysis is still a landmark in the study of the relationship between intraregional economic and social distinctions and speech patterns.

8. Mitchell's personal correspondence reveals the consciousness with which she depicted intraregional divisions within the Southern experience in the novel. In reply to Julia Peterkin's review of the novel, which referred to these themes, Mitchell wrote, "And no other reviewer seemed to grasp the difference between the old coast sections and the new up-country, and I wondered forlornly . . . if the fault was altogether mine in not being able to write my thoughts so clearly that they got across" (Harwell, pp. 46–48). While her letters usually portray this intraregional conflict in terms of Atlanta over against Macon or Milledgeville, she was also keen to the upper versus the lower South, or Virginia cavalier versus frontier tradition, as in her letter to Virginius Dabney (Harwell, pp. 357–59). And finally she was sensitive to even more obscure but equally important intraregional prejudices, as in her allusion to Mississippians and Alabamians. Thus, Honey Wilkes's Alabama husband "was a gentlemen and a man of some means; but to India, born in Georgia and reared in Virginia traditions, anyone not from the eastern seaboard was a boor and a barbarian" (Margaret Mitchell, *Gone with the Wind* [New York: Macmillan, 1936], p. 731; hereafter cited in text).

9. As manifested in James Boatwright's "'Totin' de Weery Load': A Reconsideration of *Gone with the Wind*," *New Republic,* September 1, 1973, pp. 29–32, there is a tendency in both popular and academic criticism to identify the novel indiscriminately with a Thomas Dixonian, Old School Southern racism. While Mitchell drew on stereotypical images of blacks, however, her attitudes are not at all identical with the Negrophobia of the preceding generation. She eschewed the violent racism of *The Clansman* and even of the revived K.K.K. of her own generation, which was associated with rabble-rousing politicians like Tom Watson, Cole Blease, "Cotton Ed" Smith, and James K. Vardaman. Reflecting a more genteel attitude, Mitchell had a paternalistic, protective respect for the integrity of black Southerners, however limited their range of action might have been within regional social norms. See also the specific analyses of notions of race in *Gone with the Wind* in the essays by Cripps and O'Brien in this collection.

10. David Donald and J.G. Randall, *The Civil War and Reconstruction,* 2d ed. (Lexington, Mass.: D.C. Heath, 1969), p. 66.

11. I am indebted to my colleague Howard Kaminsky for pointing out the medieval sources and parallels of *Gone with the Wind* and the courtly romances, and for his insights that have enriched my appreciation of the chivalric roots of Southern intellectual history.

12. Edmund S. Morgan, *American Slavery, American Freedom: The Ordeal of Co-*

lonial Virginia (New York: Norton, 1975). For the formation of the earliest attitudes about and position of women in Southern colonial society, see Lois Green Carr and Lorena S. Walsh, "The Planter's Wife: The Experience of White Women in 17th Century Maryland," *William and Mary Quarterly,* ser. 3, vol. 34 (1977): 542–71; Lorena S. Walsh, "'Till Death Do Us Part': Marriage and Family in 17th Century Maryland," in Thad W. Tate and David L. Ammerman, eds., *The Chesapeake in the 17th Century: Essays on Anglo-American Societies* (Chapel Hill: University of North Carolina Press, 1979), pp. 126–52.

13. An unexplored but illuminating expression of the place of women in society and of the importance of names and families in this period is the innovation of giving to sons the surnames of their mothers. Prior to 1720, this seems to have been a rare occurrence. A classic exception occurs appropriately in the Randolph family, that pace-setter clan which established many models for the rest of the Virginia aristocracy; they named one son Isham in the seventeenth century. The will of Robert "King" Carter represents the establishment of this practice by 1732. The practice did not seem to take hold in Charleston high society until the nineteenth century.

14. For a delineation of Southern aristocratic values in the colonial period, see Thomas Breen, "Horses and Gentlemen: The Cultural Significance of Gambling Among the Gentry of Virginia," *William and Mary Quarterly,* ser. 3, vol. 34 (1977): pp. 237–57; Carol Shammas, "English-born and Creole Elites in Turn of-the-Century Virginia," in Tate and Ammerman, pp. 274–96; and Rhys Isaac, "Evangelical Revolt: The Nature of the Baptist Challenge to the Social Order in Virginia, 1765–1797," *William and Mary Quarterly,* ser. 3, vol. 31 (1974): 345–68.

15. Thorsten Veblen presents the model of ownership of women as one of the classic and primary expressions of "barbarian society." While this seems generally appropriate, the situation in the South was skewed from this model; in the critical stage of the formation of the Southern mind in the seventeenth century, women in Virginia seemed to have attained a high degree of independence and initiative, one which was never totally subordinated and which, indeed, is one of the gender-based sources of the tension within the Southern mind.

16. In an interview Mitchell's brother, Stephens Mitchell, stresses the importance of marital relationships in the novel. Citing Ellen's and Scarlett's unfulfilled fantasies about their first loves, he calls the novel a "psychological drama" about immature women ("Personality: Keeper of the Legend," *Atlanta Constitution Magazine,* October 22, 1978, pp. 48–49).

17. Michael Kammen, *People of Paradox: An Inquiry Concerning the Origins of American Civilization* (New York: Knopf, 1972), pp. 89–90. While an interesting explanation of American Puritan civilization, the concept of "syzygy" is even more applicable to the Southern regional experience. For a brilliant examination of dualism in the Southern experience as an outgrowth of slavery, see Eugene Genovese, *Roll Jordan Roll: The World the Slaves Made* (New York: Pantheon, 1972).

18. John Peale Bishop, "War and No Peace," *New Republic,* July 15, 1936, p. 430. Interestingly, Mitchell commended this review as "very good" (Harwell, p. 59).

19. Boatwright, p. 32.

20. Robert Y. Drake, "Tara Twenty Years After," in *Georgia Review* 12 (Summer 1957): 142–50; Henry Steele Commager, "The Civil War in Georgia's Red Clay Hills," *New York Herald Tribune Books,* July 5, 1936, pp. 1–2 [reprinted in this volume]. Both essays are illuminating examinations of the novel in terms of its epic, or, in Drake's term, "Aeneid-like" qualities.

A Bibliographical Essay

The formal critical response to *Gone with the Wind* has had an important history of its own. For almost fifty years it has swung between lavish praise and disdain. Revealing shifting patterns in academic taste, the contours of this criticism also help to illuminate the shadowy corners of modern American intellectual history. The investigation of scholarly attitudes toward the novel is an inseparable part of the reexamination of the work itself. The responses fall into three fairly distinct intellectual and chronological categories, each of which is explored in turn below.

The Initial Reaction

The national press.—The introduction to this collection's first section, "The Critical Setting," and the Dwyer and Harwell essays deal with aspects of the initial response to the novel. Commager's and Cowley's reviews are, of course, outstanding examples of the earliest analyses. Others are important as well. Treated extensively by Dwyer, John Donald Adams's review, "A Fine Novel of the Civil War" (*New York Times Book Review,* July 5, 1936), sounds the main themes of the first reviews: the novel's dramatic power, fine characterization, and stylistic limitations. Elaborating on these themes in his "Books" column in *The New Yorker* (July 4, 1936, p. 48), Louis Kronenberger considered Mitchell a "staggeringly gifted storyteller" and her novel "glorious theater"—with both positive and negative implications.

Herschel Brickell's and Edwin Granberry's reviews are doubly important. The former is not uncritical in his essay "Margaret Mitchell's First Novel" (*New York Post,* June 30, 1936), particularly regarding Mitchell's style, but for him the dramatic sweep of the work and its vivid delineation of character rescue it—indeed, give it artistic merit. Granberry's treatment, another of the earliest reviews in the Eastern press, is more positive than Brickell's ("Book of the Day," *New York Sun,* June 30, 1936). He was the first reviewer to relate *Gone with the Wind* to the great epic novels of nineteenth-century European tradition. And he was the first to suggest the novel's importance in the intellectual conflict between modernist and traditionalist sensibilities that Dwyer develops in his essay. Thus, Granberry argues, Mitchell's clarity and linear narrative are not only richly old-fashioned, they also offer what he considers an alternative model to the confused, obscure, and overly complex "moodiness" of most contemporary novels.

Perhaps impressed by the generosity of these reviewers, Margaret Mitchell invited both Brickell and Granberry to write profiles of her for the national press. Given her intense sense of privacy and insistence on controlling her public image, her choice of these two writers and the sketches they produced are especially useful. Brickell's profile appeared in August ("A Talk with Margaret Mitchell about Her Book," *New York Post,* August 7, 1936), Granberry's seven months later ("The Private Life of Margaret Mitchell," *Collier's,* March 13, 1937). They make an interesting contrast, but Granberry's article is most notable, because he submitted it to Mitchell and her husband, John Marsh (who was a professional public relations agent), for their close scrutiny. Their lengthy comments, preserved in the Mitchell archives, offer important insights into how the Marshes perceived both the novel and Miss Mitchell's creative energies—and, not least of all, how they wished these to be perceived.

Stephen Vincent Benét's review, "Georgia Marches Through," *Saturday Review,* July 4, 1936, is also noteworthy. Like Brickell, he develops the idea of the "woman's angle" of the book; he also suggests the critical theme of considering the novel as "folklore." But when considering the work in the context of nineteenth-century novelists, he implies that *Gone with the Wind* is derivative, credits it therefore with being "good" instead of "great," and concludes on the measured note that "it should reach the wide audience it very genuinely deserves."

Similar to Benét's response is that of John Crowe Ransom, the Agrarian and Fugitive poet, in "Fiction Harvest," *Southern Review* 2 (1936–37): 407–8. Particularly approving of this "remarkable" first novel for its dramatic structure and architectural quality, he remarks, somewhat invidiously, that it is "a woman's book." Ransom raises questions about the "empty-headedness" of the book even while conceding this characteristic as an aspect of Southern culture.

Ransom's curiously wistful remarks echo in the much more negative analysis of still another Southern-born critic: John Peale Bishop, "All War and No Peace," *New Republic,* July 15, 1936. Without Ransom's insight that perhaps Southern society itself is vacuous, Bishop deals critically with the divided sensibility of the novel: neither wholly sentimental nor wholly realistic, the work is flawed by its inability to come down squarely on the side of any one issue. For Bishop, it lacks morality altogether.

Bishop's insights about the book's "moral ambiguity" reverberate in another important early analysis, Evelyn Scott's "War Between the States," *The Nation,* July 4, 1936. Scott was almost the only critic to note the work's "petty Nietzscheanism" and the "undigested influence of that literature of pessimism" that pervaded the twenties. Even so, the book "worked" for her because of "the whole-heartedness with which [Mitchell's] imagination yields itself. . . . [She] makes the reader's absorption into a narrative sprinkled with clichés and verbal ineptitudes a contagious growth."

Placing the novel within the cultural milieu of the twenties, as suggested by Scott, is the theme of one of the best and most perceptive early analyses of the book, Belle Rosenbaum's "Why Do They Read It?," *Scribner's* 99 (1937): 23–24, 69–70. She has the highest praise for Mitchell as storyteller, asking, "If you wonder why *Gone with the Wind* is so popular, think what a Dickens, a Thackeray, or a Fielding could do for America, . . . [for] people yearning for a tale well told, for the sake of its telling, by a teller who loves the tale and the art of telling it." But Rosenbaum is also keen to the book's other qualities, suggesting that it "retained a touch of Joyce, Hemingway, Fitzgerald," and that Mitchell interprets the aftermath of the Civil War "in modern terms with Scarlett O'Hara emerging as the modern prototype of Thackeray's immortal Becky Sharp."

The Left and the South.—Although the general consensus among reviewers, when *Gone with the Wind* first appeared, was that the book had genuine merit, some held a contrary view. The strongest negative responses were from the American Left.

Among American Communist reviewers, the most simplistic—but not the least relevant—source of negativism was the "party line." This is illustrated in Howard Rushmore's "Life on the *Daily Worker,*" *American Mercury* 50 (June 1940): 215–21. Party fiat, however, was rooted in moral and political concerns, chiefly interest in American blacks. This governed the Left's response to *Gone with the Wind.* The novel quickly became the American Left's primary symbol of capitalist, Anglo-Saxon racism and of the influence of the reactionary South on American life and letters. The Left waged a long-term campaign against Mitchell's opus. Between 1936 and 1944, no journal in the United States paid as much attention to the novel and its cinematic avatar as did *New Masses.* In these years, *Gone with the Wind* was one of the primary points of reference for any discussion of black issues in *New Masses*—lightly, as in "Southern Belle" (October 4, 1938), or more seriously, as in Samuel Sillen's "History and Fiction" (August 3, 1943), which was a refined effort to define legitimate historical fiction for the Left. This linking of racism and "Southophobia" with *Gone with the Wind* also influenced the non-Communist Left's attitude toward the work. This is apparent in Malcolm Cowley's analysis (reprinted in this collection); it also figures in Heywood Broun's review in his syndicated column, "It Seems to Me," *New York World Telegram,* September 19, 1936.

Rob F. Hall's "Wrestling with Jim Crow," *New Masses,* August 3, 1943, introduces an important variation on leftist criticism of the novel. Hall was a Southerner, and for all his denunciation of regional racial mores, economic reaction, and repressive politics as symbolized in *Gone with the Wind,* his essay is as Southern as grits. Northern urban radical opposition to the South is significantly transformed in his hands; he goes to the mat not only with Jim Crow but with an entire phalanx of Southern traditions, customs, and folkways. Not least of these is his sense of his people's gut romanticism. For him, "realism" became a moral, emotional, and highly personal commitment.

Hall's attitude was not unique by any means. As Richard King suggests in his essay in this collection, realism, more or less passionate, was a critical aspect of Southern intellectual history in this period; it certainly colored the response of various Southern intellectuals to Mitchell's work. It influenced John Donald Wade's curiously mixed review, "Romance Permitted," *Virginia Quarterly Review* 12 (December 1936): 618–20. But realism is best illustrated in the attitudes of W.J. Cash and Lillian Smith—and with it, the problems of a romantic attachment to realism.

As King has noted, Cash and Smith both panned the work because of its romantic elements. King also touches upon Cash's re-

period, Robert Drake's "Tara Twenty Years After" (*Georgia Review* 12 [Summer 1957]: 142–50), fresh and nonpolemical especially for the time, is still useful, even more so now with Drake's scholarly coda to his original piece (see below). Drake argues that the best literary context for understanding *Gone with the Wind* is the primitive epic, and that this form is most appropriate for Southern society—itself unself-conscious and traditional. One of the Vanderbilt students of Agrarian Donald Davidson, Drake employs Davidson's categories of tradition versus "antitradition" to understand the basic conflicts in the book, which, in turn, account for its chief or underlying dramatic tension. Conflict exists on several levels and in a variety of forms: North versus South, Melanie/Ashley versus Scarlett/Rhett, and, not least, Scarlett versus herself. Although Drake gives "tradition" his own meaning, he concludes that *Gone with the Wind* is about the ways in which the past continues.

Another Donald Davidson student also produced a significant study of the novel during these years. Reta Margaret Anderson's "*Gone with the Wind*: An Evaluation" (master's thesis, Vanderbilt University, 1956) is an internal analysis that emphasizes the work's "unique features" within the genre of the Southern Civil War novel: its urban and frontier settings and the variety of its social types. On stylistic considerations, Anderson notes Mitchell's skillful alteration of dialogue to suit the personalities of specific characters and her special focusing technique, which, like that of a motion picture cameraman, begins with grand scenes but quickly zooms in to individual actors. While Anderson's analysis is most original in these aspects, she also offers useful insights into the ways individual characters function in the novel: the idea of Scarlett as the novel's "central intelligence" (citing Allen Tate's and Caroline Gordon's use of that concept), and a very Davidsonian interpretation of the work as an affirmation of tradition and the old way—*Gone with the Wind* as a morality tale set against the New South.

Edward F. Nolan, in "The Death of Brian Lyndon: An Analogue in *Gone with the Wind*," *Nineteenth Century Fiction* 8 (1953): 225–28, briefly compares an episode from Mitchell with one from Thackeray. The article's chief importance lies in its indication of the direction that later scholars would take with more detailed comparisons to other works. One of these was Merlin G. Cheney in his

1966 master's thesis at Brigham Young University, "*Vanity Fair* and *Gone with the Wind*: A Critical Comparison." Although Cheney is simply wrong in his judgment that Mitchell used Thackeray's work, his thesis is otherwise useful, intelligent, and still fresh. His treatment of Mitchell's pessimism and realism is a good antidote to the dominant interpretation of her romanticism that was current in these "dark ages." His suggestions about Mitchell's debts to Dos Passos and Hemingway are also good. He associates Thackeray's sardonic narrative with the ironic character of Rhett Butler. He makes illuminating comparisons of the two authors' characters and, in comparing scenes, argues that Mitchell is Thackeray's superior in her ability to build character and mood indirectly through dialogue where Thackeray falls back on description by the narrative voice.

The last piece, James Matthews's "The Civil War of 1936: *Gone with the Wind* and *Absalom, Absalom!*," *Georgia Review* (1967): 462–69, is an essentially uncritical "review of reviews" of these two novels.

This period also saw the beginning of work, both scholarly and popular, on Margaret Mitchell herself. Ethel M. Bearden's 1957 master's thesis at Duke University, "Margaret Mitchell and Her Place in Atlanta," was a weak start in the direction of biography. Based exclusively on secondary sources, mostly from public clipping files, it adds nothing even to the folklore of Mitchell's life.

Although she did not have access to Mitchell's papers, Patsy Evans Darwin in her master's thesis, "The Theory of the Creative Personality and Its Application to Three Georgia Women Journalists—Lollie Belle Wylie, Emily Woodward and Margaret Mitchell" (University of Georgia, 1965), offers information on how Mitchell wrote, citing several original interview sources.

The popular biography by Finis Farr, *Margaret Mitchell of Atlanta* (New York: Morrow, 1965), is useful, if limited. It has no notes and lacks a historical or cultural framework but, even so, provides one of the most accessible sources of material on Mitchell and her ideas about herself and her work. However guarded, some of Mr. Farr's interpretations of the sources of Mitchell's creativity are also valuable.

The appearance of the Farr biography evoked some scholarly reassessment, most notably the review "Scarlett Fever," by David

210

Donald, in *Book Week,* January 23, 1966, pp. 5, 21, 23. Repeating Anderson's analysis, Donald was the first major scholar in twenty-five years to reaffirm the interpretation that *Gone with the Wind* was alien to the "gentle Confederate novel of the Thomas Nelson Page–type." Perhaps Donald's most important contribution was that he took both Mitchell and her novel seriously, an attitude that remained anomalous for several years to come.

Contemporary Reevaluation

The reasons for the next change in attitudes about *Gone with the Wind* are difficult to pinpoint. Among scholars, a "natural" reaction against the pieties of scholarly fathers is one possible source of revived interest, but the revival was by no means limited to academic Young Turks: there has been a popular as well as a high-cultural ground swell of interest in the novel since 1970.

Broader cultural influences came into play. Revisionism, in the air through the Kennedy era and afterward, took the form in American historiography of naming a school of thought for the historians of the fifties and then challenging its precepts. A reassessment of regionalism was part of this general spirit of revisionism; for instance, Marxist historians and critics from the North, such as Barrington Moore and Eugene Genovese, were reassessing the South in terms that ardent defenders of Southern peculiarity had used before.

The rise of black and women's studies also reflected the revisionist intellectual tradition, and they went far toward creating new bases for understanding the nation, the South, and Southern literature. The identification of the novel with Negrophobia and Southernism had been the greatest stumbling block to reexamining *Gone with the Wind.* But Martin Luther King's march in Cicero, Illinois, his identification of racism with the war in Vietnam, and the urban riots in the mid-sixties tended to deregionalize racism. These events, in turn, allowed critics to transcend traditional categories in dealing with Mitchell's work. Criticism and historical interpretation were themselves changing after the mid-sixties, and these changes eventually caught up with *Gone with the Wind.*

Reevaluative setting.—A flurry of dissertations and master's theses marked the close of the novel's "dark ages." While indicating a renewed academic interest, they also often reflected biases of the earlier criticism. These problems are neatly illustrated in two dissertations at Vanderbilt, the first in history, the second in literature.

"The Image of the Southern Plantation: A Comparison of Recent Historical and Fictional Accounts," by Anthony Owens Edmonds (1970), mostly reflects post–World War II criticism of *Gone with the Wind*. Edmonds disregards all of Mitchell's efforts at realism and, as a consequence, all of the tension between the old and new orders in her book. He is baffled by her appreciation of Cash. Although he makes passing reference to her debt to the great regionalist historian U.B. Phillips, he does not develop any coherent cultural or intellectual framework for a revised estimation of the novel.

Perry Carlton Lentz's "Our Missing Epic: A Study in the Novels about the American Civil War" (1970) is much more important and ultimately much more revealing of historical values than Edmonds's dissertation. As a critical revisionist, Lentz praises Mitchell's technique, especially her "tremendous skill of narration," her "exceedingly professional, subtle, persuasive style," and her large patterns of control. He also develops a new category for Mitchell's work: the novel of the disintegrating Southern family. He thus anticipated a new focus in Southern letters which Richard King, among others, has developed in this collection. Within this framework, Lentz considers *Gone with the Wind* in comparison with Stark Young's *So Red the Rose* (1934), Caroline Gordon's *None Shall Look Back* (1937), Allen Tate's *The Fathers* (1938), and Faulkner's *The Unvanquished* (1957).

Most useful of all is Lentz's development of a social and literary logic for these works. Central to his analysis is the question of how an aggressive representation of a profoundly regionalistic ideology like *Gone with the Wind* should have become the American *War and Peace*, "such as it was." In solving this riddle, Lentz uncovers a new aspect of the novel's style and structure—its prevailing duality: "The novel is based upon a constant shuffling between stated conventional myth and iconoclastic undercutting of that myth—so spaced that [they] exist comfortably side-by-side. . . . They coexist. Each outlook impacts upon the reader, sequentially."

Measured by sales, this paradox worked famously. Lentz concedes the artistic merit of this scheme as well, although he concludes, somewhat ambivalently, that it leaves the moral and esthetic patterns of the novel incomplete, especially in regard to racial issues. His examination of the racial implications of the novel is among the very best in *Gone with the Wind* criticism. Yet even in his final condemnation, Lentz still mirrors the novel's persistent ambivalence by suggesting that beneath the surface patterns of Negrophobia, the very presence of the exploited Negro in the novel is the source of the "deep and threatening tensions in the minds of its white 'folks'."

Also of value is a master's thesis that appeared the same year, G. Staley Hitchcock's "Tomorrow Is Another Day: *Gone with the Wind* and the American Mind" (Stephen F. Austin State University, 1970). Although the title is a misnomer, there are important correlations between Mitchell's world view and that of her era. Hitchcock also confirms and elaborates some of Lentz's notions about *Gone with the Wind*'s subtle shift from the conventions of the Civil War plantation romance. In addition, this work presents one of the most competent summaries to date of Mitchell's personal biography.

The final work in this academic flurry of 1970 was Judith Yvonne Chandler's "The Language Structures of Epic as Seen in *Gone with the Wind* and *Waters of Life*" (master's thesis, Morehead State University, 1970). Her purpose is to define the concept of the epic by analyzing the peculiar use of psycholinguistic patterns of words and structures. While the thesis is not convincing, her detailed examination of Mitchell's usage within patterns described by Samuel Reiss is more than a curiosity; it offers a structural analysis of Mitchell's extraordinary facility with words.

Although these four works were formally in the public realm upon acceptance by their respective universities, they have remained virtually unknown and uncited. They were hidden harbingers of the revisionist criticism of *Gone with the Wind*.

The new phase of public debate over the novel was inaugurated, paradoxically, with two broadsides against the work that were from the old school. More interesting still, Southerners delivered these shots. It is ironic, and perhaps a mark of the South's continuing intellectual drawl, that this "regionalist" campaign against the novel was mounted just as non-Southern academics were beginning to see its merit.

Floyd Watkins's essay, *"Gone with the Wind* as Vulgar Literature,"

Southern Literary Journal 2 (Spring 1970): 86–103, is calculatedly provocative. It virtually burlesques the old standards by which the work had been rejected since Cowley's treatment. While Watkins offers some evidence to support his contentions about the work's racism and romanticism, he declares that "pure assertion" occupies the crucial place in his criticism. Watkins is unconcerned with textual explication, and he rejects the work out of hand from very much the same position as does Bernard DeVoto (see Richard Dwyer's essay in this collection). In spite of his moral revulsion toward *Gone with the Wind,* many of Watkins's insights are keen, like his intuitive linking of the novel with female sensibilities. Also perceptive is his idea about evil in the novel; he insists there is none—except in relation to immorality, "which is only sexual" in Mitchell's world view.

James Boatwright's essay, "Totin' de Weery Load," is a more popular and personalistic companion piece to Watkins; it appeared three years afterward in *New Republic,* September 1, 1973, pp. 29–32. Boatwright makes some concessions to the novel's merit, such as its "uncanny" relationship to the monumental *Children of Pride* (Yale University Press, 1972); he affirms its "insistent dramatization" as well. His essay is also useful in identifying some of Mitchell's stylistic weaknesses—the book's clichés and its "collapse" in the second half. But more central to his argument are moral and political objections. He also associates his critical rejection with the repudiation of his own "adolescent fantasies" when he first encountered the novel. In Boatwright's analysis, the novel itself becomes a kind of coquettish Southern belle who tempts the gentleman—but will not deliver when the party is over. This very analogy is the source of Boatwright's condemnation of the novel's "moral ambiguity."

It is appropriate here to deal with Leslie Fiedler's reinterpretations. As in Boatwright's personalistic review, Fiedler reassesses the novel in the context of his own young-man fantasies. The fantasy that he abandons, however, is his proletarian idealism of the thirties, and in the process he discovers that *Gone with the Wind* is full of hard reality, especially sexual reality. Fiedler stands both Watkins and Boatwright on their heads. In his "Fiction of the Thirties," *La Revue des Langes Vivant: U.S. Bicentennial Issue* (1976): 93–104,

214

he returns to one of the motifs in the initial 1936 reviews: the novel's bitterness and unhappiness. He argues that the work is the central artifact of the thirties: it "contains the clues to the deepest meaning of the age." Developing the theme that Watkins and Boatwright intuitively label ominous, Fiedler suggests that the novel is "a kind of woman's protest against male exploitation." In his *Inadvertent Epic: From Uncle Tom's Cabin to Roots* (New York: Simon and Schuster, 1979), he underlines this theme again in treating the work as a "bitter war between the sexes," the fundamental metaphor for him of the modern era.

No less than Watkins—if from the opposite direction—Fiedler intended to be provocative. Between these two highly charged positions, Watkins and Boatwright on the one hand, Fiedler on the other, have come a wide range of reanalyses since 1971.

Genre studies.—One group of critics treats the novel within the traditional framework of the plantation romance. Earl Bargannier's "The Myth of Moonlight and Magnolias," *Louisiana Studies* 15 (Spring 1976): 5–20, is something of a transitional piece. It is not actually a study of *Gone with the Wind* but rather of the plantation-romance conventions; these reached their apex, he argues, in Mitchell's novel. His view echoes the old interpretation of the novel, and his reading is sometimes facile; for example, his casual reference to Scarlett as "beautiful" ignores one of the most famous opening lines in American literature. But Bargannier does suggest significant ways in which the novel departs from the tradition or bends that tradition in new directions, as in Mitchell's splitting of the conventional characters into their emotional subparts.

Hugh Holman offers fresher, if unfortunately brief, insights in his *Immoderate Past: The Southern Writer in History* (Athens: University of Georgia Press, 1977). Again underlining the observations of the earliest critics, he considers Mitchell one of the unsurpassed storytellers of American literature, ranking her high in relation to many of her Southern contemporaries. Unlike Watkins, Holman particularly credits her use of irony with rescuing the work from the sentimentality of the conventional romance.

A woman's work.—The best and most detailed of the new criticism of the novel avoids the traditional approach altogether. Some

215

of the richest work deals with the very issues broached more or less directly by Watkins, Boatwright, and Fiedler: women, sex, and gender.

The relationship between gender and culture is the subject of Dawson Gaillard's "*Gone with the Wind* as 'Bildungsroman': or Why Did Rhett Butler Really Leave Scarlett O'Hara?," *Georgia Review* 28 (Spring 1974): 9–28. She argues that Scarlett O'Hara's story can be read on two levels: one, a traditional morality tale of a woman who violates social norms and is punished in the end by losing her man; the other, an allegory of contemporary gender mores—losing her man frees Scarlett finally from her last childhood fantasies. Gaillard notes perceptively that at both the surface and allegorical levels the old way dies; that, as *Bildungsroman* ("novel of personal development"), *Gone with the Wind* is the record of the breaking free from a life of self-effacement that limited the Southern lady. Mitchell, Gaillard argues, wanted "to criticize the mythic social mode of behavior that had governed her area of the country and national popular literature but to criticize without offending (and also without completely admitting to herself what she was doing)." Anticipating Fiedler's position, Gaillard asserts that the allegorical purpose of the book is to attack an imbalance in the social positions of men and women.

Anne G. Jones's dissertation from the University of North Carolina and the book that grew out of that seminal work, *"Tomorrow Is Another Day": The Woman Writer in the South, 1859–1936* (Baton Rouge: Louisiana State University Press, 1981), deal extensively with Mitchell and her novel from a similar perspective with different conclusions. (Jones's essay in this collection is a version of the earlier work.) In her long survey of Southern culture, Jones sees enormous rebellion among Southern women, but, unlike Gaillard, she finds that culture, the past, and the Lady have always triumphed, even when (as in *Gone with the Wind*) that triumph is bleak and without victors, male or female. Jones's treatment of Mitchell is good; even better is the theoretical analysis in her first chapter, "Dixie's Diadem."

"The Hysterical Personality and the Feminine Character: A Study of Scarlett O'Hara," by Charles G. Wells, a psychiatrist at Vanderbilt University (*Comprehensive Psychiatry* 17 [March–April 1976]:

353–59), also fits into the Gaillard-Jones framework. It is an interesting, technically detailed analysis of the social forces of the plantation South that produced the characteristic appearances and behavior—if not the reality—of the hysterical personality.

Louis Rubin's essay reprinted in this volume appeared in 1976. Because Rubin is one of the most important critics dealing with life and letters of the cultural awakening in the interwar South, his reassessment and his bracketing of Mitchell with Faulkner—indeed, his interest in Mitchell as a significant writer (Anne Jones was his student)—has helped legitimate scholarly work on *Gone with the Wind.* Rubin helped to bridge the gap between the traditional postwar attitudes about the novel as romance and the newer approaches to the novel—with, for instance, his interpretation of Scarlett's gender role in the work.

New forms.—Feminist redefinitions of content comprise only one category of new work on the novel; still another develops new analyses of the form. The earliest, Fran Chalfant's "Mirror of Vanities and Virtues: A Reappraisal of *Gone with the Wind," West Georgia Review* (1971): 15–26, begins with the emotional bond between the novel and its readers. Chalfant maintains that this bond constitutes the critical clue to the nature of the novel: *Gone with the Wind* is an American version of Jonson's "human comedy." Mitchell's way is "that of the good natured, yet serious satirist, that of Jane Austen and Charles Dickens." Like Holman (and in sharp contrast to Watkins and Boatwright), Chalfant catalogs Mitchell's ironies in treating the plantation South in the first section of the novel. Like Boatwright, she notes Mitchell's shifting emphasis and changing narrative voice from one section to another; she argues, however, that this shift is not an accidental "collapse" but simply another means of maintaining the reader's sympathy as the characters' circumstances change. The entire effect remains unchanged: to underline the universality of human affectations, shortcomings, and shortsightedness.

Much more recently essays have appeared, almost simultaneously, that suggest a thoroughgoing revision of post–World War II literary interpretation of the novel. The broadest analysis is Dieter Meindl's "A Reappraisal of Margaret Mitchell's *Gone with the Wind," Mississippi Quarterly: The Journal of Southern Culture*

(Fall 1981): 414–34. Meindl deals with the novel's critical reception and the problems of its failure to fit neatly into one literary school or another. He rejects the interpretation of nostalgia as the central motif. Instead, he develops the idea that the novel is about primitive or "elemental regeneration." He also argues that the work is "a fine novel of manners." In this regard, his definition of the South as a society of very intricate rules, especially regarding gender, sexuality, and women, is a particularly significant interpretation. In his wide-ranging analysis Meindl links the novel to the culture of the twenties—for instance, the literary milieu of *A Farewell to Arms*—much as Evelyn Scott and Belle Rosenbaum did in their 1936 and 1937 reviews.

Blanche Gelfant, more narrowly literary, makes even larger claims for the novel's significance in her "*Gone with the Wind* and the Impossibilities of Fiction," *Southern Literary Journal* 13 (Fall 1980): 3–31. Her starting point is the novel's obsessive symbolism of closed doors. Secrets, she argues, "are *Gone with the Wind*'s explicit concern—hinted at, withheld, hunted and exposed." Using a complex "psychology of meaning," she proposes that the novel's ultimate secret is the reconciliation of irreconcilable desires: the coexistence of child and adult, parent and offspring, black and white, prince and pirate. It is a secret that *Gone with the Wind* shares with all great fiction, and, in this regard, Gelfant suggests that the novel "may also prove [to] be our most complex—crude, undoubtedly, and styled by clichés, but nonetheless intricate and relevant to our understanding of the mysterious motives of fiction."

The third in this trio of reinterpretations is Harold K. Schefski's "Margaret Mitchell's *Gone with the Wind* and *War and Peace*," *Southern Studies* 19 (Fall 1980): 243–60. This critic takes a commonplace comparison posed in the 1936 reviews and develops it in detail. He deals not only with the "epic sweep" that the first reviewers saw to be common between the two works, but also with form, theme, subject, characterization, methodology, structure, and style. He concludes that both novels are family chronicles and *Bildungsromanen* as well as historical novels; both take an outsider's (or unhistorical) view of historical events; each emphasizes the theme of survival; each contains similar character types; and, finally, each personifies a city. Only in structure and style does

218

Schefski find more dissimilarities than correspondences: Mitchell is insistently linear in her narrative; Tolstoy uses a tripartite structure of war, peace, and philosophy, with battle scenes providing crucial links. In the process of his comparison, Schefski presents the Tolstoyan formula for "true art" that hinges on "accessibility," and, he argues, by this yardstick the Russian himself would have approved of Mitchell's work.

Three other fields of recent scholarship indicate changing academic attitudes about the novel: popular culture, history, and biography.

Popular culture.—A new discipline without clear methodology or even goals, popular culture overlaps traditional disciplines, frequently calling on techniques and vocabulary from history, literary criticism, and anthropology. The field constitutes a useful general category, in which criticism often takes the work itself as a given, focusing instead on the public response to the work. Jerome Stern's essay "*Gone with the Wind:* The South as America," *Southern Humanities Review* 6 (Winter 1972): 5–12, is concerned exclusively with the popular response to *Gone with the Wind*. Stern hypothesizes that the South is a projection of national values and that the "regional art" of *Gone with the Wind* localizes American concerns, specifically Negrophobia, nostalgia for a lost, Edenic past, and obsession with the mythos of the family. The novel's popularity, he concludes, stems from "its accuracy as a dramatization of American attitudes."

This collection has focused primarily upon Mitchell's novel but has frequently contrasted it with the film version. One characteristic of popular culture studies, as reflected in Stern's essay, is to examine the "GWTW *phenomenon,*" thereby diminishing differences between the two media. Several significant works fall into this framework and deal specifically with the film but refer to the larger "popular culture" setting. Two such books appeared close together in the mid-seventies on the same subject. Although neither is a scholarly work, they both represent the general public's reawakening interest in *Gone with the Wind* after 1970: Gavin Lambert's *GWTW: The Making of "Gone with the Wind"* (Boston: Little, Brown, 1973) and Roland Flamini's *Scarlett, Rhett and a Cast of Thousands: The Filming of "Gone with the Wind"* (New York: Macmillan, 1976). Both books stop as the cameras cease rolling, and neither analyzes the content of the film. This is a subject that awaits its own monograph, although Thomas Pauly has inaugurated the examination of the film's content—and the meaning of the *Gone with the Wind* phenomenon—with his fresh and innovative "*Gone with the Wind* and *The Grapes of Wrath* as Hollywood Histories of the Depression," *Journal of Popular Film* 3 (Summer 1972): 203–18. In remarks that are as applicable to the novel as to the film, Pauley emphasizes the film's redemptive metaphors of the soil and the agricultural way of life (rather than mere nostalgia for lost tradition). Like Stern, and like Wood in this collection, Pauley treats the centrality of the theme of family experience for the *GWTW* phenomena.

Two other scholarly studies are useful for understanding the general place of the film in American cultural history: Jack Temple Kirby's *Media-Made Dixie* (Baton Rouge: Louisiana State University Press, 1978) and Edward D. C. Campbell's fuller treatment, *The Celluloid South: Hollywood and the Southern Myth* (Knoxville: University of Tennessee Press, 1981). The notes to the essays by Wood, Cripps, and O'Brien in this collection refer to still more detailed essays on various aspects of the film.

Reviewed widely, Flamini's book provoked a particularly important notice in the *Times Literary Supplement* (London), September 10, 1977, p. 1094: Peter Conrad's "In Praise of Profligacy." This is less a review of the book itself than a definition of the cultural or sociological setting for the novel and film. Unhampered by the preconceptions that have blinkered American critics, Conrad proposes that the appropriate cultural setting for understanding the film comprises the implosive tendencies of late capitalist society in the West. This Marxist-informed treatment is also taken up in the unpublished works of two American scholars. Anthropologist Richard Busch of Reiter College in New Jersey deals mainly with the film in his "Legitimations of Class and Mobility in *Gone with the Wind*." But in emphasizing the absence of class conflict, the invisibility of "white trash," and the positive emphasis upon the unifying qualities of human sentiments and American values, his study of the film delineates by implication the differences between the film as the "American" work and the novel as the "regional" one. Historian

220

Elizabeth Fox-Genovese's studies of *Gone with the Wind* as the reflection of the bourgeois mind in the interwar period in the United States accomplish these same goals even more felicitously: "Margaret Mitchell and the Culture of the Bourgeoisie" and "Comment: *Gone with the Wind*" (papers presented to South Atlantic Modern Language Association, November 1978, and the Organization of American Historians, New Orleans, April 1979).

Richard Harwell has not produced an analysis of "popular culture" per se, but his *"Gone with the Wind" as Book and Film* (Columbia: University of South Carolina Press, 1982), a "scrapbook" of scholarly and popular writing on the novel, Mitchell, and the film, brings together useful material including, notably, the Pauly essay.

History. —That historians have been late in examining *Gone with the Wind* reflects this discipline's difficulties in dealing with artworks as historical documents. The broadly cultural or ideological analysis by Fox-Genovese—a professional historian—is one resolution of the problem. Although more factual and specific, Willie Lee Rose's approach is similar in her *Race and Region in American Historical Fiction: Four Episodes in American Popular Culture, An Inaugural Lecture Delivered before the University of Oxford on 4 May 1978* (Oxford: Clarendon Press, 1979). This work is slated for republication in the paperback edition of her collected essays, *Slavery and Freedom* (New York: Oxford University Press, 1982). Like Fiedler in *Inadvertent Epic,* Rose compares four cultural "events" in American history: *Uncle Tom's Cabin,* Thomas Dixon's *Clansman* and D. W. Griffith's *Birth of a Nation,* Alex Haley's *Roots,* and *Gone with the Wind.* Her work is also related to popular culture studies, since she uses Mitchell's novel and Selznick's film as documents of changing patterns in American social life. In contrast to Watkins (and to another historian treated below, Robert F. May), Rose argues that racism in particular underwent a significant transformation in *Gone with the Wind.* She also notes that Mitchell's "economic realism" significantly altered the traditional plantation romance. Finally, she ties her study specifically to Southern history. By treating the economic order of the post–Civil War South, Rose underlines the tension in the region, in its desire for commerce and industrialization. This tension, she suggests, is most appropriately represented in the characters of Melanie and Scarlett, who become the contradictory—but historically accurate—representations of the two faces of the New South movement. Rose treats the novel as an intellectual document of the South's ambivalence about its past and its commercial future. Her analysis relates to the King and Rubin essays in this collection.

Unlike Rose, Robert May reads the novel not as a document but as straight history in "*Gone with the Wind* as Southern History: A Reappraisal," *Southern Quarterly* 17 (Fall 1978): 51–64. May's essay is strongly colored by Watkins's criticism, which dismisses the work out of hand as "sensational propaganda" for the plantation South and the Lost Cause. Basing his opinion on recent historiography, he concludes that *Gone with the Wind* is fundamentally false. He divides the novel into three historical periods, treating the historical authenticity of each in relation to current modes of scholarship on the region. He faults Mitchell's prewar South with "sketchiness" and her plot with the failure to develop the reality of regional, political, urban, or intellectual life or the lives of slaves. The wartime section he finds "surprisingly" true, but the Reconstruction period, he argues, has no relevance to modern historiography, and he suggests that Mitchell sinks to the "lowest levels of racism." His work has its own distortions, however. If Mitchell grossly errs in her treatment of political Reconstruction, May misses an even greater historical fallacy: the fundamental irrelevance of politics to Mitchell's postwar world, a matter treated significantly by the Kenneth O'Brien essay in this collection.

With many of the same objectives as May's essay, Jane Turner Censer's unpublished article "Scarlett and Her Southern Sisters" focuses more narrowly on Mitchell's historical accuracy in her images of Southern aristocratic women. She, too, finds that Mitchell generally misses the mark in her treatment of history. In delineating what Mitchell misses—especially regarding the insignificance of religion in the novel—Censer limns hidden values in the work that make it more clearly a document of the twenties if less of 1861.

Two other historical analyses take a different tack and reach conclusions opposite to May's and Censer's. Although concerned more with a historical event rather than with the novel, Daniel E. Sutherland appraises Mitchell's treatment of emigration of Confederates after the war, finding it accurate in detail and feeling, in "Southern

Carpetbaggers in the North; or, Ashley Wilkes, Where Are You Now?," *McNeese Review* 24 (1977–78): 9–17. Donna DeBlasio likewise finds the novel historically accurate within a related context of New South industrialization and commercialization in the region. While sharply revisionistic about the traditional interpretations of *Gone with the Wind* as a glorification of the past, DeBlasio's "'You Never Gave a Damn About the Late, Lamented Confederacy': Scarlett O'Hara and the New South," *Illinois Quarterly* 42 (Spring 1980): 12–22, misses critical nuances of the "New South Creed" as originally described by Paul Gaston. The South was of two minds about industrialization, and DeBlasio's too ready equation of Scarlett with the triumph of bourgeois values obscures the ambivalence both in the region and in the novel—as suggested by Willie Rose.

Biography.—It is fitting, perhaps, that the novel be rediscovered before its author, yet the paucity of scholarly biographical analyses is still extraordinary, especially in view of the flood of legend and folklore about Margaret Mitchell. A turning point was Richard Harwell's edition of her correspondence, *Margaret Mitchell's "Gone with the Wind" Letters, 1936–1949* (New York: Macmillan, 1976). Although the editor maintains that this compilation is as near to true biography as can be written, his limiting of the correspondence to outgoing letters of the public Mitchell—The Author of the Novel—imposes a significant bias. Mitchell's letter writing (like her personality) had an extraordinary plasticity, as indicated, for example, in her adaptation of style, tone, and content to "fit" her correspondent. Thus, without knowing her specific correspondent it is difficult to weight accurately her judgments and values.

The publication of Mitchell's correspondence precipitated a notable flurry of criticism on the author and her work. Blair Rouse's short "*Gone with the Wind*—But Not Forgotten," *Southern Literary Journal* 11 (September 1978): 173–79, introduces the idea that the novel contains much more than is apparent in the easy generalizations about its popularity. Rouse also deals with some of the mystery of its appeal that Gelfant treated later in detail. Still more useful is Robert Drake's review of the letters in *Resources for American Literary Study* 7 (Spring 1977): 98–101, in which he develops some of the observations in his 1957 essay. He finds that the letters confirm his notion of Mitchell's novel as "the tale that is told, the

223

oral narrative, which is the very stuff of the classical epic which does indeed hold children from play and old men from the chimney corner, so irresistible is its narrative power."

There are still other, more strictly biographical studies. A 1978 dissertation attempts to cast new light on Mitchell by analyzing her relationship with one of her old Atlanta associates: Kathleen Ann DeMarco's "Medora Field Perkerson: A Study of Her Literary Career and Especially of Her Friendship with Margaret Mitchell" (University of Georgia). This slim work is basically flat and descriptive and adds little to existing knowledge of Mitchell. It does contain, however, some new material in personal correspondence to DeMarco from Lois Dwight Cole, a woman with whom Mitchell was much more engaged than Perkerson.

My own biographical essay, "Margaret Mitchell: First or Nothing," *Southern Quarterly* 20 (Spring 1982): 19–34, develops the thesis that Mitchell's creativity grew out of nearly irreconcilable psychological and cultural tensions produced by being a woman in her particular household at a unique time in Southern history. This thesis provides the context for a larger biographical study I am working on.

Anne Edwards, author of the solid and interesting popular work on the heroine of David Selznick's film, Vivien Leigh, is also working on Mitchell. Her forthcoming biography will develop more personal themes, particularly regarding Mitchell's relationships with her friends and her marriages.

The future.—More detailed analyses of *Gone with the Wind*'s style, especially of its structure, seem called for—the technical sources, for example, of that dramatic power which even hostile critics have noted. The relationship between the novel and the film seems a ready object for study. The *Gone with the Wind* phenomenon itself seems almost infinitely open to examination. Perhaps the richest field of study, however, is that proposed by Leslie Fiedler: the novel as an important artifact in the culture of the interwar years. By the same token, studies of the novel and its author can be important additions to the study of American and Southern intellectual history in this formative period in our civilization.

Index

Absalom, Absalom! (Faulkner): Charles Bon, 87, 88, 92, 101; Ellen Coldfield, 85; Goodhue Coldfield, 91; Rosa Coldfield, 85, 91, 169; Quentin Compson, 91, 92, 98, 99, 100, 101, 169; Quentin Compson, Sr., 168; and *GWTW*, 36, 98, 210, 212, 217; narrator issue in, 87, 91, 98, 99, 100–101; racial issues in, 87–88, 92, 100; reviewed, 24, 82; as Southern history, 92; Thomas Sutpen, 84–85, 87, 91, 92; Sutpen's Hundred, 100. *See also* Blacks, in *Absalom, Absalom!*

Adams, Henry, 30, 185

Adams, J. Donald, 22, 23, 30–31n1, 75, 82, 203

Afro-American, 146

Agee, James, 167

Agrarians, Nashville, 21, 22, 168, 169

Alexander, Holmes, 27

Allen, James S., 142

Amsterdam News, 146

Anderson, Eddie, 143

Anderson, Reta Margaret, 209, 211

Anna Karenina (Tolstoy), 35, 69–71, 75, 76

Antaeus, 34, 57, 58, 59, 67, 68

Archie, 161, 189

Atlanta: Mitchell's excessive focus on, 171; New South city, 90, 95, 170; and slavery, 193; vulgarity of, 16, 61–62, 64, 75. *See also Gone with the Wind*, New South values in; New South; O'Hara, Scarlett, and Atlanta

Austen, Jane, 217

Balzac, Honoré de, 76

Bargannier, Earl, 215

Battleground, The (Glasgow), 12, 23

Beard, Charles and Mary, 5

Bearden, Ethel M., 210

Becker, May Lamberton, 76

Benét, Stephen Vincent, 11, 13, 26, 54, 204

Benteen, Will, 66, 189–90, 195

Berghe, Pierre vanden, 175

Bernd, Aaron, 50

Big Sam (Everette Brown), 67, 144, 160, 177, 193

Birth of a Nation (Griffith): family values in, 125–26, 127; historical verisimilitude in, 127, 135; public response to, 124–25; racial dimension of, 125, 153, 147, 148, 175; social content of, 126, 127–28, 132; technical innovations in, 124. *See also* Blacks, response of; *Gone with the Wind* (film), compared to *Birth of a Nation*

Birth of a Race, The, 125

Bishop, John Peale, 6–7, 10n3, 25, 196, 201n10, 204–5.

Blacks: in *Absalom, Absalom!*, 87, 88, 92, 98–99, 100, 175–76; and American left, 145, 146, 148, 205–6; response of, to *Birth of a Nation*, 124–25; and New Deal era, 119, 137–39, 191; in Southern romance, 120, 154–57, 175–76. *See also Birth of a Nation*, racial dimension of; Faulkner, William, on racial issues; Slavery; Southern romance, racial conventions in

—in *Gone with the Wind* (film), 143, 144; and racial turning point, 119, 125, 137, 139, 140–41, 144–45, 149; response to, 144–47; stereotypes of, 117, 118–19, 140–41

—in *Gone with the Wind* (novel): irrelevance of, 100, 162–63, 192–93; Negrophobia, 110, 118–19, 137, 156–58, 159, 160, 177, 213, 219, 222; nurturing roles of, 67; restricted roles of, 35, 36, 77–78, 157, 176–77

Boatwright, James, 8, 196, 197, 199n9, 214, 215, 216, 217

Bowers, Claude, 6

Boyd, James, 27

Brickell, Herschel, 5, 203, 204

Brier, Royce, 27

225

Brooks, Cleanth, 92
Broun, Heywood, 206
Brown, Everette, 144
Brown, Katharine, 139, 142
Brutus, 58
Butcher, Fanny, 50
Butler, Bonnie, 113, 114
Butler, Rhett (Clark Gable): ambiguity
  in characterization of, 115, 130,
  164–65, 177, 196–97, 209; as embodiment of maleness, 110, 111–
  13; and father's death, 191; as nurturer, 66, 125; and origins of *GWTW*,
  45; as realist, 178; and rape scene,
  111, 162, 180; related to narrative
  voice in *Vanity Fair*, 210
Butsch, Richard, 220

Cain (and Abel), 57
Caldwell, Erskine, 46
Calhoun, Floride Calhoun, 194
Calhoun, John C., 194
Campbell, Edward D. C., 220
Carmer, Carl, 22
Cash, W. J.: and Mitchell, 139, 177,
  206–7, 212; and New South ideology,
  121, 169, 171, 191; on rape complex,
  175; realism of, 169, 173, 206
Catholicism, 59, 63
Catonism, 168, 172, 174–75
Cease Firing (Johnston), 22
Censer, Jane Turner, 222
Chafee, G. A., 22
Chalfant, Fran, 217
Chandler, Judith Yvonne, 213
Charleston, S.C.: in *GWTW*, 114, 177,
  190–191; in Southern history, 187–
  88, 192
Cheney, Merlin G., 209
Chicago Defender, 146
Children of Pride, 214
Churchill, Winston, 27
Clansman, The (Dixon): family values
  in, 125–26; historical verisimilitude
  of, 127; progressivism of, 124, 128–

29, 131, 132; social ideology of, 124,
  125, 221
Cleveland Call and Post, 148
Cole, Lois Dwight, 75, 224
Commager, Henry Steele, 44–45,
  139–40
Communist Party: and American cul-
  tural values, 7, 28; blacks and, 119,
  145, 146, 148, 205–6; opposed
  GWTW, 6, 145, 205–6. *See also*
  Daily Worker; New Masses
Conrad, Peter, 220
Cowley, Malcolm: cultural biases of,
  7–9, 206; and Faulkner, 100; describes French admiration for
  GWTW, 10n8; and Mitchell, 10 (nn4,
  8), 186; modernist sensibilities of, 8,
  10n10; criticizes plantation legend,
  19–20, 25, 51, 120, 140, 153–54,
  185, 187
Crime and Punishment (Dostoevsky),
  58
Cripps, Thomas, 118–19, 220
Crisis, 143, 145, 147, 148
Cukor, George, 142, 144
Culture, American interwar, (1918–
  41): elitism, 28, 29–30; historical values, 5–6; misogyny, 7, 8, 19, 26,
  214–15; pessimism, irony, realism, 8,
  9, 30, 124, 133–34, 205, 214–15. *See
  also* Modernism

Dabney, Virginius, 186–87, 199n8
Daily Worker, 145, 146, 205. *See also*
  Communist Party
Darwin, Patsy Evans, 210
Davidson, Donald, 209
Davis, Ben, 148. *See also* Communist
  Party
DeBlasio, Donna, 223
DeMarco, Kathleen Ann, 224
DeVoto, Bernard: in opposition to
  GWTW, 26–27, 33, 214; in opposi-
  tion to Modernism, 10n10, 28
Dickens, Charles, 20, 205, 207, 217

227

15, 23, 120, 128, 142, 154–57; racial
reality of, 141, 142, 222. *See also*
Southern romance
—in *Gone with the Wind*: criticized, 6,
19, 36, 94–95, 153, 222; importance
of, 75, 90, 157; as justification for
Scarlett's transformation, 15, 89; ro-
manticization of, 157–61, 193
Reconstruction romance. *See* Southern
romance
Red Rock (Page), 119, 154–56, 162
Regionalists. *See* Southern regionalists
Reiss, Samuel, 213
Romance, Southern. *See* Southern ro-
mance
Roosevelt, Eleanor, 138, 143
Roosevelt, Franklin D., 138
Roots (Haley), 221
Rose, Willie Lee, 221, 223
Rosenbaum, Belle, 205, 218
Rouse, Blair, 57, 223
Rowan, Charles, 148
Rubin, Louis D., Jr., 29, 35, 36, 37, 121,
217, 222
Rushmore, Howard, 145, 205. *See also*
Communist Party

Sandburg, Carl, 133
Sarris, Andrew, 153
Sartre, Jean-Paul, 10n8
Savannah, Ga., 188, 190, 191, 195
*Scarlett, Rhett and a Cast of Thou-
sands* (Flamini), 1, 219
Scarlett Fever (Bridges and Pratt), 1–2
Schefski, Harold K., 21, 218–19
Schickel, Richard, 153
Scott, Evelyn, 47, 205, 218
Selznick, David: biography of, 1; racial
values of, 137, 143; shifts perspective
of *GWTW* (film), 118, 119, 124, 126,
131, 140, 185, 221; and Southern cul-
ture, 141
Sillen, Samuel, 206. *See also* Commu-
nist Party
Slavery: in *GWTW*, 64–65, 67, 78, 94,

100, 159, 191, 192–93; in Southern
history, 93, 192
Smith, John, 193
Smith, Lillian, 169, 172, 176, 206, 207
Smith College, 39, 40, 74
Smith-Rosenberg, Carroll, 181, 183n15
Socialist Appeal, The, 145
So Red the Rose (Young), 12, 22, 23,
172, 212
South: dualism and divisiveness in, 11,
12, 121–22, 187–88, 193–95, 197,
200; gender roles in, 36–37, 105,
114–15, 122, 193–94, 200n, 216–17;
social history (antebellum) of, 92–
93, 153, 191–92
—interwar (1918–41): literary renaissance during, 21–22, 167; and
nostalgia, 168, 169, 172, 174–75; and
realism, 168–69, 206; social history
of, 83–84, 102, 191, 222. *See also*
Southern Regionalists; Agrarians,
Nashville
South, New. *See* New South
Southern Regionalists, 21, 168–69, 173
Southern romance: class conventions
in, 156; gender conventions in, 156;
GWTW alters conventions of, 120,
161–65, 186–87, 211; *GWTW* as, 12,
19, 94, 120, 157–61, 185, 208, 215,
222; literary tradition of, 27, 154;
nostalgia of, 97, 174, 175; racial con-
ventions in, 154–56, 162. *See also*
New South; Page, Thomas Nelson;
Red Rock
Southophobia, 7–8, 153, 205–6, 207–
8, 211
Stern, Jerome, 219, 220
Still, William, 141
Stowe, Harriet Beecher, 117
Stravinsky, Igor, 58
Sutherland, Daniel E., 222

Tara: contrasted with Sutpen's Hundred,
87; as object of Scarlett's desire, 16,
59, 109; as symbol of Earth, 64, 65,